A LINGUISTIC DESCRIPTION AND COMPUTER PROGRAM FOR CHILDREN'S SPEECH

PRIMARY SOCIALIZATION, LANGUAGE AND EDUCATION

Edited by Basil Bernstein

University of London Institute of Education
Sociological Research Unit

I

Social Class, Language and Communication
Walter Brandis and Dorothy Henderson

II

A Linguistic Description and Computer Program For Children's Speech
Geoffrey J. Turner and Bernard A. Mohan

III

Talk Reform
Dennis and Judy Gahagan

IV

A Question of Answers
W. P. Robinson and S. J. Rackstraw

A Linguistic Description
and Computer Program
for Children's Speech

GEOFFREY J. TURNER

and

BERNARD A. MOHAN

London

ROUTLEDGE & KEGAN PAUL

First published 1970
by Routledge & Kegan Paul Ltd
Broadway House, 68–74 Carter Lane
London E.C.4
Printed in Great Britain
by Clarke, Doble & Brendon L'd
I.S.B.N. 0 7100 6611 2

CONTENTS

PART TWO

A COMPUTER PROGRAM FOR ASSISTING THE
LINGUISTIC ANALYSIS OF CHILDREN'S SPEECH   155

Bernard A. Mohan

ACKNOWLEDGEMENTS

We should first like to acknowledge the sympathy, encouragement and specific assistance of Professor M. A. K. Halliday of University College, London. The present authors alone, however, are responsible for the linguistic description presented in this monograph, which is based on the early work of Professor Halliday.

Secondly, we must thank our colleagues, Dr. W. P. Robinson (Deputy Head of the Sociological Research Unit 1965–6), Misses J. A. C. Nicholls, S. J. Rackstraw, A. C. Scott, and Mr. J. N. H. Pellowe, for their useful advice and criticism at the time of the compilation of the coding frame.

We should also like to express our gratitude to our present colleagues for their comments on earlier drafts of parts of this monograph: Dr. R. Hasan, Miss A. Hakulinen, Mrs. S. Taylor, and Messrs. P. R. Hawkins and R. E. Pickvance. Special thanks are due to Mr. B. N. Lewis (Deputy Head of the Sociological Research Unit 1966–8) for many enjoyable discussions from which we have greatly benefited.

We wish to thank the Director and staff of the University of London Institute of Computer Science for providing facilities which have enabled us to develop this work, and particularly Mr. D. F. Hendry for his encouragement and advice in the application of BCL to linguistic analysis.

Finally, we must express our deep indebtedness to Professor B. B. Bernstein for his inspiration and guidance throughout the period of the work.

INTRODUCTION

In this volume we are presenting a detailed account of the application of Professor M. A. K. Halliday's Scale and Category Grammar to the analysis of the speech of five-year-old children. This application was carried out by G. J. Turner in association with colleagues in the linguistic section of the Sociological Research Unit. This volume also contains the computer program designed by B. A. Mohan, who also worked with Mr. Turner on the coding frame for the linguistic analysis. Mr. Mohan would wish me to acknowledge the Unit's debt to Mr. Hendry of the Institute of Computer Science who acted as consultant throughout the period of the writing of the program. Mr. Brian Lewis, Deputy Head of the S.R.U., worked closely with Mr. Mohan in the final stage of writing up the program so that it could be made available in its present form. In terms of the various Unit activities we would all agree that the development of the computer program by Mr. Mohan and the grammatical analysis by Mr. Turner (in association with his fellow researchers) represent major achievements in the history of our research.

I would like in this introduction to outline briefly some of the problems which lay behind the development of the grammatical analysis. When we started in 1963 we were faced with the initial difficulty that there existed no precedents for the work we were doing. Very little was known about the speech of five-year-old children and certainly no major *grammatical* analysis had been reported in the literature of the speech of English children. We also had little idea of the influence of social class, sex of the child and ability upon such children's speech. We were also confronted with the problem of the selective effect of the various tasks which comprised the first language sample (see Brandis W. and Henderson D., Social Class, Language and Communication; Routledge and Kegan Paul, 1969) upon the nature of the choices the five-year-old children would take up. Finally we were also concerned to produce a grammatical description which would enable us to examine the speech of the children when they were older.

The only guides we had were the limited studies of the speech and written language of ten-year-old and fifteen-year-old children. A Nuffield Grant (1963–5) provided the Sociological Research Unit with the opportunity to carry out a grammatical analysis, using Halliday's Scale and Category Grammar, of sixty children's written language. Mr. Turner joined this project in 1964 and his work on the grammatical description became the basis of his report in this volume. We were also concerned to ensure that the grammatical analysis would enable us to relate the children's choices to various social antecedents. The developing theory with which I had been struggling had never been applied to the speech of very young children. Indeed even in the case of older children it had yielded only very general expectancies of the grammatical choices which would be taken up in different social contexts. I am distinctly conscious of the bewilderment I felt at the onset of this research when I was called upon to make decisions about the inclusion or exclusion of sub-systems within the grammar and even more to judge the degree of delicacy of the analysis at any level of the rank scale. I write this so that the reader is aware not only of the nature of the unmapped territory we were about to explore but also so that the reader will be aware of the significance of Mr. Turner's and Mr. Mohan's contribution.

We decided to set up a fairly broad and in part delicate grammatical description and apply this to all tasks within the first speech schedule. We used as our sample, the children in the factorial design reported elsewhere. This sample contained 110 children matched for various attributes like social class, sex, ability and according to an index of the mother's verbal communication to her child. This analysis together with the construction of the grammatical description took Mr. Turner and four assistants one year to carry out. We considered that such an intensive analysis might open up the directions to follow in more specialised analyses.

Mr. Mohan was faced with the problem of writing a program which included about 250 speech elements and also numerous types of possible maze phenomena in speech, (false starts, grammatical and lexical substitutions etc.). The precision required by the program brought about a continuous dialogue between Mr. Turner and Mr. Mohan.

In this account the reader will find reference to the 'middle-class' and the 'working-class'. We would not like to give the impression that the linguistic behaviour of either parents or children are as homogeneous or as different as these terms would appear to indicate. Indeed a paper written (unpublished) in 1962 and further papers since that date have moved further and further away from the crude ascription of particular uses of language to broad social class groups. This is *not* to say that broad social class correlates of non-dialect uses of language do not exist (our research is witness to their existence) only to say that as the theory developed in generality, the social antecedents of these uses of language became rather more precise, and modes of restriction and of elaboration were introduced.

It remains to be seen whether the speech of mothers and children we have collected will allow these later theoretical developments to be tested for their usefulness.

We hope that the approach to the grammatical analysis of children's speech, although developed for a specific research inquiry and following a specific linguistic theory, will be of interest to any workers concerned with the speech of children.

Basil Bernstein

PART ONE

A LINGUISTIC APPROACH TO CHILDREN'S SPEECH

Chapter 1

AIMS AND APPROACH

In a paper called 'Syntax and the Consumer', Halliday (1964) puts forward the view that 'different coexisting models in linguistics may best be regarded as appropriate to different aims, rather than as competing contenders for the same goal'. The aim of the grammar developed by Halliday and his colleagues is 'to show the patterns inherent in the linguistic performance of the native speaker'. The description involves 'a characterisation of the special features, including statistical properties, of varieties of the language used for different purposes ("registers"), and the comparison of individual texts, spoken and written, including literary texts. This in turn is seen as a linguistic contribution towards certain further aims, such as literary scholarship, native and foreign language teaching, educational research, sociological and anthropological studies and medical applications.' As Halliday points out: 'The interest is focused not on what the native speaker knows of his language but rather on what he does with it; one might perhaps say that the orientation is primarily textual and, in the widest sense, sociological.'

Our own particular aim was to make a statistical comparison of linguistic features in the speech of a sample of five-year-old working-class and middle-class children. Our main interest was in isolating social class differences in usage, those social class differences which Bernstein's theory of elaborated and restricted codes (e.g. Bernstein, 1965) implies are of educational consequence. It was necessary to take fairly large samples of children (450 children in all) in order to be able to say anything useful about the influence of social class. Furthermore, it was necessary to obtain speech from each subject in a variety of situations, in order to obtain some kind of check on the influence of the situation and to see whether particular situations favoured one or other of the social classes. It can be seen that there is a basic compatibility between our aims and those for which Halliday regards his type of grammar as appropriate.

Marshall and Wales (1966), in a critique of Halliday's paper, argue that the study of linguistic performance should be preceded by a study of linguistic competence, competence being the tacit knowledge of the language user. They write: 'It has always been accepted that, once the outlines of a competence model are fairly clear, we can then explore the manner in which this competence is realised in performance (Chomsky and Miller, 1963).' If we carry on performance studies without a competence theory, 'we are left without a norm against which to evaluate the results of such performance studies'. For a study of certain aspects of language performance a prior study of competence would indeed be necessary or at least highly desirable, for example, for a full examination of 'maze' behaviour, that is, false starts, substitutions etc., of grammatical deviations, and so forth. However, for most of our work it is not necessary to attempt to characterise the underlying competence of the speaker. Bernstein (1965) writes: 'The code which the linguist invents in order to explain speech events is capable of generating n number of speech codes.' The language code is a set of options. It is 'a set of rules to which all speech codes must comply, but which speech codes are generated is a function of the system of social relations'. The form of the social relation regulates the options which the speakers take up. Speech codes are distinguished in terms of the relative frequencies with which particular options available in the language code are taken up. As Bernstein (1964b) puts it: 'Speech . . . is constrained by the circumstances of the moment, by the dictate of the local social relation and so symbolises not what can be done, but what *is* done with different degrees of frequency.' The social class differences in speech and writing that have been found by Bernstein (1962b) and Lawton (1963, 1964) have been differences in relative frequency. There has been no suggestion in the above studies that there is any fundamental difference in the tacit knowledge of the middle-class and working-class language user. What is of primary importance to Bernstein is not the difference between 'competence' and 'performance' but the difference between performances that have been influenced by different social relations.

We might point out, theoretical considerations apart, that it would have been an enormously difficult task, in terms of time and manpower, to have attempted a systematic study of underlying competence in samples of subjects large enough to be representative of the different social classes. The difficulties of obtaining evidence about underlying competence may be gathered from this quotation from Chomsky (1964): 'If anything far-reaching and real is to be discovered about the actual grammar of the child, then rather devious kinds of observation of his performance, his abilities and his comprehension in many different kinds of circumstances will have to be obtained, so that a variety of evidence may be brought to bear on the attempt to determine what is in fact his underlying linguistic competence at each stage of development.' It was not feasible for us to approach large samples of subjects in this way.

Almost all of the linguistic description to be presented in this Monograph consists of a modified and much simplified version of the description made and at present being developed by Professor M. A. K. Halliday, University College, London. It should be pointed out that the categories for the present description were worked out in 1965. For practical purposes it was necessary to 'freeze' the description at that time; as we were coding a large body of data there was not time available for incorporating revised or new categories into the description and for re-working the data once the main analysis had begun. Considerable changes have been made in Halliday's description since that time. Some suggestion of these changes may be gauged from the name that is now used to refer to the description, 'systemic', rather than 'scale-and-category' (relating to the scales 'rank', 'exponence', 'delicacy' and later 'depth' and the categories 'unit', 'structure', 'class' and 'system') or 'system-structure'. Briefly, much greater emphasis has been placed on paradigmatic relations (the realm of the category 'system') and much less emphasis on syntagmatic relations ('structure'), the latter now being fully derived from the former. Our work came too early to draw fully on the new forms of description. So whilst we describe systems, not all the structural representations we give are related to underlying systemic choices. For this reason we shall refer to the grammatical description we used as 'scale-and-category' rather than 'system-structure' or 'systemic' description. Although our main purpose is to describe the grammatical categories that we used, we shall mention, wherever it seems appropriate, the more recent categories, and comment on their usefulness.

The modifications and simplifications mentioned above were made for four main considerations, namely, our sociological interests, computational convenience, the age of the subjects, and coder reliability. From the point of view of the sociological theory certain parts of the grammar were of much more interest than other parts, so, for example, the choices of number and person in the personal pronouns are much more important than, say, the choice of number in the noun. One great advantage of 'scale-and-category' grammar is that it does allow the linguist to vary the amount of detail he goes into in his description by making use of the scale of delicacy. The second consideration was that we intended to make the frequency counts with the aid of a computer. In order to keep the program of a reasonable length, a number of economies were made in the description; for example, tables were restricted to ten entries. It should be added, however, that these restrictions were quite consonant with our general aim which was to make a broad general survey of the data in order to see which were the special areas of promise, worthy of a subsequent more delicate analysis. Some modifications were made because we were dealing with five-year-old children. According to Inhelder and Piaget (1958) children of this age are still generally at the stage of 'preoperational intuitive thinking'. They do not reach the stage of 'formal propositional thinking' until they are eleven years and upwards. We used the divisions of Piaget as a guideline. So, for example, in our sub-classification of binders (subordinating conjunctions), we did not consider it necessary to have separate sub-classes for *granted (that), insofar as, provided that, assuming*

5

(that), etc. Instead, a general category, 'other binders', was set up, just in case binders such as these occurred. In general, then, we were less detailed in our description of those areas of grammar that we did not consider would be exploited by five-year-old children. It should be stressed, though, that we used the divisions from Piaget's theory of cognitive development only as a guideline. We do not mean to imply a complete acceptance of Piaget's position, which would seem to be that language follows cognition rather than precedes it; that language depends on the development of thought processes. We would stress the interdependence of language and cognition, and argue that certain varieties of language may facilitate or inhibit the child's cognitive development. As Bernstein (1961) writes: 'The Piagetian development sequence from concrete to formal operations may not be inevitable for a child restricted to a public language. The child may well be limited to limited concrete options.' Finally, we had to consider the question of coder reliability; there were in fact five researchers coding the data. We did not use any category which did not achieve 80% coder agreement in the tests which were run before the main analysis began. Final coder agreement over categories varied between 80% and 100%.

The chapter which follows gives a brief outline of the linguistic theory on which the present description was based.

Chapter 2

OUTLINE OF THE LINGUISTIC THEORY

2.1 Introductory

The linguistic theory underlying this study is that constructed by Professor M. A. K. Halliday (see especially Halliday, 1961). The theory requires that linguistic events should be comprehended at several different levels as different kinds of patterning are involved. There are three primary levels: substance, form and context. The substance is the raw material of language: 'phonic' (audible noises) or 'graphic' (visible marks). The form is the internal structuring of the substance; its organisation into meaningful events. The context is the relation of form to non-linguistic features in the situations in which language is used. We reproduce below the table given in Halliday, McIntosh and Strevens (1964) which summarises the complete framework of levels:

Subject concerned	Phonetics		Linguistics		
Level (general)	SUBSTANCE (phonic or graphic)	relation of form and substance	FORM	CONTEXT (relation of form and situation)	situation (non-linguistic phenomena)
Level (specific)	PHONETICS	PHONOLOGY	GRAMMAR & LEXIS (vocabulary)	SEMANTICS	
	SCRIPT	'GRAPHOLOGY' (writing system)			

Form, it may be observed, is made up of two 'demi-levels': grammar and lexis. The distinction between these two requires some comment. It is based on recognition of the fact that at different places in the language there are different ranges of possibilities. Grammar accounts for those places where there are closed system choices, that is, those where there is a

7

small fixed number of contrastive possibilities and a clear line between what is possible and what is not; the choice of 'active' or 'passive' in the verbal group is an example of a closed system. Lexis accounts for those places where there are open set choices, that is, those where there is a very large number of possibilities and no clear line separating what is possible from what is not; in a clause such as 'she is a very . . . girl', the blank may be filled by a choice from a very large range of items, including old, sensitive, athletic, domineering, etc.: it is items such as these that are handled by lexis.

Our description is grammatical in the majority of cases; just occasionally it relates to other levels, particularly those of phonology and context. It will be enough to describe the phonological and contextual categories as they occur in the coding frame, but the description of the grammatical ones will benefit from a prior consideration of the grammatical theory underlying them.

2.2 The categories of the grammatical theory

'Scale-and-category' grammar has four theoretical categories, and from these theoretical categories are derived the descriptive categories which are needed for the description of a particular language. The four fundamental categories are: unit, structure, class and system. Each of these will now be explained and illustrated with examples from English grammar, particularly aspects of grammar that are relevant to our work.

2.2a Unit

The category 'unit' is set up to account for the stretches of language that carry grammatical patterns. The units of grammar form a taxonomic hierarchy. In such a hierarchy there is a fixed relation among the members and each member is assigned a place in order in the hierarchy. The relation is one of constituency, such that, going from the highest (largest) to the lowest (smallest), an occurrence of a unit consists of one, or more than one, complete occurrence of the unit next below it. For a description of the English language we require five types of unit: sentence, clause, group, word and morpheme. The sentence consists of one or more complete clauses, the clause of one or more complete groups, and so on. The units that are required for the description of a language are in fact ranged on a scale, the scale of rank. We shall have more to say about this scale, especially when we discuss the categories 'structure' and 'class'.

Now we shall exemplify the five types of unit that are needed for a description of English. We shall take the following sentence:

(1) That dog is trying to escape.
     111   That dog   1   is try+ing   1   to escape   111

8

The boundary symbols are those given by Halliday *et al.* (1964). Briefly, 'that dog is trying to escape' is a sentence which consists of one clause. The clause consists of three groups 'that dog', 'is trying' and 'to escape'. Each group consists of two words. Each word consists of one morpheme, except 'trying', which comprises two morphemes 'try' and 'ing'.

Our system for denoting unit boundaries is based on the Hallidayan system. The two are reproduced alongside below:

Halliday et al.	*Type of Boundary*	*Present writers*
111	sentence boundary	/3
11	clause boundary	/2
1	group boundary	/1
(space)	word boundary	(no space) or/
+	morpheme boundary or fusion of morphemes	not analysed
[[ ]]	boundary of rankshifted clause	〈 /2〉
[ ]	boundary of rankshifted group	〈 /1〉
(( ))	boundary of included clause	(/2)

It should be remembered that in both forms of notation a boundary symbol of higher rank dominates one of lower rank, so, for example, /3 dominates /2. That is why in the example above the clause boundary symbol does not appear: in a sentence which consists of only one clause, the clause boundary symbol is dominated by the co-extensive sentence boundary symbol, so:

not   11   111   or   /2   /3
but   111   /3

In our analysis we carried these boundary symbols two stages further. We recognised /4 'task boundary' and /5 'interview boundary'. So the last sentence in a task received the /4 boundary and the last one of the interview received /5.

Usually, then, a unit operates as part of the unit next above it on the rank scale. However, the theory allows for rankshift. This happens when a unit is shifted down the rank scale, to operate as part of a unit of rank lower than or equal to itself. In the example which follows, 'who are getting married' is a clause acting in group structure:

Those are the people who are getting married.

The clause in question does not add a comment on the whole of the first clause, but rather defines which people are being referred to.

2.2b Structure

We said that the category 'unit' accounts for stretches of language which carry grammatical patterns. 'Structure' is the category with which these patterns are described. 'The patterns take the form of the repetition of like events' (Halliday, 1961). These patterns or structures emerge from the way in which units of the same rank are combined in order to make one unit of a higher rank. Not all possible combinations are used, but each unit above the morpheme displays a range of structures. The morpheme does not have any structures, as the morpheme itself occupies the lowest rank on the rank scale; in other words, there are no units of a lower rank to combine to make morpheme structures.

We say that structures are made up of elements of structure; each element of structure represents a different value, e.g. subject, complement, and this is the value or function that a unit of lower rank has within the structure of a unit of higher rank. In English, position in sequence is an important consideration for determining what value a unit has in a higher unit; the subject and complement, for example, may be efficiently distinguished by this criterion. Sometimes the class of the item is a consideration, for example, *I* may be described as being in the 'subjective case' and *me* as in the 'non-subjective case'

Here are some examples of structures:

(2) He | is climbing | on the train
    S | P | A

(3) She | is buying | some apples
    S | P | C

(4) Railway picture
    Z

(5) He | wants | to start | the train | moving
    S | P | P | Z | P

These are clause structures: five elements of clause structures are mentioned, namely S (Subject), P (Predicator), C (Complement), A (Adjunct) and Z (Z-element). These structural elements and others will be discussed in later sections of the monograph.

When describing structure it is very useful to employ the concept of 'delicacy'. 'Delicacy' is concerned with the amount of detail we choose to go into in our description. Delicacy is a scale (technically, a 'cline', or continuum) upon which different degrees of delicacy may be distinguished. Primary delicacy pertains to the minimal amount of detail; thus Halliday (1961) writes: 'Primary structures are those which distinguish the minimum number of elements necessary to account comprehensively for the operation in the structure of the given unit of members of the unit next below.' So we say, for example, that the nominal group has three primary elements of structure: modifier, head and qualifier.

	M	H	Q
(6)	The	car	over there (i.e. not the one here)
(7)	The	lady	I was telling you about

If we desire to go beyond the minimum amount of detail, to make further differentiations and distinctions, we may move along the scale of delicacy and distinguish secondary elements of structure, and then tertiary elements and so on. Making a move along the scale of delicacy does not imply making a shift on the rank scale: we hold rank constant when we make more delicate statements. The modifier, for example, may be broken down into five secondary elements: deictic, ordinative, epithet, nominal and intensifier. Here are some examples:

(8)	those	two	blue	police	cars	
	M	M	M	M		primary delicacy
	D	O	E	N		secondary delicacy

(9)	some	very	beautiful	trees	
	M	M	M		primary delicacy
	D	I*	E		secondary delicacy

2.2c Class

The category 'class' is used to describe those sets of items that have the same possibilities of operation in the structure of the unit next above on the rank scale. In general, to each element of structure corresponds a different set of items of the rank below. The 'B' (Bound) element in sentence structure is the place of operation of the 'bound clause' class of clauses, whilst the 'F' (Free) element is the place of operation of the 'free clause' class, and so on. Occasionally there is sufficient overlap in the membership of the classes to justify conflating more than one class into one class. Thus, the subject and complement elements in clause structure may be regarded as having the same class in common – the 'nominal group' class.

It will be useful at this point to say something about the relationship between structure and class and the rank scale. Halliday distinguishes between downward and upward movement on the rank scale: 'syntax' is the name given to the downward relation and 'morphology' is the one for

* Our decision to treat the intensifier (or 'submodifier') as being of the same status as the deictic, etc. represents a simplification of the Hallidayan description. Strictly, *very beautiful* is a word complex. cf. Huddleston (1965).

the upward relation. Syntax yields 'classes' and morphology 'types'. Syntactic classes are derived 'from above' (or 'downwards'), and morphological types (structures) are derived 'from below' (or 'upwards'). The following diagram will help to make this clearer:

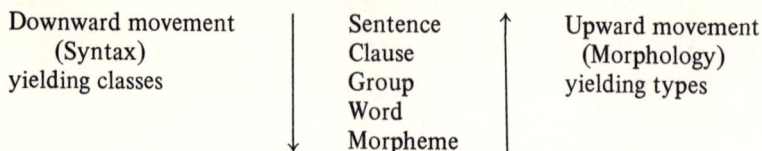

Downward movement (Syntax) yielding classes	Sentence Clause Group Word Morpheme	Upward movement (Morphology) yielding types

So far we have not mentioned that there is a special scale in the theory for relating the categories of the theory to each other and to the stretch of language under description: this is the scale of exponence. Using this scale we may make such statements as: the predicator element is expounded by that class of group called the verbal group. More recently Halliday has preferred to use the term 'realization' instead of 'exponence'*. In keeping with our older form of description, we have generally retained the older name, but have occasionally used the newer one where it seemed stylistically preferable.

If classes are the exponents of elements of structure, then a move in delicacy in the description of the elements necessitates also a move in delicacy in the description of the classes. So, whilst the primary element of structure 'modifier' is expounded by the primary class 'pre-substantive', the secondary elements of structure 'deictic', 'ordinative', 'epithet', 'nominal' and 'intensifier' are expounded by the secondary classes 'determiner', 'numeral', 'adjective', 'noun' and 'sub-modifier' respectively.

2.2d System

Classes of items may be broken down into secondary classes or sub-classes, so that it is possible to say that within a class there exists a choice between a finite number of sub-classes. It is the category 'system' which accounts for such a choice. A system may be recognised whenever there is a small fixed set of mutually exclusive possibilities occurring within a class. By way of illustration we may mention that Halliday (1966b) has recognised sixteen systems operating in the verbal group: these include voice, polarity and tense. Some examples are now given:

---

* cf. Halliday (1966a): 'I use Lamb's term "realisation" instead of the earlier "exponence". Lamb's term is more widely known; it also corresponds closely to my own use, whereas as Palmer (1964) pointed out my use of "exponence" differed materially from that of Firth.'

VOICE →	⎡ passive,	realised by presence of *be/get* + x^{n*} in verbal group, e.g. John was hit, John got hit.
	⎣ active,	realised by all other verbal groups which do not have above, e.g. Bill hit John.

POLARITY →	⎡ negative,	realised by presence of *not* or *n't* in verbal group, e.g. Bill didn't hit John.
	⎣ positive,	realised by all other verbal groups which do not have above, e.g. Bill hit John.

TENSE →	⎡ past,	realised by presence of x^d in verbal group, e.g. Mary cooked yesterday.
	⎢ present,	realised by presence of x^s in verbal group. e.g. Mary cooks to-day.
	⎣ future,	realised by presence of *will* + x^d in verbal group, e.g. Mary will cook tomorrow.

It is the category 'system' that has been developed most in Halliday's recent work. It is the basis for a 'systemic' description. We may refer to Halliday (1967c) for an introduction to this kind of description: '. . . the grammar takes the form of a series of "system networks", each such network representing the choices associated with a given constituent type: clause system network, nominal group (noun phrase) system network and so on. A system is a set of features one, and only one, of which must be selected if the entry condition to that system is satisfied; any selection of features formed from a given system network constitutes the "systemic description" of a class of items. Such a "selection expression" is then realised as a structure, the structural representation being fully derived from the systemic; each element of the structure is a point of entry into a further system network, so that constituency is based on the concept of "rank", with minimal bracketing.' There is not space here to attempt to explain all the new terminology, but it is hoped that it is sufficiently clear that there is an essential compatibility between the concept of system presented by Halliday above and the older formulation which we have given. There is no basic conflict between the two stages in the development of the theory.

---

* This symbol, x^n, and the three symbols given below, x^d, x^s and x^o, are explained in Section 6.2.

2.3 Multivariate and univariate structures

A distinction has to be made between those structures which comprise two
or more different grammatical relations and those which consist of
re-iterations of the same grammatical relation. The former are called
multivariate structures and the latter univariate. Here are some examples:

(10) He │ worked │ hard
    S │ P   │ A

(11) He │ intended │ to start │ to work │ hard
    S │ P   │ -P   │ -P   │ A

(12) He │ worked │ and played │ hard
    S │ P   │ +P   │ A

(10) is an example of a purely multivariate structure; (11) and (12)
exemplify univariate structuring at the predicator (P). Univariate
structuring is recursive. There are two kinds of recursion to be
distinguished: paratactic and hypotactic.* Parataxis is a proportionate or
transitive relation, such that if aRb and bRc, then aRc. Hypotaxis is the
non-proportionate or non-transitive relation, such that if aRb and bRc,
then not aRc. Parataxis may be sub-divided into co-ordination and
apposition. Both co-ordinate units and apposed units may be linked; the
linkers involved are different in either case, *and*, *but*, *or*, etc., being
common markers of co-ordination and *that is* a common marker of
apposition.

    A note must be added here about one of the descriptive conventions we
adopted. We decided to indicate that a recursive structure occurred at a
particular element by repeating the element and preceding it with a
symbol which indicated the particular kind of recursion involved. It was
convenient to do it this way, as the units involved, say, nominal groups,
could be referred to their relevant tables in the usual way, and this
considerably simplified the computer programming. However, it has to be
admitted that this convention, unless it is carefully understood, can be
misleading. Basically, when there is a series of elements, such as S + S + S
or S = S, there is only one value realised, here S; these are just ways of
symbolising that a number of units are realising the same value.

    The theory behind this description is set out very clearly in Huddleston
(1965). He distinguishes what he calls 'basic units' and 'supplementary
units'. Here are these units listed:

---

* In the above examples, hypotactic recursion is symbolised by the minus sign, '−',
and co-ordinate paratactic recursion by the plus sign, '+'. We should add that
appositional paratactic recursion is symbolised in our analysis by the equals sign,
'='.

'Basic unit'	'Supplementary unit'
sentence	
clause	clause complex
group	group complex
word	word complex
morpheme	morpheme complex

'Basic units have "multivariate" structures in the sense that the structures contain a number of distinct grammatical relations.' 'Supplementary units on the other hand have linearly recursive structures where there is (potentially) repetition of a single grammatical relation.' So in Huddleston's terms, then, 'intended to start to work' in (11) is a group complex.

Huddleston does point out that there may be repetition in multivariate structures, but in these structures 'it is a question of there being more than one occurrence of (what is, up to a given degree of delicacy) the same element'. He gives the following example and comment:

(13) He | lived | in London | for five years.
S | P | A | A

'What we are saying by assigning this structure is that *in London* and *for five years* have the same primary value, viz. adjunct, in the clause. We show thus what they have in common before distinguishing them at secondary delicacy as place adjunct and time (more delicately still, time-duration) adjunct respectively.'

In our analysis, recursive structures in which there is the repetition of a single grammatical relation are marked by repeating the element of structure involved and by preceding it by '+', '−' or '=', and multivariate structures in which there is more than one occurrence of the same element are marked simply by repeating the element (there being no question of preceding it with '+', '−' or '=').

2.4 Co-ordination and branching

Although what we shall say about co-ordination and branching will be more a matter of linguistic description than of linguistic theory, it will be convenient to deal with these two areas of grammar in this chapter.

Co-ordination takes place between units of the same rank, as, for example, clause and clause, group and group. Rankshifted units, we should point out, co-ordinate at the rank they are rankshifted to, so, if a clause is rankshifted to act as if it were a word, then it may co-ordinate with a word.

It is a feature of 'scale-and-category' grammar that the same item can be accounted for at more than one rank. So, the formal item 'Help!', if it is a

15

whole utterance, is one sentence which is one clause which is one group which is one word which is one morpheme. When a series of units may be accounted for at more than one rank, at what rank should we recognise co-ordination? The general rule is to keep co-ordination down to the lowest rank possible. The lowest rank possible is that at which two or more units of the same class can be generally regarded as co-ordinated *without* any other units of a different class interrupting them. We shall now consider some examples:

(14) The boy and girl.

(15) The fat boy and thin girl.

Boy and *girl* in example (14) may be analysed as two co-ordinate noun words at the head, but in example (15) the lowest rank possible for recognising co-ordination is group rank: we cannot again analyse *boy* and *girl* as co-ordinate noun words because a word of a different class, *thin*, an adjective, interrupts them. This rule at first sight may have the appearance of being arbitrary but in fact there are good reasons for it. Let us consider another example:

(16) The boy and thin girl.

If we analysed *boy* and *girl* as co-ordinate nouns at head, and *thin* as modifier, we would be implying that both the *boy* and *girl* are *thin*, whereas in fact the structure expressly distinguishes them. Examples in which the adjective precedes the second noun are unambiguous, but those in which the adjective precedes the first noun are ambiguous:

(17) The thin boy and girl.

In cases such as this, one has to look for clues in the surrounding language or in the non-language context to disambiguate the structure. If the meaning is 'both the boy and girl are thin' then the structure is 'two co-ordinate nouns at head', but if the meaning is 'the boy is thin, but not the girl' then the structure is 'two co-ordinate nominal groups'.

Above we defined 'the lowest rank possible' in terms of interruption. It may be further specified in terms of the concept of presupposition or branching. Branching occurs when an element of structure (a value) operates in more than one unit. Consider this sentence:

(18) I went home and sat down.

In this sentence *I* has the structural value 'subject' in both clauses: it is actually present in substance only in the first clause, but it is regarded as being branched in relation to the second clause. The unbranched version of the sentence is as follows:

(19) I went home and I sat down.

16

What is the relation between co-ordination and branching? Briefly, we can say that if there is a branching relation, units are co-ordinated at the same rank as the unit which is involved in a branching relation with them, provided that there is not an item of a different class interrupting them. Here are some further examples to make this clearer:

(20) Boys and girls.   two co-ordinate nominal groups; no branching.

(21) A boy and girl.   one nominal group with two co-ordinate nouns; *a* is branched in relation to *girl* because *girl* could not occur without it. The co-ordination is at word rank because the branched item, *a*, is a word.

If there is an item of a different class interrupting them, then the co-ordination has to be at one rank higher than that of the branched item, so:

(22) A fat boy and thin girl.   two co-ordinate nominal groups; *a* is branched, but *thin* interrupts.

The convention adopted in our analysis for showing branching is to mark in the branched item but to precede it by an asterisk (*), so:

(23) A | fat | boy | and | thin | girl.
     D | E | H | +*D | E | H

A further convention is that elements preceded by an asterisk are not to be subclassified. In the above example the first 'D' element would be subclassified ('D8' in fact) but the second one would not be.

Before concluding this discussion of co-ordination and branching, we shall first comment on the status of linking items, *and*, *but*, *or*, etc. and *that is*. In our analysis when these items linked word and word, or group and group, they were regarded as purely structural markers. In other words, they were regarded as items signalling either co-ordinate or appositional structures but not themselves actually entering into these structures. However, when they linked clause and clause, they were analysed as entering into the structure of the second clause. This analysis is essentially arbitrary, but a number of reasons can be given in support of it. One reason is that if there is likely to be any variation in the linking items used (that is, if there are likely to be any items other than *and* used), then this variation, in five-year-old children's speech, is much more likely to be associated with clause linkage than with group or word linkage. Moreover, this variation is not an isolated phenomenon: to a certain extent it parallels variation that occurs elsewhere, particularly in the binding items. This kind of parallelism may be illustrated by *although* and *but* in the following two sentences:

17

(24) Although I am busy, I will do it.

(25) I am busy, but I will do it.

These, then, are reasons for regarding the items which link one clause to another as operating at a clause element and for distinguishing subclasses of them, just as we do in the case of items which bind one clause to another.

2.5 Summary

So far we have discussed the choice of the linguistic theory (Chapter 1) and have outlined its main features (Chapter 2). We have already introduced some descriptive decisions. The main aim of the next five chapters is to give the descriptive decisions we reached for five main areas of grammar: the sentence, the clause, the nominal group, the verbal group and the adjunctival group. In each area the descriptive categories are explained and their relevance for the present research discussed. Wherever possible an attempt has been made to relate the linguistic categories to sociological and psychological categories, thus, for example, certain linguistic patterns are associated with certain modes of social control and/or certain modes of cognition. The discussion in the nature of things is bound to be speculative at times. The purpose of including such discussion is to stimulate further research in these areas.

Chapter 3

THE SENTENCE

3.1 Introductory

Many previous investigators, including McCarthy (1930), Day (1932), Davis (1937) and Templin (1957), have come to the conclusion that length of sentence or response is the most useful and reliable measure of linguistic development. Bernstein (1959), postulating some of the characteristics of a public language and some of those of a formal language (later Restricted and Elaborated Codes respectively), makes several references to features of the sentence. The public language has 'short, grammatically simple, often unfinished sentences, a poor syntactical construction with a verbal form stressing the active mood'. There is 'simple and repetitive use of conjunctions (*so, then, and, because*)'. Moreover, 'the individual qualification is implicit in sentence structure'. In the formal language almost the opposite is the case, as 'logical modifications and stress are mediated through a grammatically complex sentence construction, especially through the use of a range of conjunctions and relative clauses'. 'Individual qualification,' Bernstein writes, 'is verbally mediated through the structure of relationships within and between sentences. That is, it is explicit.'

3.2 Definition of the Sentence

It has often been pointed out that it is extremely difficult to define a sentence. Though, certainly, there has been no shortage of attempts at definition; Fries (1952) considers numerous conceptions before presenting his own (in which he replaces *sentence* by utterance). But Fries himself is described by Sledd (1955) as boxing a 'noisy but inconclusive round' with traditional notions of the sentence. Bernstein (1962b) in one of his experimental studies excluded a comparison of differences in sentence length 'as no reliable method for distinguishing the samples on this measure was available'. A measure of sentence was included by Lawton (1963) but he regarded it as of doubtful validity for two reasons: 'first, no-one has provided a definition of a sentence which would eliminate the investigator's subjective judgment' and 'second, mean sentence length masks very important differences in internal sentence structure.' For it is possible to produce long sentences simply by joining many clauses together, loosely, by *and* and other common conjunctions.

The scepticism of previous investigators was shared in large measure by the present researchers, but we were encouraged by some recent doctoral work by Hasan (1964). Hasan's definition of the sentence is primarily grammatical. She postulates two primary elements of sentence structure: the 'presupposing' and the 'non-presupposing' elements. Basically, the presupposing element cannot stand by itself. It demands the presence of another element which could stand by itself in order to make a complete sentence. The element that can stand by itself is, of course, the non-presupposing element. Thus, a stretch of language such as

(1) I'll come if I can

can be described as having two sentence elements, one 'non-presupposing' ('I'll come') and one 'presupposing' ('if I can'). A similar description can be given to the following:

(2) I'll come and I'll bring some drinks.

There is, of course, a big difference between 'if I can' and 'and I'll bring some drinks'. In traditional terms the former is a subordinate clause and the latter is a co-ordinate main clause. One way of distinguishing the two classes of clause is in terms of their potentialities for recursion. Recursion is to do with the repetition of a grammatical relation. Hasan defines two kinds of recursive structure in the sentence:

'i, Recursive structure where primarily sequence does not determine the presupposed – presupposing relationship between elements. This is called "dependence recursion".

'ii, Recursive structure where sequence primarily determines the presupposed – presupposing relationship. This is called "linking recursion".'

Hasan sets up a scale of depth in order to describe dependence recursion, the terms being B, C, D etc. By using examples from her texts, she demonstrates two things: one, that structures such as $\overleftrightarrow{BCF}$, $\overrightarrow{BFB}$ and $\overleftarrow{FBCD}$ are possible (where the 'F' symbol stands for the 'non-presupposing' or 'free' element and where the arrows indicate the direction of the presupposition relation), thus showing how 'dependence recursion' is independent of sequence; and two, that structures such as FBC + C are possible (where the '+' sign indicates that the second 'C' element is related by 'linking recursion' to the first 'C' element), thus showing that at any place on the scale of depth of 'dependence recursion', the dependence recursion may be arrested and linking recursion begin. Here are some example sentences from Hasan to illustrate these points:

20

(3) Even when the twins Fred and Joe
(who dealt so deviously in scrap . . .)
were fetched away by two giraffe-like policemen,
the drama had dwindled down into defeat.

Sentence structure $\overrightarrow{\underline{B}\ (\underline{C})}$ F
(where the brackets indicate inclusion)

(4) I think
we had a kind of faith
that the policemen would be gone
and that nothing would embarrass us.

Sentence structure F B C + C
We may update Hasan's terminology a little and replace it by Halliday's. Instead of 'linking recursion' and 'dependence recursion' Halliday talks of parataxis and hypotaxis. Parataxis, as we mentioned in section 2.3, is described as a transitive relation, such that, if aRb and bRc, then aRc, whereas hypotaxis is non-transitive, so that, if aRb and bRc, then not aRc. Parataxis may be subdivided into co-ordination and apposition. Co-ordination is markable by the insertion of *and*, whilst apposition is markable by the insertion of *that is*.

To return to the definition of the two classes of clause that can occur in sentence structure, we may say that a clause that can operate at the 'non-presupposing' element, that is, a clause that can stand by itself, is a free clause, and a clause that operates at a 'pre-supposing' element which is in a relation of hypotaxis is a bound clause. Following Hasan we call the 'non-presupposing' element 'Free' (F) and the hypotactic 'presupposing' element 'Bound' (B). Any clause at the 'presupposing' element which is in a paratactic relationship with a free clause is either a co-ordinate free clause or an appositional free clause, whereas any clause which is in a paratactic relationship with a bound clause is either a co-ordinate or an appositional bound clause. These clauses operate at elements '+F', '=F', '+B' and '=B' respectively.

To sum up, a sentence may be either simple or compound. A simple sentence consists of one free clause (F). A compound sentence consists of one free clause plus one or more free clauses which are attached to it in a paratactic relation, i.e. either co-ordinate (+F) or appositional (=F), and/or one or more bound clauses (B) which are bound in a hypotactic relation. Moreover, in the case of the bound clauses the hypotactic relation may be arrested and a paratactic relation begin between bound clause and bound clause (+B or =B).*

It is possible to measure the amount of recursion in a sentence by means of a scale of 'depth'. It is usual to represent paratactic recursion by

* In subsequent Unit work, this notion of a sentence was expressed in more concrete terms and an algorithm was devised for instructing the coders.

21

means of Arabic numerals, 1 2 3 etc. and hypotactic recursion by means of letters of the Greek alphabet, α β γ etc. (cf. Huddleston, 1965). We could have included these measures (with different symbolism) but we decided not to, as it was thought that five-year-old children would be unlikely to use much depth of the kind we were particularly interested in, that is, depth in hypotactic recursion.

That such a measure would be useful for older children is suggested by such work as that of Lawton (1963, 1964). Lawton actually made use of the Loban Weighted Index of Subordination (Loban, 1961), which divides all subordinate clauses into four categories, and assigns points according to their order of dependence and according to other information. This use of weighting is suggestive, and it is hoped that it might be possible eventually to arrive at scales of complexity for other areas of grammar, for example, clause structure and nominal group structure. One difficulty with weighting systems, as Lawton points out, is that an individual could score highly simply by using a lightly weighted category a sufficiently large number of times. This is one of the problems that has to be overcome.

3.3 Contextual function of the sentence

It is possible to classify sentences according to their contextual function. Sinclair (1965) suggests four contextual types of sentence: statements, questions, commands and responses. He gives the following examples of these classes:

(5) I have to go before Bill gets here.   Statement

(6) Did you say I was to switch it off?   Question

(7) Move along a bit if you can, please.   Command

(8) Maybe on Tuesday, which suits me fine.   Response

As these examples illustrate, it is the first clause, the free clause, which correlates with the contextual type; the bound clause is not related in most cases. We shall see when we discuss the clause that it is the 'mood' system in the free clause which provides the relevant options. Halliday (1967d) writes: 'Mood represents the organisation of participants in speech situations, providing options in the form of speaker roles: the speaker may inform, question or command; he may confirm, request confirmation, contradict or display any one of a wide range of postures defined by the potentialities of linguistic interaction.' Later he adds: 'Given the clause as domain . . . mood is the grammar of speech function.' From this it would follow that a discussion of contextual function is best left until we describe the clause. However, for purposes of processing the data for the computer it was found convenient to handle two of the contextual functions we were interested in as part of the sentence

22

information. We were interested in response sentences ('answers') and textshifted sentences ('direct speech'). The response sentences are answers to questions which are systemically and structurally dependent on the interviewer's question, e.g.

(9) Interviewer: What are they doing?
       Subject: Walking down the street.

The textshifted or 'direct speech' sentences occur when a subject indulges in role-play, e.g.

(10) Mummy said, 'Who's eaten our dinner?'

We shall discuss each of these contextual types in turn, and delimit the conditions under which sentences were regarded as being dependent on the interviewer's question or as expressing a particular kind of role-play.

3.3a Response sentences

In the interview situation the children were asked about 30 questions, almost all of which are of the WH-word type (that is, of the information-seeking rather than the confirmation-seeking type) and almost 20 probes were available for when the child either completely refused or only partially attempted to reply to the original questions. Part of the Trotin Coloured Picture Cards task will illustrate this. First, the child was given time to look at the picture and to make unsolicited comments, and then he was asked:

What is going on in this picture?

The interviewer, after having given the child time to make a response, next asked:

What's happening?

If the child said very little, the interviewer gave the following probes in turn:

Tell me what you can see.
What are they doing?
What else is going on?

The questions and probes on the Trotin task are typical of the Speech Schedule. The majority of them in the Speech Schedule began with *what* and have *is/are + -ing* in the verbal group, that is, they select 'present in present' tense. The structural value of *what* is not the same in all the questions; in fact three values are realised:

Subject, as in

What's happening?

Complement

What are they doing?
cf. They are doing what?

Prepositional Complement

What are they talking about?
cf. They are talking about what?

When *what* is either complement or prepositional complement, the person answering may omit at least the subject and part of the predicator (the auxiliary verb) from his reply, for these may be quite legitimately presupposed from the question put to him. For example,

(11) Interviewer: What are they doing?
     Subject: Walking down the street.
                  cf. They are walking down the street.

(12) Interviewer: What are they talking about?
     Subject: Their holidays.
                  cf. They are talking about their holidays.

It is possible for the child to make two main types of error: one, omission of the subject when *what* has this value, and, two, failure to maintain tense concord. Examples of these errors are now given:

(13) Interviewer: What's happening?
     Subject: Walking down the street.

(14) Interviewer: What are they doing?
     Subject: Walked down the street.

It was thought that the avoidance of errors such as these suggested a fairly advanced linguistic control. It was also thought that the use of a response sentence could at times have positive advantages — those of conciseness and precision. An example of this in the Toy Elephant task is:

(15) Interviewer: How does it work?
     Subject: By air pressure.

Having given some illustration of what we mean by a response sentence, we may now define the category more clearly and relate it to the conceptions of other linguists. In the first place it is important to stress that a response sentence is not just a sentence with a minor free clause, that is, a predicator-less clause. From the limited number of examples given in Sinclair one might get the impression that — although the minor

24

clause is associated with all four of the contextual functions and some more which he labels 'unmarked', namely, a title, an exclamation, an introduction – the contextual function 'response' is associated with the minor clause only.* We do not limit our category 'response sentence' in this way, as can be seen from the examples we have discussed above.

The question arises: whether a response sentence ever has a minor free clause. To answer this question, it is first necessary to re-iterate the distinction previously made between substance and form. Substance is either 'phonic' or 'graphic': in the former case it is audible noises and in the latter visible marks. Form is two related demi-levels: 'grammar' and 'lexis'. Grammar, with which we are essentially concerned, is that level of linguistic form at which operate closed systems. Now, from the point of view of linguistic substance, certain response sentences may be regarded as having the same item in substance as a sentence with a minor free clause, e.g.

(16) Interviewer: Tell me what you can see.
      Subject: A man.

But from the point of view of linguistic form these response sentences may be regarded as having an elliptical major free clause. So in the example given above 'a man' is an elliptical form of 'I can see a man', and the clause does not have the structure Z (that is, a nominal group that is indeterminate as to subject or complement status) but the structure S P C (subject, predicator, complement, where the subject-predicator part is presupposed from the interviewer's speech). Grammatically, then, 'a man' is part of a major free clause, realising certain systemic choices in the transitivity system. What we have said about 'a man' is also true for other apparently minor answers to questions. We may sum up this paragraph as follows: an elliptical clause is not a minor clause and a response sentence which has ellipsis at clause rank cannot have a minor clause.

Hasan (1968) as part of her account of grammatical cohesion provides an extremely valuable description of ellipsis, which is one of the four major ways of securing cohesion in a text. (The other ways are by reference, substitution and conjunction). In a chapter on 'Clausal Ellipsis' she deals with the contextual function 'answer'. It will be helpful to present her summary chart of the different types of answers at the outset of our discussion.

---

* Relationships between sentences are beyond the scope of Sinclair's work, as he points out on page 1: 'Our grammar starts with the sentence as its largest unit. There are patterns of a grammatical kind which link one sentence to another, patterns like the reference of pronouns, the linking of items like *therefore*, *well*, *ah!*, and the intricacies of questions and answers. But we are not going to deal with these in this book.'

```
                                                        ┌Affirmation
                                       ┌Direct────→     ├Negation
                                       │                └Specification
                    ┌Answer────→       │
                    │                  │                ┌Implicit
      ┌Response ──→ │                  └Indirect────→   │            ┌Refusal
      │             └Rejoiner                           └Explicit→│
      │                                                          └Disclaimer
Statement→│
      │             ┌Non-sequitur
      └Non-response→│
                    └Connected
```

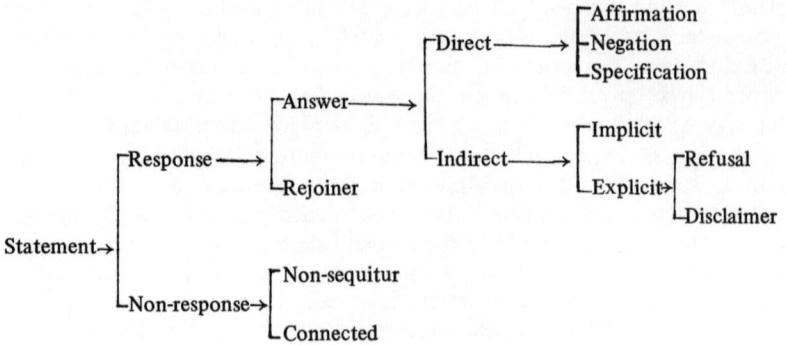

Briefly, the treatment is to sub-divide statements into 'response statements' and 'non-response statements'. At least two active participants in the linguistic activity are required for a response statement, e.g.

> (17) Leave me alone!
>   I won't.

Just one active participant is characteristic of a non-response statement, as in, e.g., a narrative text. A non-response statement may occur, though, when there are two participants if the second participant makes no reference to the immediately preceding speech of the first participant. Both the response and non-response statements are sub-divided by Hasan, but we shall concentrate on the response sub-categories as these are the ones that are directly relevant to our study.

A response statement may be an answer or a rejoinder. Of these two sub-categories it is the answer one that interests us. An answer always makes a reference to a preceding *question* whereas a rejoinder is not so limited. Furthermore, the answers to a given question may be predicted by making reference to the features of the question clause, but rejoinders are not predictable in this way. Here are two examples given by Hasan:

> (18) Did he call on me yesterday?   Question clause
>   Yes, he did.   Answer

> (19) It looks as if it's going to rain.
>   I mustn't forget my umbrella when I go out.   Rejoinder

An answer may be sub-divided into 'direct answer' and 'indirect answer'. A direct answer may be an affirmation, negation or specification of the question. Affirmation and negation relate to confirmation-seeking questions only, the 'yes/no' type. As we have mentioned above, almost all of the questions in the interview schedule are not of this type, but are the information-seeking WH-word type. It is the specification answer that relates to this type: it specifies that which is questioned by the

WH-interrogative item in the question clause. The following example of a specification answer is given by Hasan:

(20) Why didn't you tell John?
     He wasn't there.   Specification answer

It should be noted that 'He wasn't there' is elliptical, the non-elliptical parallel being 'I didn't tell John because he wasn't there.'

An indirect answer may be implicit or explicit, and if it is explicit it may be a refusal or a disclaimer. We shall not consider the implicit ones here, as only confirmation-seeking questions may be answered implicitly. Of the explicit indirect answers it is the refusal rather than the disclaimer that is likely to be used by the children in our interview situation. Here are some examples of the sorts of refusal that the children give to a question such as: 'What is the boy saying?':

(21) I don't know.

(22) I can't say.

(23) I haven't any idea.

These refusals express such things as lack of the required knowledge and inability or unwillingness to impart such knowledge.

To summarise this discussion, then, two of the six types of answer that are described by Hasan seem of particular relevance to our research. These two types are the specification direct answer and the refusal explicit indirect answer. We shall now briefly consider the kinds of ellipsis that are associated with these two types.

Concerning the first type, Hasan writes: 'Specification answers are elliptical only if they are represented by a group whose function in the answer clause is the same as that of the WH-item in the query clause.' She draws special attention to those questions with what she calls pro-verb *do*, e.g.

What did he do?

This is of special interest to us, as on four of the six tasks in the interview schedule the children are asked at least one question of this type:

What are they all doing?

Now they're sitting at table, what are they doing? (Model room)

What are they doing?   (Trotin)

What do you think he/she did?

Tell me *all* about what he did for the whole day.   (Story completion)

. . . I want you to tell me what the elephant is doing.
                                             (Toy elephant)

The interesting thing about questions of this type is that *do what* together form a specification query for the verb. The elliptical clause in answer to such a query must have a verb in it and it may or may not have a complement, e.g.

(24) Interviewer: Tell me *all* about what he did for the whole day.
     Subject: Just played.

Hasan points out that this type of answer ellipsis is the only ellipsis in English where the subject alone can be presupposed.

A clause such as 'What are they all doing?' is potentially ambiguous: *do* may be interpreted as a pro-verb, as in (24), or as a lexical verb. If the latter interpretation is put on it, then a group with the function of complement in the clause could be given in answer, so:

(25) What are they all doing?
     Their jobs.
 cf. They are all doing their jobs.

The second type of answer we are interested in, the refusal, has the options of reportage ellipsis and zero ellipsis available to it. These types of ellipsis are exemplified by the following two answers that may be given as replies to 'What's the man saying?':

(26) I don't know what.   Reportage ellipsis.

(27) I don't know.   Zero ellipsis.

Having outlined this recent work by Hasan on answers and answer ellipsis, we shall now give our own treatment. Generally, wherever a feature or value was presupposed from the interviewer's speech a response sentence was recognised (coded as S3): the exceptions to this statement will be discussed below. The presupposed could pertain to the sentence, e.g. a free clause; the clause, e.g. the subject and predicator; and the group, e.g. the preposition in a prepositional group. As our aim was to make a broad survey of the data we did not sub-classify the response sentences into various types.

We treated inadequacy signals (Hasan's refusals) and elliptical specification answers of the type 'complement with pre-supposed subject and predicator' differently from the above. They are the exceptions.

There were two main reasons why we treated these differently. In the first place the facts concerning ellipsis were not fully known at that time. If we were making a study of ellipsis now, Hasan's description would be a valuable reference work. Secondly, there seemed certain practical advantages to be derived from not coding the above phenomena under the response sentence category. We shall now discuss each of the phenomena in turn.

In our description the inadequacy signals were sub-divided into two types: 'I don't know' (or 'Dunno') versus the rest, e.g. 'I don't know

28

what', 'I don't know what he's saying', 'I haven't any idea'. We found it convenient to code 'I don't know' as a sub-class of tag clause and to code the rest as a sub-class of free clause (more precisely a sub-class of statement). This was just a coding convenience: we did not mean to imply that 'I don't know' was a tag.

We regarded the inadequacy signals as indicating an inability or unwillingness to answer the interviewer's question; in other words to give the required information. It did not seem appropriate to code this speech in the same way as we coded the speech that actually gave the information desired. So we did not mark the child who said 'I don't know', 'I don't know what', etc., as displaying his elliptical competence, but only as refusing for some reason or other to answer the question. These refusals, by the way, prompt the question whether it is possible to over-credit a child with linguistic competence. We may ask, for example, what is the non-elliptical parallel of 'I don't know' when it is given in answer to 'What do you *think* he might be saying?'. Presumably, the non-elliptical parallel is 'I don't know what I think he might be saying' or 'I don't know what to think he might be saying'. Intuitively, it perhaps seems a little unsatisfactory to credit the child with presupposing all these features.

The elliptical specification answers of this type 'complement with presupposed subject and predicator' were not coded as response sentences for a number of reasons. One, it seemed difficult to imagine that a child could make a wrong choice here: for example, there is no question of having to make a particular tense selection, to maintain tense concord. Two, on the Trotin task the children are asked 'Tell me what you can see'; in reply to this request the children sometimes give a list of nominal groups. Sometimes a number of such lists are given, either consecutively or with other clauses intervening. If we were to assign the first list of nominal groups the value complement in respect of their relationship with *see*, what value should we assign to the other lists of nominal groups, especially those occurring after intervening clauses? In other words, what sort of span should be allowed for the presupposition relation? We did not resolve these questions. In our analysis, we coded as Z ('absolute nominal') and not as C ('complement') the nominal groups that were given in response to such questions and probes as the following:

What's your favourite programme — your best programme?

Tell me what you can see.

and the *do* questions when *do* was interpreted as a lexical verb.

A special word has to be added about the treatment of the answers to the following two questions which were asked together on the Trotin task:

What shall we call this picture?

What name shall we give it?

The most usual reply to these questions is a nominal group such as 'A wedding'. The nominal group specifies *what* and/or *what name* and so, it could be argued, has the value 'complement' in an elliptical clause. A more delicate description would have to mention that 'A wedding' has the value 'objective complement' or 'appositional direct object', depending on whether it is regarded as replacing *what* or *what name*. This analysis was not adopted here. We did not regard such answers as response sentences for two reasons. The first reason has already been given in our earlier discussion of this 'complement with presupposed subject and predicator' construction: there seemed little possibility of a child making an error here. The second reason is rather more complicated: basically, it was thought that if we decided that in most cases answers to these questions were assigned the value complement, we would have to recognise many more rankshifted clauses than seemed justifiable. So, such answers as 'At the market' and 'Going to the market' would be regarded as rankshifted clauses operating at the complement element. We were reluctant to analyse items such as these as rankshifted clauses, as we wished to associate rankshift with difficulty, and there seemed nothing particularly difficult about these answers. We thought that they were best regarded as quotations – quoted titles. One way of capturing this feature was to analyse them as textshifted sentences, i.e. S2. So, for example, 'A wedding' would be described as a textshifted sentence consisting of a minor free clause with the simple structure Z.

Before concluding this section we may perhaps mention the distinction that Lyons (1968) makes between contextual completeness and grammatical completeness. Lyons argues that *John's if he gets here in time* (which might occur after *whose car are you going in?*) and *Got the tickets?* are both elliptical, that is, 'shorter forms of some longer version of the same sentence', but they are 'elliptical' in a different sense. *'John's, if he gets here in time* is grammatically incomplete; that is to say, it is not a sentence, and therefore is not to be described directly by the grammar, but by supplementary rules (if such rules can be established) which account for the deletion of contextually-determined elements in the sentences from which the utterances of connected discourse are derived. On the other hand, *Got the tickets?* (in British English at least) is a sentence (and in that sense it is 'complete'); the ellipsis that is involved in its derivation from the alternative version of the same sentence *Have you got the tickets?* is purely a matter of grammar and is independent of the wider context.' There is not space here to enter into a discussion of the points that Lyons' analysis raises. The main points of difference in the treatment of the response type of ellipsis are perhaps clear. In Hasan's terms *John's if he gets here in time* is a sentence; it is grammatically complete, its incompleteness being at the level of substance, not at the level of form.

3.3b Textshifted sentences

Our main interest in the textshifted sentences was their connection with role-play. It has been suggested by Bernstein that the middle-class home environment tends to make children more sensitive to different roles. It has also been suggested that the Elaborated Code may be defined in relation to the range of options within a role and that it may be a product of access to a wide variety of roles. For these reasons, it was considered that it would be worthwhile examining to what extent role-play was indulged in by the two classes.

For our initial survey, here, we restricted our analysis to what we might call 'role-play speech'; this occurs when a child purports to give or report the speech of others. We restricted ourselves to this type of role-play for the initial analysis partly because it is relatively easily defined and partly because in two parts of the Speech Schedule the children were explicitly prompted to give this type of speech. In the Model Room task the children were asked:

What are they talking about?
(that is, when the mother and father dolls are sitting in the armchairs) and

What are they saying to each other?

What are they talking about?
(when the family are sitting at table).

Also, in the Picture Story task, they were asked five questions of the 'what does X say?' kind (concerning most of the principal characters of the stories). Furthermore, on this task, if a child said 'I don't know', he was probed with 'What do you think he *might* be saying?' The children, of course, had the option of using role-play speech spontaneously on other parts of the Speech Schedule. In a more delicate analysis, a comparison of the relative proportions of the spontaneously uttered role-play speech and the probed role-play speech would be of considerable interest.

There are two ways of presenting the speech of others: one may do it directly or indirectly. We may quote Jespersen (1924) on this distinction: 'Either one gives, or purports to give, the exact words of the speaker (or writer): *direct speech* (oratio recta), or else one adapts the words according to the circumstances in which they are now quoted: *indirect speech* (oratio obliqua).' The difference between the two kinds may be illustrated by the following two sentences:

(28) She said: 'You are very naughty boys.'

(29) She said they were very naughty boys.

We decided to distinguish the two in our description by treating the

31

former kind, that is, direct quoted speech, in terms of 'textshift',* and the latter kind, that is, indirect reported speech, in terms of 'rankshift'. So, in (28) 'You are very naughty boys' is a textshifted sentence following the (introductory) sentence 'She said'. Whilst in (29) 'they were very naughty boys' is a rankshifted clause occurring as complement in the clause 'She said they were very naughty boys'.

Jespersen distinguishes two kinds of indirect speech, which he calls 'dependent' and 'represented'. The dependent kind is illustrated in (29). The represented kind, which has also been called 'erlebte rede' by Lorck and 'style indirect libre' by Bally, is characteristic of literary language, particularly of the novel and short story. Jespersen quotes Thackeray to exemplify this type of speech:

> (30) '. . . he thought of what he had done . . . his wounded tutor, his many duns, the undergraduates of his own time and the years below him, whom he had patronised and scorned – how could he bear to look any of them in the face now?'

To throw further light on the three kinds of speech we shall present the last clause in the above quotation as it appears in each of the three forms:

(31) Direct speech: How can I bear to look any of them in the face now?

(32) Dependent speech: He wondered how he could bear to look any of them in the face now.

(33) Represented speech: How could he bear to look any of them in the face now?

It was thought that the third kind could be discounted for five-year-old children's language, as it represents a sophisticated literary usage. So no category was incorporated into the description to cover it. At the same time, it must be admitted, we would not have been surprised if some inexperienced children, mixing up direct and dependent speech, had produced some very close approximations to represented speech. However, there is no point in calling such anacolutha represented speech.

Now taking the two kinds of role-play speech that we recognised, are there any reasons for thinking that one kind is more difficult than the other? In our opinion, there are such reasons. It will be remembered that in his definition of indirect speech Jespersen mentions that one adapts the words according to the circumstances in which they are being quoted. It is thought that these adaptations make indirect speech relatively more difficult than direct speech. In English these adaptations are effected by the following means:

* The term 'textshift' is borrowed from Halliday, but for purposes of the present analysis we have restricted its scope to the sentence.

The person is shifted,

The tense is shifted,

The form of the question is changed,

The form of a command or request is changed.

It will be sufficient here just to illustrate these adaptations by means of examples; for a fuller discussion the reader is referred to Jespersen. Here are some examples:

Shift of person

(a direct first person is turned according to circumstances to an indirect second person or an indirect third person, etc.)

(34) Direct statement (A speaking to B):
'I am glad of your agreement with him' (i.e. C).

(35) Indirect (A speaking to C):
He said I was glad of his agreement with you.

(36) Indirect (B speaking to A):
You said you were glad of my agreement with him.

(37) Indirect (B speaking to C):
He said he was glad of my agreement with you.

(38) Indirect (C speaking to A):
You said you were glad of his agreement with me.

Shift of tense

(39) I am unhappy.   (Direct)

(40) He said he was unhappy.   (Indirect)

(41) I met John the other day.   (Direct)

(42) He said he had met John the other day. (Indirect)

Briefly, if the reporting verb is in the past tense, the verb in the reported clause is often shifted into a past tense form. This is, however, by no means always the case (see Palmer, 1965).

Questions in indirect speech

(43) 'Where's Peter?'   (Direct)

(44) He asked where Peter was.   (Indirect)

Notice the lexical verb, *ask*, and the change in sequence in the reported clause, the subject occurring before the predicator.

Commands and requests in indirect speech

	(45)	'Go away!'	(Direct)
Either	(46)	He ordered (commanded, asked, requested, etc.) her to go away.	(Indirect)
or	(47)	He said she was to go away.	(Indirect)

Commands and requests are signalled in indirect speech either by a lexical verb, e.g. *order*, *ask*, etc., as in (46) or by a modal, especially *to be*, as in (47).

There is another difference between direct and indirect speech that is not mentioned by Jespersen. It is possible to adapt a sentence containing indirect speech to a change of circumstances, in a different sense from that suggested by Jespersen. One can indicate what the consequences of a particular speech act were; compare:

(48) He said: 'You are wrong, Jane.'

and (49) He persuaded Jane that she was wrong.

Austin (1962) calls utterances of the first type, represented by (48), 'locutionary acts' and those of the second type, represented by (49), 'perlocutionary acts'.

It is hoped that this section has indicated the value of examining role-play speech and of distinguishing that which occurs in a direct quoted form from that which occurs in an indirect reported form. The information for coding the former kind is given in section 3.5 and for coding the latter in section 6.7.

3.4 Sentence complexity

All sentences were subdivided in terms of nine generalised types. As it was expected that the response sentences would have a more restricted range of structures than the non-response sentences, they were given a separate table. This, then, yielded two tables of nine types.

The nine types were regarded as being graded in difficulty. The grading was done largely intuitively, and the intuitions exploited were probably psychological rather than linguistic. The classification was not just intuitive, however, as there is considerable evidence in the literature that indicates that sentence length and subordination are useful indices of linguistic development (e.g. La Brant, 1933, on subordination, and Heider and Heider, 1940, on sentence length; for a general review, see McCarthy, 1954). The nine types are now listed in order of supposed difficulty:

F		
Fn		
B		
FB	or	FnB
BF	or	BFn
FBn	or	FnBn
BnF	or	BnFn
BFB	or	BFnB
BnFB	or	BnFnB

There are a number of points concerning the generalised types which require clarification. 'F' occurring by itself means just one free clause, and 'F' accompanied by 'n' means more than one free clause. Likewise, 'B' by itself stands for just one bound clause, and 'B' with 'n' means more than one bound clause. It can be seen, then, that a type such as the last one represents a highly generalised statement that may cover a number of different cases, e.g.

BB F B
BBF + FB
FB + F + BBF

Clearly, some of the structures might be more difficult than others: the generalisation, then, is an oversimplification. Nevertheless, it is justified by the infrequency of these categories in children's speech.

There is another consideration that should be borne in mind. The bound clauses represented by 'B' in these structures were of two classes only: conditioning and additioning. These are very largely equivalent to the traditional adverb and non-defining adjective clauses. The clauses more or less equivalent to the noun clauses and defining adjective clauses were treated as rankshifted clauses, that is, clauses not operating in sentence structure. These latter clauses, therefore, do not figure in the sentence types listed above. The reasons for this decision are discussed in the section on bound clauses (4.2b.i).

Basically three intuitions have been exploited, intuitions about number, class and position. The directions of difficulty, from less to more difficult, are now given:

Number

One ⟶ more than one clause

Class

Free ⟶ bound

35

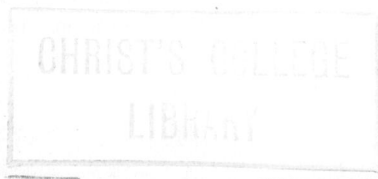

Bound after a free clause → bound before a free clause.

These are just the basic notions; some of the sentence types given above represent rather more complicated notions. In these sentence types, number, class and position are also ordered in difficulty with respect to each other, so, for example, one of the implications of the BFB type is that a sentence with a bound clause before and a bound clause after a free clause is more complex than one with more than one bound clause either before or after a free clause (but not before and after). The reason why this notion is not listed along with the others is that not as much faith is put in this hypothesis as in the others. With this sort of hypothesis (much more than with the others) one would have to make qualifications, for example, about particular sub-classes of bound clause. Such qualifications are superfluous here because it is obvious that five-year-old children do not use such structures with any real frequency.

Of the notions we have mentioned, number, class and position, it is the last one that is likely to be most controversial. But there are a number of reasons for thinking that in English a bound clause preceding the free clause it presupposes might be associated with more difficulty than one following its free clause. Quirk (1962) has pointed out that 'the typical and unremarkable English utterance has a light subject followed by the verb with the heavily modified parts then following; this pattern applies also to the disposition of subordinate clauses: they generally follow a part of a sentence which can be seen as in some way nuclear, thus conforming with the broad underlying pattern of the main fabric of the structure taking shape before the qualifications are added'. One effect of varying the order, of putting the qualifications first, is to give them greater 'emphasis' or 'prominence' or the like. These terms are taken from Sinclair (1965), who discusses these contrasts. He gives these examples:

(50) He'll come if you call

(51) If you call, he'll come

'If you call' has greater prominence in (51) because of its initial position; moreover, this clause is on a different tone group from 'he'll come' (as is indicated by the presence of a comma) and this has the effect of also giving the clause more prominence, thus reinforcing the prominence gained by it being in initial position. Yngve (1960) suggests a reason why bound clauses in the initial position are more infrequent than those in non-initial position. He postulated a depth limit of about 7 for 'regressive' structures (those in which the bracketing is associated with the left) while allowing 'progressive' structures (those in which the bracketing is associated with the right) to be infinitely expanded. Now the bracketing associated with

36

bound clauses preceding their free clause is leftward, whereas that of bound clauses following their free clause is rightward. To illustrate the two kinds of bracketing we will give Yngve's own examples:

(52) *Regressive*
If what going to a clearly not very adequately staffed school really means is little appreciated, we should be concerned.

(53) *Progressive*
We should be concerned if there is little appreciation of what it really means to go to a school that clearly isn't very adequately staffed.

Whilst preferring not to accept all Yngve's descriptive details, it is thought that he is probably right when he suggests that regressive structures put a greater tax on immediate memory and thus are more difficult to handle than progressive ones. We may mention, by the way, that Martin and Roberts (1966) quantified sentence complexity according to Yngve's index and, holding sentence length constant, found that sentences of lesser indexed complexity were recalled significantly more frequently than sentences of greater complexity, thus indicating the value of Yngve's model and hypothesis. It is for these reasons, then, that we have made the assumption that bound clauses preceding a free clause are more difficult than those following a free clause.

3.5 Coding information

The information for coding the data in a form acceptable to the computer is given at the end of each of the chapters which deal with the linguistic description.

CHILD'S CODE NUMBER
The child's code number consists of four digits, e.g. 1234. The first digit refers to the grouping of the school the child attended: there were five groups. The second digit refers to the particular school within the group: the number of schools within a group ranged between three and five. The third digit refers to the sex of the child, 0, 1 or 2 being male, 3 and 4 female. The final digit in conjunction with the third digit gives the child his particular number. So for example in a school with twenty-one boys their names would first be ranked in alphabetical order, then the first on the list would be assigned the number 00, the second 01, ... the eleventh 10, and the twenty-first 20. A similar list would be made for the girls, the first girl on the list being assigned the number 30, the second 31 ... the eleventh 40 and so on.

The child's code number is placed on a line by itself.

TASK NUMBER

There are six tasks. One task, the game explanation, is subdivided into four sections. It was decided to collect together all the non-task speech that a child uttered and to treat it as a seventh task. Here are the possible numbers:

10 Model room
20 Picture story
30 Trotin
40 Story completion
51 Game: Hide-and-seek
52 Game: Musical chairs
53 Game: Ring a ring a roses
54 Game: Any other
60 Toy elephant
70 Non-task speech

The task number is always placed on a line by itself, the first task number occurring immediately below the child's code number.

SENTENCE NUMBER

Sentences are numbered according to task. Up to ninety-nine sentences per task are allowed for. These are numbered thus: 01, 02, 03 . . . 99.

The sentence number always begins a new line. The first sentence number occurs immediately below the first task number.

TABLE 01 'SENTENCE CLASS'

The sentence number is obligatorily followed by one of the following compound symbols: S1, S2, S3 and S4. These symbols form Table 01 'Sentence class'. Here is the table reproduced below:

Symbol	Class
S1	Non-response, non-textshifted sentence
S2	Non-response, textshifted sentence
S3	Response, non-textshifted sentence
S4	Response, textshifted sentence

The sentence symbol immediately follows the sentence number.

SENTENCE BOUNDARY

After the sentence class information, the clause and group information is coded, according to the rules to be given at the end of the clause and group sections. When the end of the sentence is reached, a boundary symbol has to be added. Here are the relevant symbols:

Symbol	Type of boundary
/3	non-final sentence
/4	task-final sentence, that is, the last sentence of a task
/5	interview-final sentence, that is, the last sentence of the last task.

SUMMARY

In terms of the chart of allowable transitions (given in full in Part 2, Diagram 8) we have so far covered the following stages:

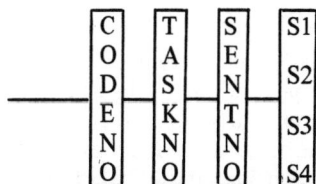

C O D E N O	T A S K N O	S E N T N O	S1
			S2
			S3
			S4

In terms of the rank scale we have coded the information relating to the sentence rank. The next step is to move down to the rank below the sentence, which is the clause rank.

Example

We shall give an example to illustrate these coding rules. The sentence is a concoction, but let us suppose that it is the first sentence that a child utters on the first task. Here is the sentence:

That lamp has fallen in front of the television.

Coding

1234	i.e. CHILD'S CODE NO.
10	TASK NO.
01S1	SENTENCE NO., SENTENCE CLASS

We shall continue the coding of this sentence in sections 4.7, 5.9, 6.8 and 7.9.

Chapter 4

THE CLAUSE

4.1 Introductory

A clause may be non-rankshifted or rankshifted. The normal place of occurrence of a unit is in the structure of the unit next above on the rank scale, so a clause normally operates in the structure of the sentence: this is its non-rankshifted position. If a clause operates in the structure of a unit below itself, it is regarded as being rankshifted. In the present description we shall deal first with the non-rankshifted clauses and then with the rankshifted ones.

To avoid possible misconceptions it will be as well to make two points clear from the outset. One, the clause in 'scale-and-category' grammar may be either finite or non-finite, e.g.:

    (1) <u>Whilst I was walking down the street,</u> I met John.
            (finite)   (finite)

    (2) <u>Walking down the street,</u> I met John.
          (non-finite)   (finite)

In (1) the underlined part is a finite clause and (2) the underlined part is a non-finite one. Both (1) and (2) are sentences consisting of two clauses. And two, the clause may be either major or minor. The defining criterion is the presence or absence of a predicator. A clause with a predicator is major, and one without a predicator is minor. Here are some examples:

    (3) We are going home. (major)

    (4) Goodbye!   (minor)

4.2 Non-rankshifted clauses

Non-rankshifted clauses may be subdivided into three classes: free, bound and tag. The distinction between free and bound clauses has already been mentioned in section 3.2 when we defined the sentence. The tag clause class has not been referred to previously in this description. We shall now describe each of these three classes in turn.

4.2a Free clauses

In section 3.3 we mentioned that it is the free clause which correlates with the contextual function of the sentence, the bound clause not being related in most cases, and we said that it is the 'mood' system that provides the relevant options. We shall now examine the mood system and its relationship to contextual functions.

4.2a.i Mood

The system of mood has three terms: affirmative, interrogative and imperative. Below we present the system diagrammatically and give the clause structures which expound the terms in the system:

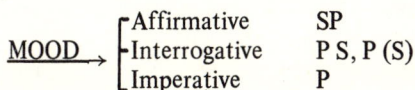

$$
\underline{\text{MOOD}} \rightarrow \left[
\begin{array}{ll}
\text{Affirmative} & \text{SP} \\
\text{Interrogative} & \text{P S, P (S)} \\
\text{Imperative} & \text{P}
\end{array}
\right.
$$

In the affirmative clause the subject is the nominal group which precedes the verbal group at the predicator, with no other nominal group in between, e.g.

(5) Bill | has gone
    S |P

In the interrogative clause the subject is the nominal group which follows the first word of the verbal group at the predicator, so if the verbal group contains more than one word the subject will be included within it (this is the significance of the brackets), e.g.

(6) Have | you | any bread?
    P |S |C

(7) Did (you) have | any bread?
    P (S) |C

The imperative clause has a predicator, in the appropriate form of the verbal group, but no subject, e.g.

(8) Go | away!
    P | A

The imperative clause, we may add, may have a vocative element, e.g.

(9) Go | away, | John!
    P | A | V

(10) You | go | away!
     V |P | A

4.2a.ii Contextual functions of free clauses

The usual contextual functions for the affirmative, interrogative and imperative clauses are statement, question and command respectively. We also may mention that the main ones for the minor clause (sometimes called the 'moodless' clause) are exclamation and address (e.g. What a pity!; John!). As we have indicated above (section 3.3a), when ellipsis is taken into account, it is not true to say that the minor clause is associated with the contextual function 'answer'.

These contextual categories are, needless to say, very crude. Sinclair (1965) regards statement, question, command and response as being the primary classes of contextual functions. More delicate subclasses could be set up; 'threats', for example, would be a subclass of statement. Philosophers, of course, might argue for more or different primary classes; Austin (1962), for instance, argues that such things as threats and promises are not statements, but are 'performatives', that is, utterances that actually perform actions when said under certain conditions. It was thought, though, that a subtle subclassification of contextual functions was beyond the scope of our broad survey of the data. Which contextual functions we decided to operate with will be discussed shortly.

First we must elaborate the relationship between the affirmative, interrogative and imperative clause classes and the statement, question and command contextual functions. These are the usual functions for these clause classes. But even at this degree of delicacy it is by no means always the case that the clause classes and contextual functions are paired in the way suggested above. For example, a clause with the interrogative structure PS may occur without a questioning function (a) when the clause begins with an adjunct; (b) when the clause follows direct speech (cf. Sinclair, 1965). Examples of these uses now follow:

(11) Here comes the bus.

(12) There goes my last penny.

(13) 'We'll help you,' said the man in the boat.

Moreover, it is possible to ask a question without using the PS clause structure. Using clause structure SP and rising final intonation, one can ask a question, e.g.

(14) You've finished now?

We had to ask ourselves what was likely to be most useful to our research, the purely structural information or the contextual function information. We decided on the latter. There were a number of considerations that influenced our decision. One, Bernstein (1959) gave as one of the characteristics of a public language 'Frequent use of short commands and questions'. It seemed likely that Bernstein had the contextual function rather than the structural information as such in mind. Two, there was the problem of incomplete verbal groups. It is not unusual for young children to omit part of the exponents of tense in the verbal group. This is quite apart from the question of presupposing elements of structure in the interviewer's question, though it is possible that giving such response sentences might reinforce the tendency. The most commonly omitted element is the *be* part of a *be+ing* tense, e.g.

(15) The man walking down the street
cf. The man is walking down the street

If one were being strict, one could argue that such clauses are non-finite and therefore should not be analysed in terms of the mood system. The third factor that influenced our decision was the relatively high frequency of minor clauses in the data, that is, clauses which do not contain a predicator. In most cases these minor clauses did not have the contextual function 'exclamation' or 'address'; they seemed best handled under the contextual function 'statement'.

4.2a.iii Elected subclassification of free clauses

With the above considerations in mind we divided the free clauses (including the clauses with incomplete verbal groups among these clauses) into three classes: statements, questions and commands. We did not recognise responses as separate from statements, because we had already subclassified sentences on this dimension, and it would be possible to instruct the computer to relate the sentence and clause information, if we so wished. The statement category, then, includes such structures as:

(16) A man | is walking | down the street.
    S   P   A

(17) A man.
    Z

(18) Said | the little boy's mummy.
    P   S

The question category includes the following types of structure:

(19) What | are (you) doing?
    C   P (S)

(20) Who | 's | there?
    S   P | A

(21) You | 've (never) eaten | that?
    S   P (A)   C

(22) An aeroplane?
    Z

The command category contains only one set of different structures from what the imperative category contained, the minor structures, e.g. Steady! (Z).

As our description goes beyond the purely structural description given in the mood system as outlined above, it is necessary to make some use of intonational criteria for identifying the contextual functions. Here we draw on Halliday (1963a), and anyone requiring a fairly comprehensive introduction to intonational systems in English is referred to that work. Our aim is not to give a full description but just to make use of intonational clues when the purely structural information is insufficient. Below we present the criteria for recognising the three clause classes: statement, question and command.

Statement

1. Affirmative clause structure, except when on Tone 2, i.e. either a rise or sharp fall-rise.
2. Interrogative clause structure when the clause begins with an adjunct or when the clause follows direct speech.
3. Minor clause structure when Tone 1, i.e. fall (usually glossed 'answer') or when Tone 5, i.e. rise-fall ('exclamation').

Question

1. Interrogative clause structure, except when the clause begins with an adjunct or when the clause follows direct speech.
2. Affirmative clause structure with Tone 2.
3. Imperative clause structure with Tone 2.
4. Minor clause structure with Tone 2.

Command

1. Imperative clause structure, except when on Tone 2.
2. Minor clause structure with Tone 3, i.e. low rise (usually glossed 'warning').

There was one class of statement that it seemed worthwhile to isolate from the outset. These were the clauses that signalled a refusal or inability to supply the information requested by the interviewer's question. We have already discussed these inadequacy signals in the section on response sentences (3.3a). All the inadequacy signals other than 'I don't know' were coded as F4, whilst 'I don't know' was coded as T4. Typical examples of inadequacy signals coded as F4 are:

(23) I haven't any idea

(24) I just don't know what he might be saying.

To sum up, then, we recognised four classes of free clause, making use of grammatical, phonological and contextual clues. The four classes are:

Statements	(F1)
Questions	(F2)
Commands	(F3)
Refusals	(F4)

4.2a.iv Social class influences on the use of free clauses

We shall now consider briefly the typical functions of the three main clause classes: statements, questions and commands. Our main aim is to suggest how different home environments might tend to encourage or inhibit the use of particular classes.

First of all, how are our three classes distributed with respect to Piaget's (1926) subclassification of the functions of language? Questions and commands would seem to be clear subdivisions of Piaget's 'socialised speech', that is, speech 'in which the child addresses his hearer, considers his point of view, tries to influence him or actually exchanges ideas with him'. Statements have to be cross-classified: those that contain adapted information (which occurs when 'the child really exchanges his thoughts with others'), criticism, or answers to questions are socialised, whereas those that do not contain such information are egocentric. In egocentric speech 'the child does not bother to know to whom he is speaking nor whether he is being listened to. He talks either for himself or for the pleasure of associating anyone who happens to be there with the activity of the moment. . . . He does not attempt to place himself at the point of view of his hearer.' What environmental factors are likely to be associated with differences in the use of questions, commands and statements? We shall consider questions first.

Questions

It is generally acknowledged that at a certain stage in their development young children start to ask numerous questions. Russell (1956) says that the so-called questioning age seems to begin about three years and reaches its peak about the time the child enters school. Now it is important that a child, when he shows a readiness to elaborate and perfect a skill, should receive particular help and reinforcement at that time. If the emerging readiness is not fully recognised or if help is not proffered, then the child's questioning facility may be inhibited.

In the work of the Sociological Research Unit an attempt has been made to construct a profile of the communication interaction that takes place in the family, as reported by the mother in an interview (see Bernstein and Brandis, 1969, Bernstein and Henderson, 1969 and Brandis, 1969a, 1969b). The index devised by Brandis is a measure of the mother's orientation towards communication and control. It is not the place here to go into detail about this measure which is actually based on five indices of the mother's orientation. We shall refer to two of these indices, those that are specifically related to communication, namely the 'Avoidance Index' and the 'Verbal Interaction Index'. The Avoidance Index is based on a closed schedule which consisted of five possible tactics the mother might employ in dealing with difficult questions that the child might ask. The mother was asked to give the frequency with which she used each tactic. The Verbal Interaction Index is based on a closed schedule which consisted of seven social settings in which the child initiates conversation with the mother. In each case the mother was asked what she would usually do and was given a choice of four options ranging from telling the child to be quiet to chatting with the child. The correlation between the Avoidance Index and Social Class is .36, that between the Verbal Interaction Index and Social Class is .37 and that between Avoidance combined with Verbal Interaction and Social Class is .45. Briefly, then, the higher the social class the more the mother is disposed towards answering the child's difficult questions and chatting with him, and the lower the social class the more the mother is disposed towards evading the child's difficult questions and the less she is inclined to talk to him.

In another part of the maternal interview the mothers were asked to say how they would reply to six everyday questions that children often ask. One question, for example, was:

Children sometimes ask why people have to do things.
Imagine X asking: Why does Daddy shave every morning?
What would you say?

Robinson and Rackstraw (1967) in an analysis of this data found that 'middle-class mothers differed from working-class mothers in that they evaded fewer questions, gave more accurate answers, gave more information in their answers, used fewer "noisy" items, used fewer social psychological checks of agreement and preferred certain modes of answering "why" questions'.

The evidence indicates, then, that asking questions is typically a rewarding activity for the middle-class child and typically an unrewarding one for the working-class child. In this connection it is interesting to note that McCarthy (1930) and Davis (1937) found that children of the upper socio-economic classes ask a much larger number of questions than children of the lower socio-economic levels. McCarthy (1954) comments on this finding as follows: 'This is undoubtedly due in part to the intellectual factor, but is probably also related to the satisfaction that the children are likely to get when they ask questions. A child from a superior home is somewhat more likely to get a satisfactory answer to his questions and hence will be encouraged to ask more.' It is Bernstein's view that the working-class child's low level of curiosity in certain areas is attributable in part to the unrewarding nature of the answers he receives to his early questions. In the working-class home environment, Bernstein (1958) writes, 'sustained curiosity is not fostered or rewarded, as answers to questions rarely lead beyond the object or further than a simple statement about the object'. But the middle-class child's home experience makes him 'more generally and specifically aware of a wide range of objects at any one time which will intensify his curiosity and reward his explorations'. So we might expect the middle-class child to ask more questions, provided, of course, that the tasks are of sufficient interest and complexity to justify questioning behaviour.

A serious study of children's questions would require making a number of subdivisions within the general category 'question'. An important distinction is that between the polar questions (the 'Yes/No' type, e.g. Is that a balloon?) and the non-polar questions (the 'WH-word' type, e.g. What is that?). As we have mentioned earlier, the former type is usually glossed as 'confirmation-seeking' and the latter as 'information-seeking'. Thomas (1965) shows how the polar question relates to the entire sentence, that is, questions the entire sentence, whereas the non-polar one relates to part of the sentence; it may question a noun, a verb, an adjective or an adverb. Thomas illustrates this point with a set of questions which are related to the following sentence:

(25) The small boy was sleeping under the tree.

Here are the most pertinent questions:

(26) Who was sleeping under the tree? (nominal question)

(27) What was the small boy doing under the tree? (verbal question)

(28) What kind of boy was sleeping under the tree? (adjectival question)

(29) Where was the boy sleeping? (adverbial question)

(30) Was the boy sleeping under the tree? (Yes/No question, that is, one which questions the entire sentence)

Waismann (1965), in a chapter called 'Towards a logic of questions', distinguishes between word questions and sentence questions. The former correspond to non-polar questions and the latter to polar questions. Waismann makes the interesting observation that the word questions are of two kinds, namely, those which cannot be negated (e.g. 'How old is the earth?') and those which alter their sense when negated (e.g. 'What day are you free?') whilst the sentence questions are of a third kind, namely, those whose sense remains unaltered when negated (e.g. 'Were you at home yesterday?'). Waismann wonders whether the word questions are reducible to sentence questions: apparently Carnap holds this view: 'In the strictly logical sense, to ask a question is to seek to ascertain whether a given proposition or its negation is true.' But Waismann rejects this view as too narrow. For Waismann, not every question presupposes a proposition, but what is presupposed is some definite mental background, some particular system of thought. Waismann qualifies this view too: 'We begin to realise that not every question can find an answer within the world of thought which gave it birth, that it is sometimes necessary for something quite fresh to happen, for man to pass to a new course of thought before the way to its solution can be opened up.' On a lesser plane, it seems worthwhile asking what kind of mental background the questions of a child presuppose and in what way the answers he receives may change his system of thought.

Clearly, a delicate subclassification of questions is a prerequisite for such a study. The WH-words, for example, have to be subclassified. Some useful work has been done in this area. Russell (1956) states that the earlier questions of a child are *what* questions, but *what* eventually turns into *why*. He adds that it is probably these later questions which are of most value in building concepts. Piaget (1926) reports that *why* questions appear at about 3 years but he claims that these early questions do not actually seek causal explanations. They are affective rather than intellectual. According to Piaget, children do not ask questions concerning causal relationships until they are 7 or 8 years old. Lewis (1951) essentially agrees with Piaget's view but he stresses the social function of the child's questions. He attempts to show that 'the growth of the various categories of questions depends very largely upon the replies that the child receives; that is, upon social cooperation'. He thinks that the child's real notion of causality develops out of his experience with the causal answers he receives from others. The emphasis that Lewis puts on the social factor in questioning behaviour is of particular interest from the point of view of our research. We would certainly expect that the replies that middle-class mothers give to their children's questions would facilitate the development of concepts such as causality.

Commands
Having considered questions, we shall now discuss commands and suggest how they may be associated with a particular kind of socialisation. Bernstein (1969; see also 1964a) distinguishes, at a general level, two modes of social control: the imperative mode and the mode based on appeals. The distinction is based on the range of role discretion (that is, the range of alternatives) accorded to the person regulated. In the case of the imperative mode the range of role discretion is reduced, whereas in the case of appeals, varying degrees of discretion are accorded. 'The imperative mode is realised through a restricted code (lexicon prediction): "Shut up",

"Leave it alone", "Get out" or extra-verbally through physical coercion.'
Appeals are broken down into two types: positional and personal.
'Positional appeals refer the behaviour of the regulated (child) to the
norms which inhere in a particular or universal status.' But in the case of
the personal appeals 'the focus is upon the child as an individual rather
than upon his formal status. Personal appeals take into account inter-
personal or intra-personal components of the social relationship.' Bernstein
exemplifies these two types with reference to an imaginary situation in
which a child has to visit his grandfather who is unwell and the child does
not like to kiss him because he has not shaved for some time. The mother
using a positional appeal says: 'Children kiss their grandpa'; whereas the
mother using a personal appeal says: 'I know you don't like kissing
grandpa, but he is unwell and he is very fond of you.' It seems likely that
of these three modes: imperative, positional and personal, it is the
imperative that is most associated with the use of commands. It is
interesting to note that whereas Bernstein associates positional and
personal modes with both elaborated and restricted codes, he associates
the imperative mode far more with the restricted code. It seems probable
that the families who most make use of the imperative mode are lower
working-class. Because of this it seems reasonable to suggest that under
certain conditions lower working-class children are more likely than
middle-class children to opt for using commands. In the speech schedule
the first picture story is about some boys breaking a window with a
football and the owner coming out to them: the children are asked to say
what the man is saying. It seems likely that the lower working-class would
opt for expressing an imperative mode of control in such a situation as this
and make use of commands. But it is also possible that they generalise this
learning and that they use commands more frequently than the middle-
class in other situations as well: one gets the impression, for example, that
working-class children are perhaps more likely to try to direct the
attention of the interviewer by means of commands, e.g.

(31) Look at that train there.

Bernstein (1969) makes the point that 'where control is positional, and,
even more, where it is imperative, the child has a strong sense of social
identity but the rules which he learns will be tied to specific contexts and
his sense of autonomy may well be reduced'. It may be that the two
concepts that Bernstein mentions: a sense of social identity and specificity
to context are the keys to working-class language, for not only commands
but also a number of other features that are associated with their language,
e.g. sociocentric sequences, pronouns, etc., are related to these concepts.

Statements
Finally, concerning the use of statements, are there any suggestions that
there will be any social class differences in the use the children make of

statements? It will be remembered that we crudely distinguished egocentric statements and socialised statements, making use of Piaget's distinction. It is thought that the working-class speech will tend to resemble egocentric speech in certain aspects. In egocentric speech, according to Piaget, the speaker 'does not attempt to place himself at the point of view of his hearer'. In restricted code speech, the speaker tends to assume that his hearer is placed at the same point of view as himself. Inasmuch as the speaker tends to assume identity between his listener and himself, his speech will resemble speech for himself. The middle-class speaker, being much more aware of the difference between self and others, will have a more obviously socialised form of speech. Bernstein (1969) writes: 'A restricted code will arise where the form of the social relation is based upon closely shared identifications, upon an extensive range of shared expectations, upon a range of common assumptions.' Also in the same paper: 'An elaborated code, in principle, presupposes a sharp boundary or gap between self and others which is crossed through the creation of speech which specifically fits a differentiated "other".' How these basic differences in outlook are reflected in the statements that they make is a very large question. We shall be able to examine particular aspects of it as we discuss such features as the egocentric sequence and sympathetic circularities in section 4.2c and the pronouns in section 5.4.

4.2b Bound clauses

We have explained in section 3.2 that bound clauses are defined with reference to sentence structure. We shall now proceed to subclassify them according to the restrictions that obtain on their operation in sentence structure.

4.2b.i Subclassification of bound clauses

It is usual in 'scale-and-category' grammar to subdivide bound clauses into three classes: conditioning, additioning and reported. The conditioning clauses correspond pretty well to the traditional adverb clauses, the additioning to non-defining adjective or non-restrictive relative clauses, and the reported to noun clauses. We shall consider each of these three classes in turn.

Conditioning
The conditioning clause may either precede its free clause, e.g.

(32) When I am twenty-one /2 I hope to get married to a young girl /3

or follow its free clause,

(33) I hope to get married to a young girl /2 when I am twenty-one /3

or be included in its free clause,

(34) I hope to get married (when I am twenty-one /2) to a young girl /3.

We may add that most conditioning clauses are finite and are introduced by a binder, e.g. after, although, because, before, etc. A full list of binders is given in section 7.8.

Additioning
In contrast to the conditioning clauses, the additioning clauses may occur at only two places in sentence structure: they may *not* occur in initial position. The additioning clause may either follow its free clause, e.g.

(35) It is 116 miles to Bristol from London /2, so it will be about 90–100 miles to Bristol from Didcot in Reading /2, where I live /3

or be included in its free clause,

(36) It is 116 miles to Bristol from London /2, so from Didcot in Reading, (where I live /2), it will be about 90–100 miles to Bristol /3.

There is a further difference between the two classes of clause which is pointed out by Sinclair (1965). This concerns their potentiality for interrupting a free clause, that is, for being included within it. The conditioning clause may interrupt a free clause immediately after an adjunct such as *however, therefore, thus, still, nevertheless, indeed* (that is, one which refers to a previous sentence) or after a linker such as *and, but,* and *or,* e.g.

(37) However, (when we arrived home /2), everything was all right /3.

The additioning clause may not occur in either of these positions, however.

Items which introduce additioning clauses include how, when, where, which, who, why, by which, into which, etc.

Reported
We shall now consider the last class of bound clause, the reported clause. The chief difference between this class and the other two is that this class of clause may only occur when there is a certain kind of verb in the free clause, a 'reporting' verb, in fact. This is a small class of verbs which includes say, ask, beg, demand, insist, request, require, vote, etc.

The reported clause also differs from the other two classes of clause in its potentialities of occurrence in sentence structure. In general we can say that it may either precede its free clause, e.g.

51

(38) He was retiring /2, he said /3

or follow its free clause,

(39) He said /2 that he was retiring /3

(40) He said /2 he was retiring /3

or include its free clause,

(41) The next day, (he went on /2), he was retiring /3.

Drawing mainly on Sinclair (1965), we may mention one or two qualifications to the above. Reported clauses introduced by *that* may not occur in initial position. Nor is the pre-/post-free clause reversibility possible if the verbal group in the free clause is negative, or if it contains a negative pronoun like *nobody*, or a word like *never, seldom, only*, etc., e.g.

(42) He never said he was coming

but not

(43) He was coming, he never said

In the recent work of Halliday and others, many of the clauses which were previously treated as reported clauses are now analysed as rankshifted clauses, as indeed are some of the conditioning clauses. The main criteria for recognising rankshifting of the clause are as follows:*

1. Active/passive reversibility is possible:

(44) He found what he wanted

(45) What he wanted was found

2. Co-ordination with non-rankshifted units is possible:

(46) He got what he wanted and a surprise

3. Marked theme is possible:

(47) Whether he is right I can't say.

4. Theme identification is possible:

(48) It was that she must work hard that he emphasised.

At the time of compilation of the coding frame an attempt was made to livide the reported clauses into non-rankshifted and rankshifted. It proved no difficult to achieve an adequate degree of coder reliability, so we had

A useful distinction to incorporate in future research is that which Halliday (1968) makes between 'report' clauses and 'fact' clauses. The criteria for distinguishing these clauses are given at bottom of page 53.

to abandon this subdivision. The decision, then, had to be taken whether to regard these clauses all as non-rankshifted or all as rankshifted. We decided on treating them as being rankshifted. The reason for this being that it was felt that the free clauses occurring with these clauses often seem less capable of occurring by themselves than do the free clauses occurring with conditioning and additioning clauses. This is why we treated them as an integral part of the free clause. Here are some examples to illustrate this point:

Reported

    (49) I imagine he's gone home.

    (50) I expect he's gone home.

    (51) He said he would leave early.

    (52) He asked if he could leave early.

By contrast:

(Footnote continued from page 52.)

report	fact
1. can't insert *the fact that* e.g. John says that he's left.	can insert *the fact that* e.g. John regrets that he's left.
2. can't have *it's that he's left that he says.*	can have *it's that he's left that he regrets.*
3. can't make subject, so no passive *that he'd left was said by John.*	can make subject, so can have passive *that he's left is regretted by John.*
4. can report a text, even without reporting verb: *He was leaving. He couldn't bear it any longer.*	can't report a text.
5. has quoted equivalent *John said, '. . .*	no quoted equivalent.
6. no noun as alternative – no *he said his departure.*	noun as alternative form – *he regretted his departure.*
7. if reporting clause follows, is tail, like quoting.	matrix clause can never be tail.
8. reporting verbs can't usually take C, and even when they can take C can only be *report* (or synonym), and cannot co-ordinate with reporting clause: no *he answered the question and that he'd come at once.*	can have noun as C, not restricted to fact/report class of nouns; and noun as C can co-ordinate with fact clause: *he regretted the incident and that he'd never apologised for it.*

Conditioning

(53) He left early because the roads were bad.

(54) He went to the station in order to meet his mother.

Additioning

(55) He wasn't in the office, which was unusual

(56) I was speaking to a friend, whom I've known for a long time.

4.2b.ii Social class influences on the use of bound clauses

Having outlined the subclasses for the bound clauses, we shall now briefly suggest in what respects they might be used differentially by the middle and working-class. We shall consider the conditioning clauses first.

Conditioning

In traditional grammar it is usual to subclassify the adverb clauses into the following subclasses: time, place, manner, condition, concession, cause, purpose, result, comparison. In effect we subclassified the conditioning clauses along similar lines but we did it through the binding-conjunctions introducing the finite conditioning clauses. We did not consider all the traditional categories to be appropriate to five-year-old children's speech: we just used time, cause, condition and others. Of these categories we were especially interested in those of cause and condition, as we would expect the middle-class child to have a more developed awareness of these concepts. This is because 'the child in the middle-class and associated levels is socialised within a formally articulated structure. Present decisions affecting the growing child are governed by their efficacy in attaining distant ends, affectually and cognitively regarded. Behaviour is modified by, and oriented to, an explicit set of goals and values, which create a more stable system of rewards and punishments, although the psychological implications of this may vary from one family to another. . . . Consequently, the child grows up in an ordered rational structure' (Bernstein, 1961). In the same paper, Bernstein draws on the work of Luria and Yudovich (1959): 'The child's responses are rewarded or punished until the child is able to regulate his own behaviour independent of the adult model. The child learns his social structure and introjects it from the very beginnings of speech.' Bernstein (1964) writes: 'The social structure becomes for the developing child his psychological reality by the shaping of his acts of speech.'

In the maternal interview administered to the mothers of the children in our sample just before they started school, there was a section in which the mothers were asked how they would deal with their child in six hypothetical situations, e.g.

> What would you do if ... brought you a bunch of flowers, and you found that he/she had got them from a neighbour's garden?

The mother's responses were coded in terms of a great number of categories. From four of these categories a Child-oriented Reasoning Index was constructed, and this was used as one of the five indices that make up the measure of the mother's orientation towards communication and control (Bernstein and Brandis, 1969). The Child-oriented Reasoning Index is of particular interest to us here as it is a measure of the mother's willingness to elaborate verbally reasons and rules. It is based on four categories:

(a) Simple Cognitive Child-oriented Personal Appeals:
 e.g. If you don't go to school, you won't learn to read.

(b) Complex Cognitive Child-oriented Personal Appeals:
 e.g. If you stay up you'll be tired in the morning and you won't work well at school.

(c) Cognitive-Affective Child-oriented Personal Appeals:
 e.g. If you don't go to school, you won't have any friends and you won't learn anything.

(d) Recognition of the child's intent:
 e.g. I know you meant well but ...

Briefly, in the first three of these categories the mother appeals to the child in terms of an objective explanation of the consequences of the act for him. In the third category she also invokes an emotional response in the child. In the last category the mother explicitly recognises the child's good intention. All these appeals have important consequences for the child's linguistic and cognitive development, in particular the development of his awareness of causes and conditions. Now the correlation between the Child-oriented Reasoning Index and Social Class is .326, over the total sample. In other words, the higher the social class the more the mother reasons with her child in this way.* We would expect, then, that the middle-class child would tend to have a greater comprehension of consequences and that in certain situations this would be reflected in his language performance, in, for example, his greater use of conditioning clauses of cause and condition, if these were appropriate to the context.

---

* Recent work by Cook (1968) has established that middle-class mothers, especially mothers of boys, use more clauses of condition introduced by *if* than the working-class mothers do in this section of the maternal interview. Clauses of cause have not yet been examined.

Additioning and reporting
Both the additioning clauses and the 'reporting' clauses, namely those that
are associated with reported clauses, may be used as devices for making
comments on other language material. Here are some examples:

(57) They have broken the window, *which is naughty of them.*

(58) *I think* they should pay for a new window.

Both these uses perhaps may be seen as examples of what Schatzman and
Strauss (1955) have called 'communication control'. The middle-class
speaker stands outside of his experience more than the working-class
speaker: 'It is as though he were directing a movie, having at his command
several cameras focussed at different perspectives, shooting and carefully
controlling the effect.' The extra perspective here is one of evaluation.
Labov and Waletsky's (1967) work on 'Narrative analysis: oral versions of
personal experience' is of interest here. They define a category 'evaluation', namely 'that part of the narrative which reveals the attitude of the
narrator towards the narrative by emphasising the relative importance of
some narrative units as compared to others'. They distinguish a scale of
degrees of embedding of evaluation, going from the most internalised to
the most externalised. Somewhat related to this is the work of Poldauf
(1964) on 'The Third Syntactical Plan': 'The third plan has in it
components which place the content of the sentence in relation to the
individual and his special ability to perceive, judge and assess.' We shall
discuss Poldauf's conception in more detail when we examine the
sociocentric and egocentric sequences.

4.2c Tag clauses

Under the general title 'tag clauses' we bring together a number of
different linguistic entities, not all of which are technically tags. They are
brought together as exponents of certain functional categories, which we
shall now describe.

Bernstein (1961) gave as a characteristic of a *public* language (later
Restricted Code) the following:

'A large number of statements/phrases which signal a requirement for
the previous speech sequences to be reinforced: "Wouldn't it? You see?
You know?" etc. This process is termed "sympathetic circularity".'

In his experimental study, Bernstein (1962b) found clear social class
differences on the use of sympathetic circularities, the working-class
groups using more. In his discussion he comments: 'The meanings signalled
by the code tend to be implicit and so condensed, with the result that
there is less redundancy. A greater strain is placed upon the listener which
is relieved by the range of identification which the speakers share.' The
sympathetic circularities act as checks: 'It is as if the speaker is saying

"check – are we together on this".' As Rackstraw and Robinson (1967) remark, they are 'tests of similarity of viewpoint, a check on shared subjectivity'. They reinforce the closely-shared and self-consciously held identifications of the group and tend to inhibit the expression of individuated messages. More empirical evidence for the sympathetic circularities as a characteristic of the Restricted Code is provided by Robinson and Rackstraw (1967). This study relates to the speech of adults, and a clear tendency is revealed for the working-class subjects to use more sympathetic circularities.*

In the paper cited, Bernstein (1962b), the sympathetic circularities are also referred to as 'sociocentric sequences'. These are in contrast with the 'egocentric sequence', 'I think'. This is characteristic of the Elaborated Code. The Elaborated Code is more explicit; there is less need for the speaker to include special signals checking on whether the listener is following his train of thought and is agreeing with him. The language is more explicit, because 'the orientation of the individual is based upon the expectation of psychological difference, his own and others' (Bernstein, 1962b). The utterance of an egocentric sequence is indicative of this expectation of difference. As Rackstraw and Robinson (1967) write: 'Egocentric sequences show an awareness of points of view other than one's own and, hence, imply an objective frame of reference.'

We may mention that Rackstraw and Robinson (1967) include in their discussion a careful comparison of Bernstein's concepts 'egocentric sequence' and 'sociocentric sequence' and Piaget's (1926) concepts 'egocentric speech' and 'socialised speech'. Briefly, Piaget's 'socialised speech' and Bernstein's 'egocentric sequence' are rather similar, in that both concepts imply objectivity, speech for others. And Piaget's 'egocentric speech' and Bernstein's 'sociocentric sequence' are somewhat similar, in that both imply subjectivity, speech for self or for others of an assumed identical viewpoint.

Having distinguished the two types of sequence, we shall now look at the egocentric sequence in more detail. We shall examine it from the point of view of phonology, more particularly from the point of view of tonicity. Tonicity refers to the placing of the tonic, or nucleus (Halliday, 1963a). With 'I think' the tonic may fall on either *I* or *think*†; thus:

(59) *I* think it's an aeroplane.

and

(60) I *think* it's an aeroplane.

* Further evidence pertaining to the speech of adults is provided by Cook (1968), who finds a greater use of sympathetic circularities (sociocentric sequences) in the working-class mothers and a greater use of the egocentric sequence in middle-class mothers.

† cf. Hymes's (1968) comment on Cazden (1966).

Now clearly at one level there is a difference in meaning between these two sentences: (59) emphasises that it is a particular person that is making the assertion, and (60) emphasises the tentativeness with which the assertion is being made. It is thought, though, that both could be said to show an awareness of other possible points of view. We believe that middle-class speakers tend to use both kinds, depending on the circumstances. Clearly, there are times when a speaker wishes to state that a certain proposition is a personally held conviction and there are other times when he wishes to convey the tentativeness with which he puts forward a particular proposition. As we did not expect the egocentric sequence to occur frequently in five-year-old children's speech, we did not subdivide them according to this phonological criterion in our initial analysis. It can be expected, however, considering the nature of the tasks that the children were set to do, that the majority of occurrences of the egocentric sequence will be of the tentative kind. It is thought that the middle-class children will follow a similar pattern to Loban's subjects (1966). Loban reported as follows:

'Those subjects who proved to have the greatest power over language by every measure that could be applied ... were the subjects who most frequently used language to express tentativeness. ... Those most capable speakers often use such expressions as the following:

It might be a gogher, but I'm not sure.
That, I think, is in Africa.
I'm not exactly sure where that is.

The child with less power over language appears to be less flexible in his thinking, is not often capable of seeing more than one alternative, and apparently summons up all his linguistic resources merely to make a flat dogmatic statement.'

Both the egocentric sequence and the sociocentric ones may be seen as examples of what Poldauf (1964) calls the 'Third Syntactical Plan'. 'The third plan has in it components which place the content of the sentence in relation to the individual and his special ability to perceive, judge and assess. An individual has some particular sort of concern in the content of a communication.' We may say that in the case of the sociocentric sequences the individual involved, 'the one having concern', as Poldauf puts it, is the listener, whereas in the case of the egocentric sequence it is the speaker who is involved. With the egocentric sequence the involvement seems to be of the sort which Poldauf describes as follows: 'He feels that the matter communicated is what we might call his "mental property".' The speaker is conveying his own attitude to the facts communicated. 'With these expressions', according to Poldauf, 'the idea is ... expressed in the subordinate element, while the governing expression introduces into the sentence the person presenting his evaluation.' Poldauf's work is highly suggestive, and his concept of 'the Third Syntactical Plan' seems a useful one for drawing together such diverse entities as 'modals of possibility', 'attitudinal adjectives', 'manner adverbs', etc. Some examples are:

(61) It may be an aeroplane.

(62) He was very careless.

In general we would expect the middle-class to make more use of the third syntactical plan than the working-class except in the case of sociocentric sequences.

In our analysis we divided sociocentric sequences into two groups, the mirror image type and the non-mirror image type. The mirror image type is the true tag. The subject of the tag must be a pronoun referring back to a previous subject (the subject to the previous predicator), e.g.

(63) It's a man, isn't it?

(64) That man isn't going to catch his train, is he?

The commonest tag is the reversed polarity tag, that is one where, if the verbal group of the SP is positive, the verbal group of the PS is negative, and vice-versa. Sinclair (1965) writes that 'the contextual meaning of a sentence with such a tag clause is of a question which predicts a confirmatory answer.' This interpretation accords well with that of Bernstein (1962b): 'On the whole the speaker expects affirmation.' The non-mirror image type of sociocentric sequence includes 'you know', 'you see', 'see'. These may come at the end of a sentence, but they may also occur at the beginning of it or interrupt it quite freely.

The egocentric sequence was coded differently according to whether it was associated with an elliptical clause or not. If it occurred with such a clause it was coded under T3 in the Tag Clause table; examples of these clauses are now given:

(65) An airship, I think.

(66) The Eiffel Tower, I think.

If it did not occur with such a clause, it was marked by means of the lexical element in the verbal group. This type may be exemplified by the following:

(67) I think that it is an airship.

(68) I think it is an airship.

(69) It is an airship, I think.

This arrangement gives three entries in the tag clause table: mirror image sociocentric sequences, non-mirror sociocentric sequences and the egocentric sequence associated with an elliptical clause. It was also decided

59

that it would be useful to employ a further entry in the table for marking the brief inadequacy signal, 'I don't know' (or 'Dunno').

4.3 Rankshifted clauses

Rankshifted clauses occur at four main places, at M, H and Q in the nominal group, and at V in the adverbial group. Section 5.2 on the nominal group and 7.3 on the adverbial group should be consulted for a description of these places. It is convenient to refer to rankshifted clauses operating in these places as modifier, head, qualifier and vortex clauses respectively. We shall consider each of these in turn.

Modifier clauses
The most likely use of a modifier clause in the speech of a five-year-old child – even this use is probably not very likely – is as a means of specifying the theme of clause. In the examples which follow, the modifier clauses are those within angle brackets.

(70)	John	wants	to meet	you.	
	S	P	-P	C	Theme unspecified

(71) ⟨It's⟩	John that*	wants	to meet	you.	
	S	P	-P	C	S-Theme specified

(72)	I	want	to meet	John	
	S	P	-P	C	Theme unspecified

(73) ⟨It's⟩	John	I	want	to meet	
	C	S	P	-P	C-Theme specified

(74)	They	're sailing	tomorrow		
	S	P	A		Theme unspecified

(75) ⟨It's⟩	tomorrow	they	're sailing		
	A	S	P		A-Theme specified

Head clauses
These occur as head of nominal groups operating at subject and complement in the clause and as complement to a preposition in the prepositional group. Those that occur at the complement include those that have been referred to as reported clauses in the discussion above. The verbs that are associated with such clauses include reporting verbs, e.g. *say*, *announce*, *murmur*, verbs of cognition, e.g. *think*, *suppose*, *know* and verbs of perception, e.g. *perceive*, *see*. Here are some examples of head clauses:

* The description of this item, *that*, is too complicated to be dealt with here.

60

at Subject

(76) ⟨What we want⟩ is Watneys

at Complement

(77) They're ⟨what we play with⟩

(78) You have to find ⟨where they are⟩

as Prepositional Complement

(79) It doesn't look like ⟨what we want⟩

Qualifier clauses
These clauses include the traditional defining adjective clauses or restrictive relative clauses, and also the traditional noun clauses in apposition. We did not make any subdivisions as it was not thought that these clauses would be a very frequent choice in five-year-old children's speech. Here are some examples illustrating something of the range of these clauses:

(80) The argument ⟨when we were leaving⟩

(81) The argument ⟨which John started⟩

(82) The argument ⟨that age is important⟩

Vortex clauses
These are rankshifted clauses which have the value 'adjunct' in clause structure, e.g.

(83) It's ⟨where you left it⟩
    cf. It's there.

Of these four types of rankshifted clause it is the head type and qualifier type that we would most expect to show social class differences. We would predict that the middle-class would use more of both these types: more head clauses because of their association with (a) the egocentric sequence, 'I think', (see section 4.2c) and other verbs of cognition, especially those implying suspension of judgement (section 6.7) and (b) indirect role-play speech (sections 3.3b and 6.7); and more qualifier clauses because they are, among other things, a useful means of defining the referent of a nominal group. In an example such as (81) the determiner, *the*, is cataphoric to the qualifier clause, that is, it points forward to this clause, which identifies which argument is being referred to. These, then, are the main reasons why we would expect the middle-class to use more of these types of rankshifted clauses.

61

4.4 Clause elements

In our description of the clause we recognised eight elements of structure:

S Subject
P Predicator
C Complement
A Lexical Adjunct
B Binding-conjunction
L Linking-conjunction
Z Z-element ('absolute nominal')
V Vocative

We have already mentioned most of these elements in the preceding description, for example, in our discussion of the free clause classes. For a more detailed treatment of S, P, C, A and Z, the reader is referred to Sinclair (1965). Here it will only be necessary to consider the relationship of A, B and L to each other and the relationship of Z and V.

Strictly, A, B and L should be subdivisions of one element, adjunct. The adjunct breaks down into 'grammatical adjunct' and 'lexical adjunct' (here A). The grammatical adjunct must always precede, and can never be included in, or follow, the subject and predicator in the clause in which it occurs. The lexical adjunct cannot precede the grammatical adjunct but it can precede, or be included in, or follow the subject and predicator complex in the clause in which it occurs. Below is given an example of a prepositional group that can operate at the lexical adjunct in all these three positions:

(84) *After that day* | his parents | treated | him | like a proper child.
    A   S   P   C   A

(85) His parents | *after that day* | treated | him | like a proper child.
    S   A   P   C   A

(86) His parents | treated | him | like a proper child | *after that day.*
    S   P   C   A   A

The grammatical adjunct is broken down into 'linking-conjunction' (L) and 'binding-conjunction' (B) according to whether it is the first element in a co-ordinate clause or in a bound clause, e.g.

(87) One day in the summer a boy called Fred ran away from home, *and* set out into the country, *because* his parents were cruel to him.

In the above sentence, *and* is operating as a linking-conjunction and *because* as a binding-conjunction.

Also, strictly, Z and V should be subdivisions of one element, called Z by Halliday and others. This Z breaks down into three elements Z-

62

(Z-negative or absolute), Z+ (Z-positive) and Z^V (Z-vocative). Our Z covers the first two elements. These two are in complementary distribution. Z-negative may be characterised as 'either subject or complement' as it occurs in predicator-less clauses, where the subject/complement opposition is neutralised, e.g.

(88) John!
     Z

Z-positive may be characterised as 'both subject and complement' as it occurs in clauses with more than one predicator, and it acts, as it were, as complement to one predicator and as subject to another, e.g.

(89) I | want | him.
    S | P | C

(90) He | will mend | it.
    S | P | C

(91) I | want | him | to mend | it.
    S | P | Z | P | C

Z-vocative may be characterised as 'neither subject nor complement': it is the vocative in imperative clauses. We use the element 'V' to cover this use, e.g.

(92) Be | fair, | John!
    P | C | V

4.5 Clause complexity

All clauses were subdivided into twelve generalised types, these types being the product of the interaction of three basic clause types and the number of adjuncts present. The three basic clause types are minor clause, clause with a predicator, and clause with a predicator and a subject. There are four possibilities for the number of adjuncts present: none, one, two and three. Differences in the ordering of the subject and predicator elements and in the ordering of the adjuncts are not taken account of in this classification. The idea underlying this classification is that the adjunct is optional in clause structure. Basically, choosing it involves going beyond the minimal structure of a clause. Hasan (1964), considering the weighting of clause complexity, makes a number of interesting suggestions: 'The weighting of a minimal "compound" pattern e.g. of SP, P((S)) ... can be lower than that of SPA, P((S))A etc., where the presence of A is irrelevant to the types' ability to expound a particular class. Similarly though successive A elements may be weighted highly, their value when occurring in a moodless (independent) clause may be considered lower

63

than that in other clauses.' That clause structure should always be considered in relation to the class of the clause is important. In this respect our clause types are considerably less than the ideal perfection; for example, we do not distinguish command free clauses from non-finite bound clauses, or non-response statement free clauses from response statement free clauses. However, it is thought that these clause types are a useful starting point, and that the patterns that emerge might suggest fruitful subclassifications. The table for the twelve types is now presented:

Minor	Minor A	Minor 2A	Minor 3A
P	P A	P 2A	P 3A
S, P	S, P A	S, P 2A	S, P 3A

4.6 Systemic choices in the clause

The above description of the clause deals with systemic choices only in the case of the mood system. Nothing is said of the other two important clause systems, transitivity and theme. It was thought that basic information about the latter two systems could be gained by means of a supplementary program and a second run-through of the data. The computer could be instructed to count, in the case of transitivity, such things as the number of complements in the clause (that is, none, one or two), the kind of complement in the case of single complements (the single intensive complement is marked by means of the subclass of lexical verb in our analysis), and, in the case of theme, whether there is an initial complement or adjunct.

Such an analysis of transitivity and theme as outlined above is clearly quite limited. Any future work will have to take as its starting point Halliday's recent work (Halliday, 1967c, d). To give some idea of the scope of this work, we may quote the following from Halliday (1967d):

'The English clause ... can be regarded as the domain of three main areas of syntactic choice: transitivity, mood and theme. Transitivity is the set of options relating to cognitive content, the linguistic representation of extralinguistic experience, whether of the phenomena of the external world or of feelings, thoughts and perceptions. Mood represents the organisation of participants in speech situations, providing options in the form of speaker roles: the speaker may inform, question or command; he may confirm, request confirmation, contradict or display any one of a wide range of postures defined by the potentialities of linguistic interaction (Halliday, 1967e). Theme is concerned with the information structure of the clause; with the status of the elements not as participants in extralinguistic processes but as components of a message; with the relation of what is being said to what has gone before in the discourse, and its organisation into an act of communication. . . . None of these areas of meaning is restricted to the clause; but for each the clause provides a significant range of options, and it is these clause options for which the terms "transitivity", "mood" and "theme" are here being used: given the clause as domain, transitivity is the grammar of experience, mood is the grammar of speech function and theme is the grammar of discourse.'

4.7 Coding information

TABLE 02 'CLAUSE CLASS'
The sentence class information is immediately followed with a symbol from Table 02 'Clause Class'. The table is given below:

Symbol	Class
F	Free clause
B	Bound clause
T	Tag clause

TABLE 03 'FREE CLAUSE CLASS'
If symbol 'F' is chosen, it has to be followed immediately with a selection from Table 03 'Free Clause Class'.

Symbol	Class
1	Statement
2	Question
3	Command
4	Inadequacy signal

TABLE 04 'BOUND CLAUSE CLASS'
Likewise if symbol 'B' is chosen, it has to be followed immediately with a symbol from the Table 04 'Bound Clause Class'. Here is the table:

Symbol	Class
1	Conditioning
2	Additioning

Co-occurrence Restrictions
    The additioning clause (B2) may never come immediately after a sentence class symbol (S1, S2, S3, S4) or a linker (LL1, LL2, LL3, LL4) or sentence adverb (AV5).

TABLE 05 'TAG CLAUSE CLASS'
If symbol 'T' is chosen, it has to be followed immediately with a symbol from Table 05 'Tag Clause Class'.

65

Symbol	Class
1	Sociocentric: mirror image
2	Sociocentric: others
3	Egocentric
4	Inadequacy signal

Co-occurrence Restrictions

The sociocentric (mirror image) tag (T1) may never come immediately after a sentence class symbol (S1, S2, S3, S4).

INCLUDED CLAUSE

If a clause is included in another clause, a round bracket '(' is put before the included clause. The bracket is followed immediately by the number of the 'Clause Class' table, '02'. The clause is then coded as usual, that is, sentence element, clause class, etc. The end of the included clause is signalled by '/2' and by closing the brackets, ')'.

TABLE 06 'ELEMENTS OF CLAUSE STRUCTURE'

If a tag symbol was previously selected, then no selection is made from Table 06, 'Elements of clause structure'. In other words, we treated the tags, e.g. isn't it?, you know, I think, I don't know, as if their clause structure were fully predictable.

If a free clause or bound clause symbol was selected, then a selection must be made from Table 06. Here is the table:

Symbol	Element
P	Predicator
S	Subject
C	Complement
Z	Z-element
V	Vocative
A	Adjunct
B	Binding-conjunction
L	Linking-conjunction

Co-occurrence Restrictions

Only a co-ordinate clause may contain a linking-conjunction, and only a bound clause may contain a binding-conjunction.

SUMMARY

In terms of the chart of allowable transitions (Diagram 8 in Part 2), we have now covered the following stages:

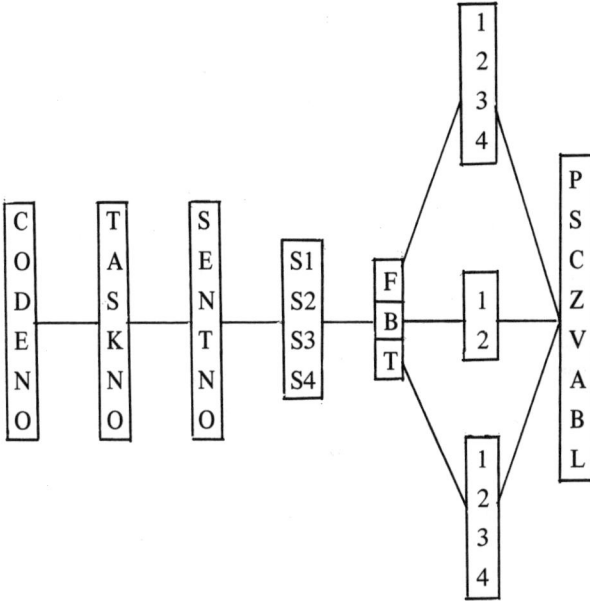

CODE NO — TASK NO — SENT NO — S1 S2 S3 S4 — F B T

```
                                1
                                2
                                3
                                4
 C    T    S                              P
 O    A    E    S1                        S
 D    S    N    S2   F                    C
 E    K    T    S3   B    1               Z
 N    N    N    S4   T    2               V
 O    O    O                              A
                                          B
                                1         L
                                2
                                1
                                2
                                3
                                4
```

Example

Here is the example sentence again (previously given in section 3.5):
    That lamp has fallen in front of the television.

Coding

1234	i.e.	CHILD'S CODE NO.
10		TASK NO.
01S1F1S		SENT. NO., SENT. CLASS, FREE CLAUSE STATEMENT, SUBJECT

We have now coded the clause information. Our next move is to examine the groups that make up clauses.

Chapter 5

THE NOMINAL GROUP

5.1 Introductory

The nominal group is that class of the unit 'group' which operates at the subject, complement, Z-element (or 'absolute nominal') and vocative elements in clause structure, and also certain subclasses operate at the adjunct. The reason why only one class is set up to account for the first four elements is that there is a large degree of overlap in the exponents of these elements. It is therefore economical to establish only one class.

The justification for regarding certain subclasses of nominal group as operating at the adjunct is given by Halliday (1963b). Some examples will suffice here. In the four sentences which follow, 'this morning' has the structural values S, C, Z and A respectively:

(1) This morning promises to be sunny.

(2) I've set this morning aside for working in the garden.

(3) I'd like this morning to last a bit longer.

(4) I arrived later than ever this morning.

Other nominal groups that behave like 'this morning' are those with 'time' nouns, e.g. day, night, afternoon, evening, week, month, year, yesterday, today, tomorrow; those with 'place' nouns, e.g. home, downstairs, upstairs, and nouns expressing 'distance', feet, yards, miles; and finally, those with 'manner' nouns, e.g. way.

Carroll (1964) gives the approximate conceptual meaning of the nominal class as the class of experiences that includes 'objects, persons, ideas, and relations whose location or distribution in space, actually or metaphorically, can be specified'. By contrast, the verbals refer to 'events, relationships, or states whose location or distribution in a time dimension can be specified'. Although one may question aspects of Carroll's formulation, it does seem that he points to the basic difference between nominal and verbal expressions.

Halliday (1967a, 1967b), has indicated that to a large extent the early conceptual structure of the child is determined by the choices available in the nominal group, choices such as mass/count, singular/plural, abstract/ concrete, animate/inanimate, etc. Moreover, the nominal group normally operates in clause structure, and one of its chief functions there is to associate participants (possessing any of the features mentioned above) with a process, and to state, as required, particular attributes and circumstances of the process and participants. The nominal group can realise various participant roles, including 'initiator', 'actor', 'goal', 'attribuant' and 'beneficiary'. These functions are described by Halliday (1967c, 1967d).

5.2 The primary structure of the nominal group

At primary degree of delicacy, the nominal group is treated as a multivariate structure, that is, one that contains more than one structural value. An inventory of its primary elements of structure is: modifier (M), head (H) and qualifier (Q). The position in sequence is fixed. Sequence is conceived of as from right to left, so Q may not precede H, and H may not precede M. Only the head is an obligatory element, the modifier and qualifier being optional. There may be more than one modifier and qualifier. A nominal group that has a head and no other element has a simple structure. A nominal group with more elements than this has a compound structure. There are three types of compound structure possible, which may be symbolised in the following way:

$$MH$$
$$HQ$$
$$MHQ$$

Examples of these three types of compound structure are:

(5) university ⌐ men
    M   H

(6)   men | of great experience
             H | Q

(7) university | men | of great experience
    M | H | Q

We may express the primary structure of the nominal group in a generalised form, so:

$$(M \ldots^n) \; H \; (Q \ldots^n)$$

The brackets indicate optional elements, and the dots and superscript ^{n} indicate that there is no theoretical limit to the number of modifiers and qualifiers.

From these primary elements of structure, M, H and Q, are derived three corresponding classes of the unit 'word': 'pre-substantive',

'substantive' and 'post-substantive' respectively. Each of these elements and classes may be subdivided at secondary degree of delicacy.

5.3 The modifier

The modifier may be differentiated into four secondary elements: deictic (D), ordinative (O), epithet (E) and nominal (N). Place in sequence is crucial to the definition of these elements; going from right to left, N may not precede E; E may not precede O, and O may not precede D. These elements yield four distinct classes of word: 'determiner', 'numeral', 'adjective' and 'noun'. Some examples illustrating these elements are:

(8) the | men
    D

(9) two | men
    O

(10) the | two | fat | men
     D | O | E

(11) three | university | men
      O | N

At the same degree of delicacy we may recognise a further element, the intensifier (I). The intensifier is expounded by a class of items which includes the following: more, most, very, rather, quite, awfully, etc. These items are known as submodifiers. They operate within the modifier. Examples of this phenomenon are now given:

(12) About | ten | men (arrived there)
      I | O

(13) Very | much | food (as in: Is there very much food left?)
      I | O

(14) Some | very | beautiful | flowers
      D | I | E

Having described the modifier at second degree of delicacy, we shall not carry our description any further. It is possible to break down the deictic, ordinative, epithet and nominal into further multivariate structures, but it was thought that this would be unrewarding in our present analysis as it was not expected that the children would produce very 'heavy' modifications.

Now that we have established the five structural elements of the modifier, we shall briefly consider how they function in the modifier as a whole. The modifier as a whole may be regarded as an example of

70

left-ward branching. It branches from the head of the nominal group, as is shown in the following diagram:

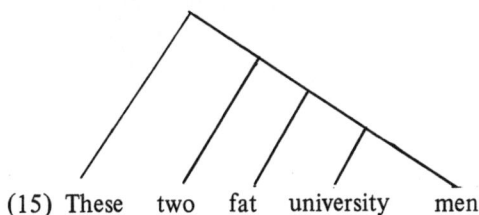

(15) These two fat university men

The effect of this branching is to yield a semantic taxonomy, which moves from the most specific on the left to the most general on the right. A series of examples will make this point clearer:

(16)   men
                                                                    H

(17)   university | men
                                                             N | H

(18)   fat | university | men
                                                E | N | H

(19)   two | fat | university | men
                                       O | E | N | H

(20)   those | two | fat | university | men
                                D | O | E | N | H

The further the branching extends to the left the more specific the classification becomes. This, it must be admitted, is a simplification of the matter, for not all items that occur in the modifier are classifying (or 'defining', as Halliday has called it) in this way. We may illustrate this latter point by referring to the adjectives: these may be differentiated into attitudinal ones and descriptive ones. The attitudinal adjectives normally occur further away from the head than do the descriptive ones; they convey subjective evaluations and are often emotive (examples are: beautiful, lovely, horrid, wicked), and they are never defining. The descriptive adjectives are more objective and concrete; they can classify the referent of the head in terms of dimensions such as size, colour, shape, material, provenance etc., (examples are: small, red, round, wooden, French); these are potentially defining. Nevertheless, to return to our original statement, it does seem reasonable to say as a generalisation that the further the branching extends to the left the more specific the classification becomes.

What perhaps is not obvious at first is the relationship of the pattern of specification (that is, most specific on the left and most general on the right) to the actual sets of items that make up the pattern. The items that occur on the left in a heavy modification, the determiners and numerals, are the most general and those that occur on the right, the adjectives and nouns, are the most specific in their reference. We might mention here what Jespersen (1924) said whilst discussing substantives (nouns) and adjectives in terms of 'specialisation': 'The adjective indicates and singles out one quality, one distinguishing mark, but each substantive suggests, to whoever understands it, many distinguishing features by which he recognises the person or thing in question.' Jespersen also wrote that 'it is really most natural that a less special term is used in order further to specialise what is already to some extent special'. What is the point of all this for our research? The main one is that we cannot really expect the children to use many, if any, long modifications involving nouns and adjectives. Such modifications are much more appropriate to, say, the language of scientific exposition on the one hand, in which it is often necessary to give precise classifications on a number of different dimensions, e.g.

(21) Simple Cognitive Child-oriented Personal Appeals.

or to the language of advertising on the other hand, in which highly emotive concatenations are often required, e.g.

(22) Natural Teak and Antique Softglow Formica decorative Laminate (quoted by Leech, 1966).

The pattern in which the most specific classes of items occur nearest the head and in which the most general classes of items occur furthest from the head is exactly parallel to another pattern, the lexical—grammatical pattern. The items that are most specific are the ones that are most easily analysed in terms of lexical classes, and the ones that are most general are those that are most easily handled in terms of grammatical classes. A further pattern is also discernible: the grammatical items are relatively few in number whereas the lexical items are immensely numerous; this, in fact, reinforces what we said earlier about the nouns and adjectives being more specific.

In our analysis we decided to subdivide the determiners as these give clear clues as to why a speaker has selected a particular nominal group, that is, what type of reference he is aiming at. There are, in fact, about 30 different determiners that lend themselves to analysis in terms of systemic choices. Here is a list of them:

the, which, what, whichever, whatever, whose, whosoever, this, that, these, those, my, your, his, her, its, our, their, one's, each, every, all, both, neither, either, no, any, a, some.

Had we been recognising a multivariate structure at the deictic, these would have been the items occurring at the first place in this structure.

Halliday has broken down the determiners into one-member classes in most instances. They are differentiated into these micro-classes by means of a multi-dimensional analysis which utilises about sixteen binary systems. We have not space to describe and explain all these systems here, but we will give a couple of illustrations. One item, *the*, is completely characterised by means of two systems, 'specification', and 'selection', the terms it realises being 'specific' and 'non-selective'. All the other items require to be characterised by means of more than two systems; *this*, for instance, requires six systems, and the terms it realises are 'specific', 'selective', 'non-interrogative', 'demonstrative', 'proximate' and 'singular'.

Halliday's use of 'specific' and 'non-specific' is, of course, precise and defined, and should not be confused with the way in which we have been using 'most specific' and 'most general' to point up a distinction between nouns and adjectives as lexical items, and determiners and numerals as grammatical items. The distinction between 'specific' and 'non-specific' is to do with the preciseness of the identification or definition of the referent of the head of the nominal group, for example, *that* in

(23) Pass me that book

is specific, but *a* in

(24) Pass me a book

is non-specific. We have to distinguish also another system, that of selection, which should not be confused with specification. It has two terms, 'selective' and 'non-selective'. The system of specification is to do with identification of referent; it does not imply choice, the choice of one referent rather than another or others. The system of selection is to do with choice. For example, we have said that *a* is non-specific, and so is *either*, as in

(25) Pass me either book

but *either*, unlike *a*, does imply a choice, a selection from two objects, and so it is 'selective' whereas *a* is 'non-selective'. We might add, by the way, that all the items that are 'specific' are also 'selective', all except one, *the*. *The* is not regarded as 'selective', because it does not make the selection itself; the selection is made elsewhere in the surrounding language, by an adjective, for example, as in the following nominal group:

(26) Pass me the pink dress.

As the form of analysis contained in the 'Centertester' program was meant to give a survey of the data, in general the procedure was to make broad initial cuts in the data which it was hoped would show up areas of promise which would receive further investigation in secondary analyses.

The programming decision was taken that no table should contain more than ten entries, and this was held to rigidly, the only exception (and this was only a partial exception) was in the case of the tense system, which in fact was made up of 4 tables of 10 entries, laid alongside each other. At the time of compiling the table for the determiners it was thought that in a table of 10 entries only 9 were available for effective use; it later became apparent that the full 10 could have been used.

It was considered that the specific and selective choices were the ones which were most easily relatable to the sociological theory. A cut was made, accordingly, between the specific and selective and the rest, the latter being referred to as 'other determiners', and entered under category D8. The specific and selective were next broken down into interrogative and non-interrogative, the interrogative items being the WH-words: *which, what, whichever, whatever, whose, whosoever*. It was expected that the middle-class subjects would tend to use these items more frequently than the working-class, as they would ask more 'information-seeking' questions (that is, the WH-kind) and would use more indirect speech. These WH-words were put in category D7.

Following Halliday, the specific and selective determiners were also subdivided into 'demonstrative' and 'possessive'. The demonstrative determiners are *which, what, whichever, what* (the interrogative) and *this, that, these, those* (the non-interrogative). The possessive determiners are *whose, whosoever* (the interrogative) and *my, your, his, her, its, one's, our, their* (the non-interrogative). It was thought that the division of the interrogative into demonstrative and possessive was too delicate for our analysis, and so it was ignored. We subdivided the non-interrogative demonstratives into two categories: 'proximate', i.e. *this, these,* and 'non-proximate', i.e. *that, those.* These were put into categories D5 and D6 respectively. There are a number of reasons for distinguishing the proximate and non-proximate demonstratives. The proximate ones are associated with the first-person mode of address, the future (in fact) and the non-past (in texts) whereas the non-proximate ones are associated with the second and third person, and the past (in fact and in texts). Clearly this crude analysis into proximate and non-proximate could not bring out these meanings; it is simply intended as a first broad cut. One hypothesis that might be worth testing in a subsequent more delicate analysis is that the working-class in conversational situations might use *this* more than the middle-class. For, as Halliday has pointed out in a lecture, *this* in a clause like 'I saw this man' has the effect of bringing *you* and *me* together, building on this opposition of 'near' and 'far'. *This* brings the listener into the shared experience. Shared experience is at the essence of the Restricted Code. Bernstein (1962b) wrote: 'A restricted code is generated by a form of social relationship based on a range of closely shared identifications self-consciously held by the members.'

Setting up these categories left five more possible entries in the

74

determiner. One was needed for marking omissions of the determiner, and so this meant that just four were available for dealing with the eight possessive items. We subdivided them into 1st, 2nd and 3rd person, and then further subdivided the 3rd person items, splitting *his, her, its* and *their* against *one's*. This was done as it was thought there would be some association of the use of *one's* and the use of the pronoun *one* as a characteristic of a formal language (Bernstein, 1959): 'The use of the pronoun "one" as subject implies the objectification of the experience which is verbalised. The subject is made general and so freed from the confines of a personal experience.' The general subdivision into 1st, 2nd and 3rd person is a traditional one, but a useful starting-point. The 3rd person items are used much more than the 1st and 2nd person ones for making anaphoric reference, that is, for referring back to previously mentioned items in the text, and so are an important device for securing cohesion in a text. However, the initial results on this measure are bound to be ambiguous, as the 3rd person items may also be used for making exophoric reference in a situation such as the one in which the present speech sample was collected, i.e. they may refer to entities in the context.

5.4 The head

For purposes of subclassifying the words that occur as head of the nominal group – the substantives – it is quite useful to refer to the classes of word we recognised in the modifier, for it is found that to a large extent the words that appear in the modifier may also appear at head. There are obvious exceptions to this, of course. *The* and *a* may not occur at head; it has been said that the head form of *the* is *that* or *it* and the head form of *a* is *one*, but this description was not used in the present analysis (see Hasan, 1967). Certain determiners change their form when they occur as head: thus, *my, your, her, our, their* become *mine, yours, hers, ours* and *theirs*. The two most obvious differences between the words that occur in the modifier and those that occur at head concern the submodifiers and the pronouns. The submodifiers, e.g. *very, quite, beautifully,* cannot occur at head. Pronouns cannot occur in the modifier at all but they are a very frequent choice at head.

It was decided, then, to recognise determiners, numerals, adjectives, nouns and pronouns. It will be remembered that in the modifier the determiners were broken down into eight different classes. It was considered unnecessary to differentiate so many classes at head, as the possessives were probably a relatively rare choice there. Three groups of determiners, however, were separated from the main category and were treated separately. These were the proximate demonstratives, *this, these,* and the non-proximate demonstratives, *that, those,* and the interrogatives, *which, what, whichever, whatever, whose, whosoever* and *who*. These eight categories, then, together with the category for marking missing heads, made up a complete table. The pronouns, however, still had not been subclassified. As these were regarded as of considerable sociological interest an additional table of nine entries was attached to them.

The chief guide for subclassifying the pronouns was Bernstein's experimental study (published 1962b) in which he found that the middle-class subjects used *I* significantly more than the working-class and that the working-class used *you* and *they* (taken together) significantly more. According to Bernstein: 'The use of "they" is not simply the result of the tension between in-group and out-group. . . . The non-specificity implied by "they" is a function of the lack of differentiation and the subsequent concretising of experience which characterises a restricted code as a whole. . . . The lack of specification also implies that there is possibly some implicit agreement about the referent such that the elaboration is redundant. In this sense "they" is based upon "we".' A similar explanation is given for the use of *you*. 'It offers a formal subject which facilitates a ready identification on the part of the listener. The content of the statement is presented in such a way that the listener can translate this in terms of his experience.' Concerning the use of *I* Bernstein suggests that 'it may be that if an individual takes as his reference point rigid adherence to a wide range of closely shared identifications and expectations, the area of discretion available is reduced and the differentiation of self from act may be constrained. . . . If individuals are limited to a restricted code one of its general effects may be to reduce the differentiation of self.' In the same paper Bernstein remarks that contrary to expectation *one* was not used by the middle-class subjects. In an earlier paper Bernstein (1959) had suggested that the use of *one* 'involves a reaching beyond the immediate experience, a transcending of the personal and brings the individual into a particular relationship with objects and persons'. In the same article Bernstein says that it is probable that in the Restricted Code *we* and *they* will serve an apparently similar function to *one*. But he comments: 'It is in fact not similar, nor is it a simple substitution; for "we" or "you" refer to the local experience, the local social relationships, the immediate normative arrangements, and are bounded by the personal.' Here, then, are the main ideas on which we based the present subclassification of pronouns. In a discussion, Bernstein stressed that it was the operation of these pronouns as 'subject' that was of chief importance. Here are the subclasses we arrived at:

P1	Subject	I
P2		you (singular)
P3		he, she, it
P4		one
P5		we
P6		you (plural)
P7		they

76

Two more entries were available; one was needed for the remaining pronouns and the other we decided to use for *there* (weakly stressed *there*). Weak *there* seemed a fairly frequent choice in our data, and as its usual function was to act merely as a 'prop subject' or 'anticipatory subject' it was decided that it would be best to isolate it so that it could be excluded from major comparisons. Examples of weak *there* are:

(27) There's a train, a station and a tunnel.

(28) There's a man walking down the street.

5.5 The modifier and the head related

The class of word at head determines to a large extent what classes of word may occur in the modifier. We shall outline briefly some of the most important patterns, namely those associated with the noun, pronoun and adjective.

The most striking feature of the noun is that normally it must occur with a determiner. Only 'mass' nouns (*sugar, bread*, etc.), 'abstract' singular nouns (*beauty, truth*) and 'generic' plural nouns (*lions are ...* etc.) and nouns following certain prepositions (e.g. *by bus*) may occur without a determiner. Nouns may also be modified by numerals, if they are 'countable', and by adjectives and other nouns. They may not usually be submodified.

Pronouns cannot normally occur with modifiers. The reason for this is that pronouns like proper names are supposedly self-identifying (e.g. *John, London*) and pronouns such as the personal ones are identified either by surrounding text or by the context of situation. The proper name pronouns need some further comment. It is because they are treated in the language as being the unique names for people and places that they cannot be modified, or qualified either; they are self-identifying and do not need determiners such as *the* and *that* to identify them. However, occasionally, as Sinclair (1965) has pointed out, they do appear with adjectives, e.g.

(29) Come to sunny Devon!

But these adjectives are not identifying or defining; they are purely attitudinal. Sinclair remarks: 'Sunny Devon is not "a kind of Devon" or "one of the Devons" as a *sunny day* would be a kind of *day*.' It is, of course, often possible in language to use the same formal item in more than one way, and we can do this with the items we have been referring to. We can use items like *John* or *daddy* either as pronouns or as nouns, e.g.

(30) John is coming home this weekend.   (pronoun)

(31) This is my John.   (noun)

(32) Give that to Daddy!   (pronoun)

(33) I was speaking to John's daddy.   (noun)

In the pronoun use the referent is treated as being unique and as not being in need of identification, whereas in the noun use the referent is regarded as a member of a class of entities and as being in need of being differentiated from the other members of the class.

It is regretted that we could not expand our pronoun analysis further, so as to include the question of reference. But we had already devoted a whole table to them, and it would have been going beyond our scope (our aim being to make a broad initial survey of the data) to have differentiated them further. Hasan (1967) points out that the pronominals may be anaphoric, cataphoric and exophoric in reference. In the anaphoric use the pronominal has a verbal referent in the preceding part of the text, whereas in the cataphoric use it has a verbal referent in the following part of the text. In contrast, the referent in the exophoric use is not in the text; it is not in the language at all, but in the situation. It is possible, by the way, to distinguish a further kind of non-language reference, namely homophoric. Whereas exophoric reference is to the context of situation, homophoric reference is to the context of culture. Examples of these different kinds of reference are now given:

(34) anaphoric   That's John. *He's* an old friend of mine,

(35) cataphoric   *It's* wrong to do that.

(36) exophoric   *He's* an old friend of mine.

(said of someone who is actually present in the context of situation)

(37) homophoric   I'm fascinated by *the* moon.

In (34) *He* refers back to *John* in the preceding sentence; in (35) *It* points forward to *to do that*; *He* in (36) points to the non-language context; and finally *the* in (37) indicates that in the context of British culture the moon is regarded as being a unique entity, which does not require to be distinguished from other moons, the ones that orbit Saturn, for example. From our point of view the two most interesting uses are the anaphoric and the exophoric. The anaphoric use is a strong device for securing cohesion in a relatively extended stretch of language. The exophoric use demands the presence of situational clues for identifying the referents; it can easily lead to imprecision and ambiguity if the speaker too readily assumes that the listener is 'with him', is following his train of thought. It is clear, then, that before anything very precise can be said about the pronouns, a further subclassification into at least 'anaphoric' and 'exophoric' is required.*

* Such a further subclassification is now being performed by P. R. Hawkins and R. E. Pickvance of the Sociological Research Unit. Preliminary findings are presented in Hawkins (1969).

Adjectives at head cannot normally be modified by any modifier except the submodifiers. An adjective is used to ascribe a quality to a previously mentioned referent. Some submodifiers define the quality in terms of a range of some kind, e.g. *almost, rather, quite, very*, whereas other submodifiers (the open-class ones, that is, those that have the morphological structure, base adjective + the suffix *–ly*) also convey an attitude towards the quality, for example:

(38) She's looking marvellously happy.

It is possible, we might add, to use some formal items as either adjectives or nouns. When such items are used as nouns they must be modified by the determiner, *the*, for example:

(39) The poor are always with us.

Having discussed some of the formal features of the modifier and the head in relation to nouns, adjectives and pronouns, we shall now suggest in what way the social classes may differ in their use of these items. We shall begin with the adjectives.

Bernstein (1962b) found a significant social class difference on total adjectives and uncommon adjectives expressed as proportions of total analysed words. It should perhaps be pointed out that Bernstein's 'total adjective' count includes numerical and demonstrative adjectives; in other words, it is largely the same as our total modifier count. The numerical and demonstrative adjectives and *other* and *another* and repetitions were excluded from the 'uncommon adjective' count. Lawton (1963, 1964) did not find significant differences on total adjectives but did find differences on uncommon adjectives, especially in the older children. Lawton's uncommon adjectives were obtained by 'excluding all repetitions of an adjective and all those which occurred in the list of the 100 most commonly used words (McNally and Murray, 1962)'. Henderson (1969), examining three tasks of the Speech Schedule, found that middle-class children, particularly those of high verbal ability, used more different adjectives than the working-class children.

There are a number of ways in which the home environment might influence a child's use of adjectives. We shall discuss two ways which seem to be important. First, though, we shall subdivide the adjectives into two classes: the attitudinal and the descriptive. As a broad distinction we may say that the descriptive ones refer to the concrete, physical and inherent attributes of entities, whereas the attitudinal ones refer to the abstract, moral, affective and non-inherent attributes. So, *round, red* and *small* are descriptive adjectives and *good, beautiful* and *unhappy* are attitudinal.

It seems likely that a mother who frequently controls her child by personal appeals of the affective kind will tend to have an influence on his stock of attitudinal adjectives. In a person-oriented appeal an explanation is offered to the child in terms of the effect of the child's behaviour on himself or on some other person. In the case of the affective person-oriented appeal, the appeal 'relies on the emotion or guilt that someone will feel if the child persists or that the child will feel' (Social Control Coding Manual). Here are some examples of these appeals:

(a) Simple Affective Parent-oriented Personal Appeals:
    e.g. That makes mummy very sad/upset/delighted/pleased.

(b) Simple Affective Child-oriented Personal Appeals:
    e.g. You'll feel miserable/upset/delighted/happy/pleased, if you go on/stop doing that.

(c) Simple Affective Other-oriented Personal Appeals:
    e.g. The shopkeeper will be very angry/sad, etc., if you take things from his shop.

It is not being suggested that a personal appeal always contains an adjective. This is certainly not the case; consider:

Daddy won't like it.
You want to please mummy.

What is being suggested is that the adjectival construction is a useful means of making a personal appeal, and that it is one that the middle-class mothers who use such appeals might employ a good deal. If this were the case we would expect that the children of these mothers would tend to exhibit a considerable number of these affective attitudinal adjectives in their speech.

What about the descriptive adjectives? What are the home conditions that might favour the use of these adjectives? It is suggested that an environment which provides a rich variety of stimuli is likely to promote the use of these words. Deutsch (1963) quotes Hunt's discussion of Piaget's developmental theories: 'The more new things a child has seen, the more he has heard, the more things he is interested in seeing and hearing. Moreover, the more variation in reality with which he has coped, the greater is his capacity for coping' (Hunt, 1961). Discussing the slum environment, Deutsch introduces the concept 'stimulus deprivation': 'By this is not necessarily meant any restriction of the spectrum of stimulation, but, rather, a restriction to a segment of the spectrum of stimulation potentially available.' The conditions that Deutsch is concerned with are much worse than those in which the typical British working-class child is reared, but we have evidence that the working-class environment, in some important respects at least, provides less variety in the events that are significant for the development of the child. In support of this claim we mention some of the differences which have been observed in patterns of reading and conceptions of the uses of toys (see Bernstein and Young, 1967, and Jones, 1966). Concerning reading, 'only 19 per cent of the working-class mothers read to their children according

80

to some regular pattern, compared with 36 per cent in the mixed-class and 71 per cent in the middle-class. Middle-class mothers who regularly read to their children offer more reasons for doing so than working-class mothers. They are also more inclined to stress the developmental and (formal) educational value of reading, rather than its value in keeping the child amused or "quiet" ' (Jones, 1966). Concerning the importance of toys, Jones reports: 'Middle-class mothers were much more selective than working-class in their choice of toys. They were more inclined to take the age and sex of the child into account. They were more sensitive to the physical properties of different toys, more aware of the different functions that toys could have, and more inclined to stress the value of toys in stimulating the child's curiosity and emotional development.' It seems highly probable that the middle-class mothers make use of linguistic items such as descriptive adjectives to increase the child's sensitivity to the physical properties of the toys. So, because of these two influences at least, we should expect the middle-class children to make more use of descriptive adjectives than the working-class children.

From a formal point of view, we may mention that although both attitudinal and descriptive adjectives may occur either in the modifier or at the head of the nominal group, the attitudinal is probably more likely at the head and the descriptive in the modifier, e.g.

> (40) That lady looks happy. (attitudinal)

rather than: (41) A happy lady is walking down the street.

> (42) She is wearing a red hat. (descriptive)

rather than: (43) That hat is red.

Concerning social class differences in the use of nouns and pronouns, we may mention briefly that Bernstein (1962b) and Lawton (1963) found that the working-class used more total pronouns. Bernstein also found that the working-class used 'you' and 'they' more (when combined) and the middle-class used 'I' more. Henderson (1969) reports that middle-class children, particularly those of high verbal ability, used more token nouns and more type nouns. Hawkins (1969), in a study which represents an extension of the analysis of the nominal group described here, reports the following: 'Middle-class children do not simply use more nouns, they also exploit the possibilities of elaborating the nominal group more widely. Their speech is, in Bernstein's terms, more differentiated. The working-class children, on the other hand, tend to use pronouns instead of nouns as "heads" which reduces the possibilities of both modification and qualification, and they rely on the listener's awareness of the situation to achieve comprehension.' For discussion of how differences in socialisation may be reflected in certain aspects of nominal group usage, the reader is referred to the discussion of the results in Henderson.

5.6 The qualifier

The qualifier, unlike the modifier, is mainly a univariate structure. Like other univariate structures it may be either paratactic (co-ordinate or appositional) or hypotactic. Here are two examples:

(44) The	man	whom we know	and whom we love
M	H	Q	+Q

Here 'whom we know' and 'whom we love' are paratactically related, actually co-ordinate. The convention adopted for showing co-ordination is the use of the '+' sign.

(45) The	journey	to the home	of Clive
M	H	Q	-Q

In this example 'of Clive' is dependent on *home* and not on *journey*. The value Q, then, is repeated in a hypotactic relation. The convention for hypotaxis is to use the '−' sign.

The class of word that occurs as the qualifier we have called the 'post-substantive'. Again for purposes of subclassification it is useful to refer to the word classes we recognised in the modifier. However, as we shall see, single-word qualifiers do not occur very frequently, and we decided that it would be sufficient for our purposes to recognise just three word classes, namely the determiners, the adjectives, and other single-word qualifiers. Examples of these are now given:

	H	Q	
(46)	we	*all*	} determiner
(47)	we	*both*	

(48)	someone	*pretty*	} adjective
(49)	nothing	*new*	

(50)	years	*ago*	} other single-word qualifiers
(51)	miles	*away*	

Usually it is a rankshifted unit that operates in the qualifier, either a group or a clause. The most usual rankshifted group is the prepositional group and the most usual rankshifted clause is what has been called the defining adjective clause or restricted relative clause in traditional grammar. Here are some examples:

	M	H	Q	
(52)	The	man	*on the train*	} prepositional group
(53)	The	lady	*with a blue hat*	

82

(54) The | man | *who is on the train* ⎤
                                          ⎬ clause
(55) The | lady | *who has a blue hat*   ⎦

5.7 The modifier and the qualifier related

It is of some interest to consider whether the difference between the modifier and qualifier is purely a matter of sequence. Even from a structural point of view, this is not the case. The modifier is a mixture of multivariate and univariate structuring and in general the bracketing is associated with the left. The structuring of the qualifier, in contrast, is generally univariate and the bracketing is associated with the right. So bearing Yngve's (1960) hypothesis in mind we might expect a long modification to be more difficult than a long qualification. However, there is a complication that needs to be mentioned: the size of the units involved is not constant, or not usually constant, in each case, the normal unit in the modifier being the word and the most usual unit in the qualifier being a rankshifted group or clause.

It may well be that these larger units are placed in the 'easier' position in the structure of the English nominal group, because it would be too taxing if they had to be stored in the pre-head position. We may mention here again Quirk's (1962) remark on English sentence structure: 'The typical and unremarkable English utterance has a light subject followed by the verb with the heavily modified parts then following; this pattern applies also to the disposition of subordinate clauses: they generally follow a part of the sentence which can be seen as in some way nuclear, thus conforming with the broad underlying pattern of having the main fabric of the structure take shape before the qualifications are added.' It is possible that a similar type of patterning occurs in the nominal group.

Having said something concerning the structural dissimilarities between the modifier and the qualifier, we may now ask whether there are any particular semantic implications specific to the modifier and the qualifier. We shall consider the one-word qualifiers first. Most of the one-word qualifiers are either those associated with pronoun head or those associated with those subclasses of nouns which can occur as head of nominal groups that can operate as adjuncts. Here are some examples:

(56) they all/both

(57) something special

(58) what else

(59) two days ago/later/after

(60) three miles away/off

83

There are two main observations to be made about the semantics of the qualifier in these examples. One, concerning those with pronoun heads, there appears to be no special meaning attached to these qualifiers: that they follow the head seems to be a purely superficial feature associated with the fact that pronouns are not usually modified. Often it is quite easy to find groups of similar meaning, but of the 'modifier—noun-head' pattern, e.g.

(61) He said, 'You both are wrong.'

(62) He said that both men were wrong.

(63) something spectacular

(64) a spectacular event

(65) something else

(66) another thing

Two, concerning such words as *ago, later, after, away, off*, it would seem that of the special functions of the qualifier, one is to locate the referent of the head along the dimension of time and space. It is not easy to find groups of a similar meaning, but of the 'modifier-head' type. It must be admitted, however, that a case could be made for treating groups of this type as prepositional groups or perhaps, more accurately, as postpositional groups; compare (67) and (68):

(67) after three days

(68) three days after

Furthermore, a case could be made for analysing these groups as adverbial groups; compare (69) and (70):

(69) much later

(70) several days later

We prefer, however, our original analysis. It enables us to bring together such groups as 'last week' and 'three days ago' as in the following examples:

(71) I saw him last week.

(72) I saw him three days ago.

In any case, our contention that it is a function of the qualifier to locate the referent of the head in time and space is supported by the rankshifted prepositional groups and clauses of time and space that are found in the qualifier. We shall now consider the rankshifted groups and clauses and the extent to which they differ in meaning from the words in the modifier.

There is no quick and easy way of deciding whether two forms are semantically equivalent or not. It is thought that some use may be made of the rules that transformational grammarians have devised for generating linguistic structures. Roberts (1964) has shown how it is possible, by using a small number of transformation rules, to reduce relative clauses (a) to participles, present (active) or past (passive); (b) to nominal groups; (c) to prepositional groups of place; and (d) to adjectives, simple and compound. These reductions are achieved by two deletion rules, known as T-del and T-del-ing. The former applies to relative clauses that contain *be*, and the latter to those that cannot contain *be*. The T-del rule is:

NP + relative pronoun + tense + be + X ⇒ NP + X

Here is an example:

(73) The man who was burning the rubbish ⇒ the man burning the rubbish

The T-del-ing rule is:

NP + relative pronoun + Aux + X ⇒ NP + ing + X

This is exemplified by:

(74) people who own property ⇒ people owning property

This by a further transformation may become:

property-owning people.

These examples suggest two main points. One, there need not be an appreciable difference in meaning between a finite and a non-finite relative clause when the subject of the finite clause is referentially identical with the head of the nominal group. Two, there is not a great deal of difference between qualifiers like 'owning property' and modifiers like 'property-owning'. Where the qualifier would seem to have the advantage is in its potentiality for adverbial expansion, e.g.

people owning property before 1st January, 1968 . . .

However, it should not be thought that the modifier construction may never have an adverbial expansion; compare:

(75) an animal which moves fast

with

(76) a fast-moving animal

We may mention, in passing, that any non-finite construction, whether it occurs in the modifier or the qualifier, offers a more limited range of options than a finite one, the latter having a wider range of tense and the choice of a modal, e.g.

(77) an animal which should have moved fast but didn't.

The modifier cannot handle choices such as these.

Before leaving the clauses we may add a word about the passive relative clauses. The finite ones may or may not have an agent, but the non-finites are more likely to have an agent than not. The adjectival equivalent in the modifier may not have an agent. Examples illustrating these points are now given:

(78) the boy who was injured (by a rock)

(79) the boy injured by a rock

(80) the injured boy.

Summarising, then, we may say that adverbial expansion, actual or potential, is a characteristic feature of the qualifier. In contrast, only certain expansions are possible in the modifier. We shall now turn our attention to rankshifted groups.

The most frequent rankshifted group is the prepositional group, and it will be sufficient for our purposes to concentrate on these. The facts are rather complicated and not always very clear, but it does seem possible to make some statements (a) concerning the relation of these rankshifted prepositional groups to certain rankshifted clauses, and (b) concerning the relation of these groups to certain nominal modifiers. Firstly, then, certain finite relative clauses, e.g.

(81) the house which is in the country

may be reduced to rankshifted prepositional groups by a simple deletion of the relative pronoun and the verb, so:

(82) the house in the country.

Likewise, certain other finite or non-finite clauses may be so reduced. Thus, both

(83) the house which is situated in the country

and

(84) the house situated in the country

may become

(85) the house in the country

by obvious deletions. In cases such as these it would seem that the most one could say is that the clause is possibly more explicit than the group.

Secondly, what can we say about the relation of these groups to certain nominal modifiers? Is there a relation of semantic equivalence between them? When we study examples, for instance,

(86) the house in the country

and

(87) the country house

two facts strike us. One, the group with *country* as a modifier is ambiguous. Two, its most obvious meaning is not that which it shares with (86). Its most obvious meaning is one which implies subclassification or subcategorisation, namely the house of the subclass known as 'country', contrasting with 'town', etc. A more extreme example will help to make this clearer. Quirk (1962) quotes the following nominal group from an iron and steel company's public notice: 'the redesign and enlargement of *the Company's eight open hearth steel melting furnaces*'. He points out that critics of this tendency in technical writing might favour something like 'eight furnaces, of a fixed type with open hearth, for the melting of steel'. Leech (1966), commenting on these two expressions, says he would claim that they are semantically different: 'Whereas the noun with premodification denotes a specific category of furnace, the same noun with equivalent postmodification describes furnaces with certain attributes in common. This rather subtle distinction is analogous to that between "black birds" and "blackbirds".'

Lees (1960) in his work on English nominalisation puts forward the view that nominal compounds are best understood in terms of eight underlying grammatical relations. He points out too that nominal compounds are often multiply ambiguous. In an appendix he shows how six of these grammatical relations underlie nominal phrases. Below we list these six relations and give examples of nominal compounds and nominal phrases ('n.c.' and 'n.p.' respectively):

1. Subject – Predicate

    (88) n.c. girl friend (= friend who is a girl)

    (89) n.p. toy soldier

2. Subject – 'Middle-Object'

    (90) n.c. arrowhead (= head of an arrow)

    (91) n.p. earth satellite

3. Subject – Verb

    (92) n.c. talking machine (= machine which talks)

    (93) n.p. flying saucer

4. Subject – Object

    (94) n.c. steamboat (= boat powered by steam)

(95) n.p.   steam-powered boat

5. Subject — Prepositional Object

(96) n.c.   gunpowder (= powder for guns)

(97) n.p.   bathroom scales

6. Object — Prepositional Object

(98) n.c.   blockhouse (= house of blocks)

(99) n.p.   tin soldier

We may abstract two points from the above which seem of special relevance to our comparison of the modifier and the qualifier. One, the qualifier, being more explicit and therefore less ambiguous than the modifier, is a very useful tool for making precise identifications and definitions. Two, it is only usually when the head of the nominal group can be associated with an underlying 'subject' term that modification of the kind we have been describing is possible. Qualification really comes into its own when the head of the nominal group can be associated with an underlying 'non-subject' term. It is precisely these patterns that the modification cannot usually handle. Here are some examples of these patterns:

(100) a point *that John wouldn't consider important*

(101) a present *Bill gave me yesterday*

5.8 Nominal group complexity

The nominal groups were collected in terms of twelve generalised types, these types representing the interaction of two variables: the number of modifiers present and the number of qualifiers. There were four possibilities for the number of modifiers, ranging from none to three, and three possibilities for the number of qualifiers, ranging from none to two. The basic reasoning was: the more modifiers and the more qualifiers a group has, the more complex and difficult it is. However, it must be admitted that this is rather an over-simplification of the facts. Ideally, one would want to know about the classes of the items that make up the structures; for example, a simple group, that is, one consisting of a 'head' element only, could be a personal pronoun (*he, she, it, etc.*), or it could be an abstract noun (*disobedience*, etc.). Nevertheless, it is thought that these twelve types are a useful starting point for an examination of complexity in the nominal group, especially in the speech of young children. Below is given the table for the nominal group types:

		Number of Modifiers			
		0	1	2	3
Number	0	H	MH	2MH	3MH
of	1	HQ	MHQ	2MHQ	3MHQ
Qualifiers	2	H2Q	MH2Q	2MH2Q	3MH2Q

5.9 Coding information

TABLE 07 'ELEMENTS OF NOMINAL GROUP STRUCTURE'
If 'S', 'C', 'Z' or 'V' is selected from Table 06, then a selection must be made from Table 07 'Elements of nominal group structure'. Here is the table:

Symbol	Element
M	Modifier
H	Head
Q	Qualifier

Co-occurrence Restrictions
'H' is the obligatory element; 'M' and/or 'Q' may not occur without 'H'.

TABLE 10 'SECONDARY ELEMENTS OF MODIFIER'
If 'M' is selected from Table 07, then a selection has to be made from Table 10 which deals with the secondary elements of structure of the modifier. The table is given below:

Symbol	Element
D	Deictic
O	Ordinative
E	Epithet
N	Nominal
I	Intensifier

TABLE 20 'CLASSES OF DETERMINER'
If 'D' is selected from Table 10, it has to be followed with a symbol from Table 20 'Classes of Determiner'. This table has nine entries:

Symbol	Class
1	1st person possessive: *my, our*
2	2nd person possessive: *your*
3	3rd person possessive: *his, her, its, their*
4	Impersonal: *one's*
5	Proximate demonstrative: *this, these*
6	Non-proximate demonstrative: *that, those*
7	Interrogative: *which, what, whose*
8	Other determiners
9	Missing determiner

WORD RANK

Units, except the morpheme, are made up of units of the rank below: the morpheme is exceptional for, as it is the unit of lowest rank, it has no internal structure. In our analysis we did not examine the internal structure (or morphology) of the word. There is consequently no table to do with elements of word structure.

TABLE 11 'CLASSES OF HEAD'

If there is no 'M' in the nominal group structure, then 'H' is selected immediately after the clause element. If there is an 'M', all the secondary elements of the modifier have to be described one after another and then '/' inserted before 'H' is put in. 'H' has to be followed immediately with a selection from Table 11 'Classes of Head':

Symbol	Class
D	Determiner, other than those under S, T and W
O	Numeral
E	Adjective
N	Noun
P	Pronoun
S	Proximate Demonstrative
T	Non-proximate Demonstrative
W	Interrogative
Y	Missing item

TABLE 21 'CLASSES OF PRONOUN'

If 'P' is selected from Table 11, then a further selection has to be made from Table 21 'Classes of Pronoun'. Here is the table:

Symbol	Class
1	Subject 1st person sing. personal *I*
2	Subject 2nd person sing. personal *you*
3	Subject 3rd person sing. personal *he, she, it*
4	Subject impersonal *one*
5	Subject 1st person plur. personal *we*
6	Subject 2nd person plur. personal *you*
7	Subject 3rd person plur. personal *they*
8	Unstressed *there*
9	Non-subject personals, proper names, and all other pronouns.

TABLE 12 'CLASSES OF QUALIFIER'

After the subclassification of 'H' or 'HP' by means of Tables 11 and 21 respectively, a '/1' is added if there is no qualifier. This is a group boundary and it signals here the end of the nominal group. If there is a qualifier, a '/'

is added and then a 'Q'. 'Q' has to be subclassified by a selection from Table 12 'Classes of Qualifier'. This table is given below:

Symbol	Class
D	Determiner
E	Adjective
O	Other single-word qualifiers

When the qualifier has been described, a '/1' boundary is added to signal the end of the nominal group.

RANKSHIFTED UNITS

If a rankshifted clause is operating at 'M', 'H' or 'Q', this is symbolised by placing an angle bracket, '⟨', immediately after the element. The bracket is followed immediately by the number of the 'Clause Class' table, '02'. This number is put in instead of the more usual sentence element (i.e. 'F', 'B' or 'T'). The internal structure of the clause is then described in the usual way. The end of the clause is signalled by '/2' and then this is followed immediately by '⟩' to signal the end of the rankshifting. If a rankshifted group is operating at 'M' or 'Q', this is shown by placing an angle bracket, '⟨', immediately after the element and then the number of the group table, '07' for the nominal group and '09' for the adjunctival group. These numbers are put in instead of the more usual clause elements (i.e. 'S', 'C', 'Z', 'A'). The end of the group is signalled by '/1' and the end of the rankshifting by '⟩'.

SUMMARY
Continuing the chart given in Part 2, Diagram 8, we may now add the tables for the nominal group. (See page 92.)

Examples
First we shall continue our description of the example sentence (previously given in sections 3.5 and 4.7):

That lamp has fallen in front of the television

Coding

```
1234
10
01S1F1SMD6/HN/1
```

So far we have coded the information for the sentence, clause, and the first group, the nominal group *that lamp*. Before we can continue the analysis we shall have to give the rules for coding the verbal and adjunctival groups (see sections 6.8 and 7.9).

Here are some more examples of nominal groups:

That big lamp
SMD6E/HN/1
That lamp I put there
SMD6/HN/Q⟨02SHP1/1 . . ./2⟩/1

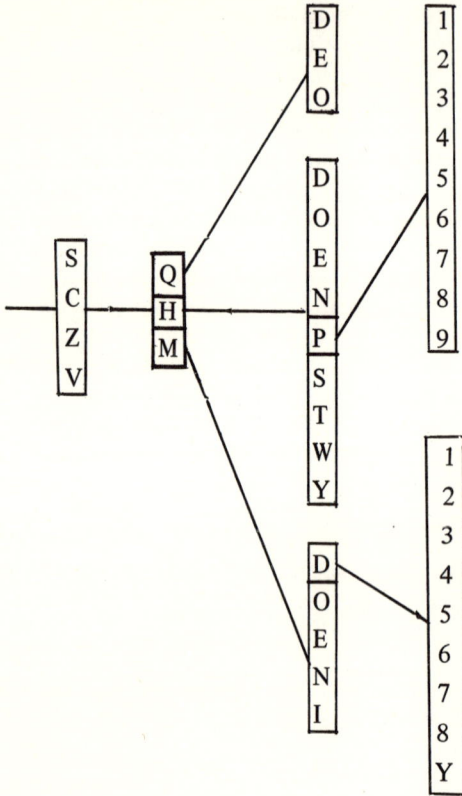

Chapter 6

THE VERBAL GROUP

6.1 Introductory

The verbal group is that class of the unit 'group' which operates at the element 'predicator' in the structure of the clause. An example is:

(1) The train is going into the tunnel

Here *is going* is a verbal group operating at the predicator. It is possible for the verbal group to consist of one word only; *went* is an example of this in the following clause:

(2) The train went into the tunnel

Halliday (1966b) in a paper which is concerned to identify the verbal group and some of its categories gives a table which shows the verbal group systems, their terms and environments. He lists sixteen systems in all. Our analysis is not so comprehensive as this. Six systems only were described: modality, tense, aspect, 'perfectability' (that is, 'to' infinitive/'zero' infinitive), voice and polarity. Of these systems three were considered of special relevance to the research: tense, voice and modality. We shall begin by outlining the tense system.

6.2 Tense

Halliday's three-term system (that is, 'past'/'present'/'future') is used here, the only modification being that *will* is not always taken as signifying the future. Both an operator *will* (future) and a modal *will* (volition, probability, etc.) are recognised. The difference may be illustrated by the following two sentences:

(3) It will snow tomorrow   (future)

(4) That will be Harry now   (probability)

This analysis, then, draws on both of the two traditions associated with the analysis of tense in English: the one that recognises a three-term tense

93

system and the one that sets up a two-term system ('past'/'present' or 'non-past') and asserts that *will* is not a tense form at all but a modal like *can* and *may*.

Major tense system

Halliday's major tense system has 36 different tenses. It is convenient to number them from 1 to 36. However, this labelling is somewhat misleading, for 'when a speaker chooses a certain tense, he is not making a sudden selection all at once from this huge inventory; he is choosing from a very small set of possibilities, namely "past", "present" or "future"' (Halliday, 1966b). Having made this selection once, he may make a second choice from the same set. He may go on to make a third choice, and so on. Some examples will make this clearer:

			Tense number
(5)	took	'past'	1
(6)	had taken	'past in past'	4
(7)	was going to have taken	'past in future in past'	13

The speaker may make up to five selections. There are not, however, 243 different tenses; there are 36. This is because there are certain combinatory restrictions. It may be helpful to list the combinations which may occur, using *take* as the model (see pages 96 and 97) and then to give the three rules ('stop rules') which prevent further combinations.

The combinatory restrictions which preclude all but the combinations listed are now given:

Rule 1. 'present' can occur only at the outer ends of the series (that is, as first and/or final choice).

Rule 2. except at a and β, the same tense cannot be selected twice consecutively.

Rule 3. 'future' can occur only once other than at a.

Halliday has devised some simple rules which permit the identification of these tenses. In these rules:

x = the stem of the lexical verb in a simple tense, and any immediately following element (other than the negative *not, n't*) in a compound tense.
o = the base form.
s = the finite form: present tense
d = the finite form: past tense
η = the non-finite present/active form ('present or active participle')
n = the non-finite past/passive form ('past or passive participle')

94

The rules are as follows:

$$x^d = \text{past}$$
$$x^s = \text{present}$$
$$\text{will} + x^o = \text{future}$$
$$\text{have} + x^n = \text{past in}$$
$$\text{be} + x^\eta = \text{present in}$$
$$\text{be going/about to} + x^o = \text{future in}$$

The first three rules pertain to the a selections and the last three to the non-a selections. Here are some examples:

(8) We had been dancing.

$$x^d \qquad\qquad\qquad\qquad \text{past}$$
$$\left.\begin{array}{l}\text{have} + x^n \\ \text{be}\end{array}\right\} + x^\eta \qquad \begin{array}{l}\text{past in} \\ \text{present in}\end{array}$$

(9) She is going to dance.

$$\left.\begin{array}{l}x^s \\ \text{be}\end{array}\right\} \text{going to} + x^o \qquad \begin{array}{l}\text{present} \\ \text{future in}\end{array}$$

(10) She will have arrived.

$$\left.\begin{array}{l}\text{will} + x^o \\ \text{have}\end{array}\right\} + x^n \qquad \begin{array}{l}\text{future} \\ \text{past in}\end{array}$$

(11) She will be arriving.

$$\left.\begin{array}{l}\text{will} + x^o \\ \text{be}\end{array}\right\} + x\eta \qquad \begin{array}{l}\text{future} \\ \text{present in}\end{array}$$

The tenses are constructed from left to right, but Halliday specifies that their names should be read from right to left, as they make more sense that way. So, for example, 'she *is going to dance*' is 'future in present'. Semantically, this means that the future is being focused on from the point of view of the present. Each additional tense selection adds a further reference point. Thus 'we *had been dancing*' ('present in past in past') means that the present is being focused on from the point of view of the past which in turn is being focused on from the point of view of the past.

So far we have considered the major system of tense; there are two minor systems to be mentioned: sequent tense and non-finite tense. These may be regarded as forming subsets of the major tense system, the former being skewed to the past and the latter to the present.

95

tε	tδ	tγ	tβ	ta	
				past	01
				present	02
				future	03
			past in	past	04
				present	05
				future	06
			present in	past	07
				present	08
				future	09
			future in	past	10
				present	11
				future	12
		past in	future in	past	13
				present	14
				future	15
		present in	past in	past	16
				present	17
				future	18
		present in	future in	past	19
				present	20
				future	21
		future in	past in	past	22
				present	23
				future	24
	past in	future in	past in	past	25
				present	26
				future	27
	present in	past in	future in	past	28
				present	29
				future	30
	present in	future in	past in	past	31
				present	32
				future	33
present in	past in	future in	past in	past	34
				present	35
				future	36

TENSE (MAJOR SYSTEM)

01 took/did take
02 takes/does take
03 will take

04 had taken
05 has taken
06 will have taken

07 was taking
08 is taking
09 will be taking

10 was going to take
11 is going to take
12 will be going to take

13 was going to have taken
14 is going to have taken
15 will be going to have taken

16 had been taking
17 has been taking
18 will have been taking

19 was going to be taking
20 is going to be taking
21 will be going to be taking

22 had been going to take
23 has been going to take
24 will have been going to take

25 had been going to have taken
26 has been going to have taken
27 will have been going to have taken

28 was going to have been taking
29 is going to have been taking
30 will be going to have been taking

31 had been going to be taking
32 has been going to be taking
33 will have been going to be taking

34 had been going to have been taking
35 has been going to have been taking
36 will have been going to have been taking

Sequent tense

Sequent tense may be used in reported speech and expressions of 'unreality'. The name 'sequent' is derived from 'sequence of tenses'. This relates to its use in reported speech. With reported speech the verb in the rankshifted clause is usually in the past tense if the verb of reporting is also in the past tense. To find out whether the verb in indirect reported speech is sequent, one has to translate the clause into direct quoted speech. If the same tense is possible in direct quoted speech, then it is not sequent; if the same tense is not possible, then it is sequent. For example:

(12) He said he saw him the day before
     (non-sequent past, because
(13) I saw him yesterday
     is possible).

But

(14) He said he had seen him the day before
     (sequent past, because
(15) I had seen him yesterday
     is not possible).

To identify the sequent tense, then, one first determines what the tense would be in direct quoted speech (here 'past') and then one simply puts the label 'sequent' (symbolised by element 'C') before it (here 'sequent past'). Here are some examples of sequent tenses:

Example Number	*Tense Number*	*Direct quoted speech*	*Indirect reported speech*
(16)	1	I saw him yesterday (non-sequent past)	He said he'd seen him the day before (sequent past)
(17)	2	I like it (non-sequent present)	He said he liked it (sequent present)
(18)	3	I will enjoy it (non-sequent future)	He said he would enjoy it (sequent future)
(19)	6	She will have arrived (non-sequent past in future)	He said she would have arrived (sequent past in future)
(20)	8	I'm reading (non-sequent present in present)	He said he was reading (sequent present in present)
(21)	9	I will be flying (non-sequent present in future)	He said he would be flying (sequent present in future)

There are three main types of expressions of 'unreality' (Palmer, 1965):

A. Tentative or polite questions and requests:

(22) 'Real'   I want to ask you about that.

(23) 'Unreal' I wanted to ask you about that.

wanted in the second example is 'sequent present'.

B. *If* conditionals:

(24) 'Real'   If he comes he will find out.

(25) 'Unreal' If he came he would find out.

came is 'sequent present' and *would* is 'sequent future'.

C. Wishes, and statements of the type *It is time* . . .

(26) I wish I knew.

(27) It's time I went.

knew and *went* are 'sequent present'.

Halliday's table for the sequent tense system is given on page 100.

Non-finite tense

This minor tense system represents a subset of the major tense system. It is skewed to the present. There are three rules which reduce the 36 tenses to 12.

Rule 1. 'Future' cannot be selected twice.

Rule 2. (. . .) past in past
     (. . .) past in present } are neutralised to tense 1
     past

Rule 3. (. . .) future in present } are neutralised to tense 3
     future

Examples

Examples of the most commonly occurring tenses are now given:

Example Number	Tense Number		
(28)	1	to have taken	having taken
(29)	2	to take	taking
(30)	3	to be going to take	being about to take

99

01 had taken
02 took
03 would take

04 (01)
05 (01)
06 would have taken

07 had been taking
08 was taking
09 would be taking

10 had been going to take
11 was going to take
12 would be going to take

13 had been going to have taken
14 was going to have taken
15 would be going to have taken

16 (07)
17 (07)
18 would have been taking

19 had been going to be taking
20 was going to be taking
21 would be going to be taking

22 (10)
23 (10)
24 would have been going to take

25 (13)
26 (13)
27 would have been going to have taken

28 had been going to have been taking
29 was going to have been taking
30 would be going to have been taking

31 (19)
32 (19)
33 would have been going to be taking

34 (28)
35 (28)
36 would have been going to have been taking

The decision was taken to regard the non-finite past/passive participle as tense 1, and the non-finite base form as tense 2. Examples are as follows:

(31) *Found* by the police, I gave myself up.
      tense 1

(32) The man *found* by the police escaped
      tense 1

(33) This makes it *go*
      tense 2

Tense and the modals

The modals themselves generally do not select for tense, *can/could, may/might, shall/should, will/would* and *is to/was to* being the exceptions. There are restrictions, too, on the tense selections in the verbal groups in which they occur. Only twelve tenses may be selected. These are the same twelve tenses as may be selected by the non-finite verbal groups. Examples are now given below and the table reproduced on page 102.

Example Number	Tense Number	
(34)	1	can have taken
(35)	2	can take
(36)	3	can be going to take.

Having described the formal categories required for analysing tense in English, we shall now give reasons why they were included in this inquiry. On the formal level, Bernstein (1962b) showed social class differences on a category he called 'Complexity of Verbal Stem'. This was a count of 'the number of units in the verbal stem excluding the adverbial negation'. Verbal stems containing more than three units were counted, and also a verb plus an infinitive was counted as a complex verbal stem. It is thought that Halliday's method of isolating the tense elements in the verbal group is a useful tool for measuring the complexity therein; an advantage of it, too, is that it also permits the making of semantic statements. The verb plus infinitive constructions, e.g.

(37) It's beginning to snow

(or Phase relations, as they are sometimes called) are treated separately in the present analysis, as they were considered best handled as a feature of clause structure.

On the semantic level there are a number of suggestive reasons for looking at tense. In his book *The Psychology of Time*, Fraisse (1964)

01 can have taken (to have taken, having taken)
02 can take (to take, taking)
03 can be going to take (to be . . ., being about to take)

04 (01)
05 (01)
06 can be going to have taken (to be . . ., being about to have taken)

07 can have been taking (to have . . ., having been taking)
08 can be taking (to be taking, being taking)
09 can be going to be taking (to be . . ., being about to be taking)

10 can have been going to take (to have . . ., having been about to take)
11 (03)
12

13 can have been going to have taken (to have . . ., having been about to have take
14 (06)
15

16 (07)
17 (07)
18 can be going to have been taking (to be . . ., being about to have been taking)

19 can have been going to be taking (to have . . ., having been about to be taking)
20 (09)
21

22 (10)
23 (10)
24

25 (13)
26 (13)
27

28 can have been going to have been taking (to have . . ., having been about to hav
29 (18)   been takin
30

31 (19)
32 (19)
33

34 (28)
35 (28)
36

draws 'a fine but necessary distinction between the temporal horizon and the notion of time'. The former is a personal, subjective way of looking at time; it is concerned with how an individual constructs his past and attempts to shape his future. The latter is more impersonal and objective; it is concerned with how we conventionally estimate time, the principal concepts being order and duration. We shall consider the temporal horizon first.

Fraisse contends that control over time is essentially an individual achievement conditioned by everything which determines personality. Age and environment are important. Summarising the literature on the influence of age (especially Gesell and Ilg, 1943), it seems clear that the temporal perspective of a five-year-old child is very much tied to his own personal experience. He is not yet interested in the pasts of others nor does he plan for a future outside the limits of his usual activities. His temporal horizon is not all that narrow, however, as his memories go back two years and he is fairly precise about future events such as Christmas and his birthday.

Concerning the influence of environment, what interests us most, of course, is the effect of a middle-class or a working-class environment on the development of a child's temporal horizon. Fraisse refers to some relevant research. Leshan (1952) found that if children of between 8 and 10 years are asked to make up stories, those invented by middle-class children cover a longer period of time than those of working-class children. Fraisse writes that the explanation of this fact is that, in the working-class, the cycles of tension and satisfaction are much shorter and people spare themselves the frustrations which result from projects with more distant perspectives. Members of the middle-class, on the other hand, can organise their lives in longer cycles and act in accordance with their projects.

The relationship of temporal perspective to academic achievement is also mentioned by Fraisse. He points out that Teahan (1958) found that children who have the most success at school think more of the future and have wider temporal perspectives than those who are at the bottom of their class.

Rather similar points to these are made by Bernstein (1958). He gives among the defining characteristics of the middle-class and associative levels 'an awareness of the importance of the difference between means and long-term ends' and 'the ability to adopt appropriate measures to implement the attainment of distant ends by a purposeful means-end chain'. The effect of this future orientation is to give greater significance to objects in the present. 'Objects in the present are not taken as given, but become centres for inquiry and starting points for relationships.' Educationally this is very fortunate for the middle-class child for 'the school is an institution where every item in the present is finely linked to a distant future, consequently there is not a serious clash of expectations between the school and the middle-class child'.

For the working-class child the situation is quite the reverse. Working-class family structure is less formally organised in relation to the development of the child. 'Present, or near present, activities have greater value than the relation of present activity to the attainment of a distant goal.' Consequently, there is no continuity between the expectations of the school and those of the child.

One point which is somewhat difficult to assess concerns the respective strengths of the influence of age and the influence of environment. It is not clear to what extent a particularly stimulating environment may overcome limitations which are due to age. However, it should be pointed out that Bernstein seems to be saying that it is not so much that the middle-class children are more advanced than the working-class but rather that they are different in their orientations.

What differences generally may we expect to find in the middle- and working-class child's tense selections, stemming from differences in their temporal perspectives? It seems reasonable to expect that the working-class child would reveal a preference for the simple present and that the middle-class child would show a preference for the future generally and in particular for those compound future tenses which carry an implication of determination or decision in the present. For example:

(38) I'm going to be a doctor,

in which the tense selected is 'future in the present'. It needs no emphasising that such an utterance could be made only in a particular kind of situation; there are many situations which would preclude saying such a remark or which would make it sound quite inappropriate. The interview situation in which the speech was collected from the children in our sample does not afford many opportunities for the child to refer to the future, and so we may not legitimately expect very frequent selections of future tense.

Pursuing the middle-class orientation to the future a little further, it is obvious that there are limits to the number of future events that may be controlled by present thought and action. Much of the future is uncertain. How can we come to terms with this uncertainty? There are two main courses available to us, one tentative and one more positive. Both rely on our knowledge of the past and the present. The tentative way is to conjure up hypotheses, to list the possibilities. The more positive way is to draw inferences from what we know and make predictions about what will probably happen in the future. It is of interest to consider what choices are available in the verbal group for making hypothetical statements and for making predictive statements.

Although we introduced this distinction whilst discussing the notion of future, it is important to point out that unlike predictive statements, which are always concerned with the future, hypothetical statements may be made about any event no matter when it occurred, nor is it necessary to list all the possibilities: we may mention just one and in this way it often reflects what we consider to be most probable. It is in this sense of 'hypothetical' that we shall discuss hypothetical statements.

A hypothesis may be expressed in a great number of different ways: children, however, cannot be expected to know how to use all these ways. When Gahagan and Gahagan (1966) set up a coding frame for a content analysis of the children's responses to the speech schedule they decided that four ways in which a hypothesis could be expressed should be considered:

(i) perhaps . . .

(ii) modals *may/might, can/could*

(iii) *if. . . then* constructions

(iv) I wonder . . .

In the verbal group, then, the modal is the chief means by which one can make a hypothetical statement. This facility will be described in a later section, which is on Modality. It is also true that making 'if . . . then' statements can have repercussions for the verbal group, as there may be a choice of sequent tense in this environment, e.g.

(39) If I were to come, he would go.

There is, however, no set of environments in which the choice of sequent tense is fully determined; compare (39) with (40):

(40) If I come, he will go.

The resources available in the verbal group for making predictive statements have been described elegantly by McIntosh (1966). By predictive statements McIntosh means statements which simply convey judgements or assessments about what is going to happen – separated from others which carry other implications as well, e.g. 'decision' or 'promise'. He shows that there are two main tense types available: the G-constructions and the W-constructions. The G-constructions are *be going to* + base form and *be going to be* + *-ing*; these are not available for prediction when the lexical verb carries the implication of 'arrangement' or 'decision'. So 'It's going to rain' is predictive but 'My daughter's going to sing for you' is not. The W-constructions are *will* + base form and *will be* + *-ing*; these are not available for prediction when the verb carries the implication of 'determination' or 'agreement'. Thus 'I'll collapse before long' is predictive but 'I'll leave tomorrow night' is not.

In Hallidayan terms the G-construction are tenses 11 ('future in present') and 20 ('present in future in present') and the W-constructions are tenses 3 ('future') and 9 ('present in future'). Examples are:

105

Example Number	Tense Number	
(41)	3	He'll cry
(42)	9	He'll be crying next
(43)	11	It's going to snow tomorrow
(44)	20	It's going to be snowing tomorrow.

As our particular interview situation is not one which is likely to demand the utterance of many predictive statements, we decided not to explicitly mark tenses 3, 9, 11 and 20 as being predictive or non-predictive. As it was not likely that many would occur we thought that it would be sufficient to do a hand count later. It was considered that the Picture Story Cards task might well be the best stimulus to this type of response, as the child may be prompted to make predictions about the outcome of events in the stories.

We shall now consider the notion of time as distinct from the temporal horizon. The principal concepts are order and duration. Order is to do with the succession of events and duration with the intervals between them. According to Piaget (1946), order presents no difficulties for a five-year-old child when it is perceived in unambiguous conditions. But if the temporal order must be distinguished from the spatial order, confusion ensues. As soon as the order has to be recalled rather than perceived, young children fail because they are not yet capable of reconstituting the sequence of their memories. As for the other concept, a five-year-old child is incapable of measuring duration. This is because he cannot form the representation of a duration independent of its contents, e.g. 15 seconds spent standing with folded arms seems longer than 15 seconds spent looking at a funny picture. When the child is about 7–8, there seems to be a fairly sudden reorganisation in his understanding of order and duration. He seems to understand the relationships between the order of events and their durations.

What relevance has the above, if any, to our study of the use of tense? Where the interest lies is in speculating whether there is likely to be any correlation between the concept of duration or a disposition towards it and the use of the *be + -ing* tenses (that is, those which select 'present in' in Halliday's terminology or 'progressive', 'continuous' or 'durative' in the terminologies of others). Looking at the matter from the point of view of encoding, can we say the more developed the concept the more frequent the choice of these tenses, or considering it from the point of view of decoding, can we postulate the greater the exposure to use of these tenses the more developed the concept of duration? The question of the meaning of these tenses is a moot point in linguistics. Palmer (1965) states: 'The progressive indicates activity continuing through a period of time – activity with duration. The non-progressive merely reports activity, without indicating that it has duration. This is shown by comparison of:

He walked to the station

He was walking to the station

The first sentence simply gives the information that he walked to the station; the second indicates that the walking had duration. There is, of course, no suggestion that there are two kinds of activity one without and one with duration, but simply that attention is drawn in the one case to its durational aspect.' Palmer does make certain qualifications concerning this interpretation but there is no doubt that he suggests that the main use of the progressive is to indicate duration. Sinclair (1965) recognises a system in the verbal group, which he calls 'event-timing'. This system has two terms: 'event-timed' which is expounded by *be* + *-ing*, and 'neutral', namely, any verbal group without *be* + *-ing*. According to Sinclair, the occurrence of *be* + *-ing* is 'the device which the verbal group has for pointing out that events occur over a period of time, however short'. The 'neutral' verbal groups 'do not say anything about the event-time, but only about the reference-time'. Halliday, of course, would interpret the meaning of the *be* + *-ing* tenses in terms of a point of focus and a point of reference, and not in terms of duration. It is difficult to know how to evaluate semantic statements. Presumably in this case one would have to test for possession of the concept and for use of these tenses independently and then correlate the results.

Bernstein wonders whether the *be* + *-ing* tenses signal incompleteness – that the action is still continuing. If this were the case he would expect the middle-class to use more of them, as such a usage would be in line with what appears to be a general tendency among the middle-class, namely, that of leaving the possibilities open.

6.3 Voice

The system of voice has two terms, 'active' and 'passive'. If one chooses passive, one has also to choose in a further system whose terms are 'be' passive and 'get' passive. Sometimes this system is called the system of mutation, with the terms 'non-mutative' and 'mutative'. As we did not expect the choice of passive to be very frequent in our data, we did not sub-divide occurrences of it into 'be' passives and 'get' passives.

Previously we gave Halliday's rules for recognising the exponents of tense in the verbal group; the rule for the passive is of a similar form:

$$\text{be/get} + x^n = \text{passive}$$

where, as before, n = the non-finite, past/passive form ('past or passive participle'). To illustrate the rule, here are some examples:

(45) Bill was hit

$$\left.\begin{array}{l} x^d \\ \text{be} \end{array}\right\} + x^n \qquad \begin{array}{l} \text{past} \\ \text{passive} \end{array}$$

107

(46) Bill had been hit

$$\left.\begin{array}{l} x^d \\ \text{have} \end{array}\right\} + x^n \\ \text{be} \left.\right\} + x^n$$

past
past in
passive

(47) Bill is being hit

$$\left.\begin{array}{l} x^s \\ \text{be} \end{array}\right\} x^n \\ \text{be} \left.\right\} + x^n$$

present
present in
passive

(48) John got caught

$$\left.\begin{array}{l} x^d \\ \text{get} \end{array}\right\} + x^n$$

past
passive

It is normal to regard the passive as the 'marked' term in the voice system. The term 'marked' has been used in a number of different ways by linguists. One, it can mean morphologically 'marked', that is, one term is realised by one (or more) morpheme(s) more than the other. For example, the plural of common nouns is realised by the addition of -s, and negation in the verbal group by *not* or *n't*. Similarly we can say that the passive is marked by *be/get* + x^n. Two, the term 'marked' can be used to mean that the opposition between two terms is not equal. Quirk (1959) writes: 'Now, in these binary oppositions, it is common to find one member regarded as more neutral or normal than the other; the contrast is relatively unmarked in one member and relatively marked in the other; in other words, the polarity is not equal between the opposing pairs.' Thus, Sinclair (1965), discussing voice, says: 'We may expect that the so-called "active" is a neutral form, in contrast with some specific meaning given by the presence of the "passive" voice.' What this specific meaning is we shall consider later. Finally, 'marked' can mean 'infrequent'. A 'marked' term is one which you do not use unless you have a special reason for doing so. Svartvik (1966) found that even in a text which was part of the group of texts with the highest occurrence of passives (the 'scientific exposition' group) the proportion of passives to actives did not exceed 1 : 3. Probably the last two meanings of 'marked' are of most interest to our research. We shall now consider further what can be established about the meaning and use of the passive.

Gleason (1965) introduces a concept which is of interest to us here – the concept of agnation. Pairs of sentences with the same major vocabulary items, but with different structures (generally shown by differences in arrangement, in accompanying function words, or other structure markers) are agnate if the relation in structure is regular and systematic, that is, if it can be stated in terms of general rules. As examples of agnate sentences he gives:

(49) He saw it.

(50) It was seen by him.

Gleason writes that agnate sentences may be classified into two groups. At one extreme, the selection is made on the basis of style, the choice being free of semantic or grammatical restrictions. At the other, 'meaning' in one of its many forms determines the choice, and there is little possibility of stylistic significance. The question to be decided, then, is whether the passive has a different meaning from the active. If it has not – if its use is just a matter of style – then it is clearly of less interest for us.

Katz and Postal (1964), who are leading transformational semanticists, make the general claim that what they call 'singulary transformations' do not alter or affect meaning; they merely re-arrange the surface structure. The passive transformation is an example of this type of transformation. There is no difference, then, in meaning between actives and their corresponding passives. What Katz and Postal say would seem to be true of examples like:

(51) He saw it,

(52) It was seen by him,

that is, those in which the agent is specified in the passive (here, *by him*). However, Svartvik (1966) has shown in his textual study that the great majority of passives in modern English have no agent.

A number of linguists have commented on this feature of the passive. Palmer (1965) writes: 'The most difficult question to be asked about the passive is why it is used rather than the active. There is only one obvious and one clear reason – that it may be used where the 'actor' is not specified, e.g.

He's been killed.

He was hurt in the crash.'

A similar point is made by Sinclair (1965), though with a different emphasis: 'The passive voice isolates an event from a performer, or actor, and refers to the event in itself.' He adds: 'Many of the typical instances of the passive voice occur where it is unnecessary or undesirable to specify a performer.' As examples of this he gives:

(53) It just can't be done in time,

(54) The specimen was placed in a tinting solution,

and others. Halliday (1967b) says that 'the desire not to specify a causer' is 'one of the principal reasons for choosing a passive'.

To return to our original question about whether the difference between a passive and an active is a matter of stylistics or semantics, we can say that in the case of passives with agents the difference is probably stylistic and in the case of passives without agents, that is, the majority of passives in fact, the difference has to do with meaning, that is, it is semantic. This is, of course, considering the whole clause, and not just the verbal group alone. Probably more debatable is Sinclair's contention that the meaning of the verbal group itself is different depending on whether it is active or passive. The passive voice isolates an event from a performer, and refers to the event in itself whereas the active voice because it sometimes implies a performer but sometimes refers to the event in itself may be considered neutral in this respect. Concerning the meaning of the verbal group alone, we might add that in the case of the mutative passives (*get* + x^n) there is no doubt at all that the meaning of the passive verbal group differs from that of the active group: there is no element in the active verbal group which can carry this meaning 'mutative'.

How does the use of the passive relate to Bernstein's theory? Bernstein (1962b) reported finding that his middle-class subjects used a significantly higher proportion of passives than the working-class subjects. Lawton (1963, 1964) also found significant differences on the passive, and in the second of these papers he includes a useful discussion on the use of the passive. He suggests that Jespersen's (1924) comments on the use of the passive are of some relevance to his study. He summarises Jespersen's five possible types of use as follows:

'(1) Where the active subject is unknown or cannot easily be stated.

(2) Where the active subject is self-evident from the context.

(3) Where there are special reasons like tact or delicacy for not mentioning the active subject.

(4) Where the passive is preferred even if the active subject is indicated because interest is focused on the passive subject (the "converted subject") rather than the active subject, e.g. "the house was struck by lightning".

(5) Where the passive may facilitate connection between one sentence and the next: "He rose to speak and was listened to with enthusiasm".'

The above list perhaps creates the impression that the use of the passive is always motivated. However, as we have suggested above, its use can be conventional, that is, more a matter of style. We nevertheless can agree with Lawton's comment: 'All five of Jespersen's categories are examples of fairly sophisticated usage requiring a high degree of control over the language forms, and although it might be argued that in theory anything could be expressed in English without ever using the passive voice, in practice, its absence or low frequency is probably symptomatic of a limited control over language use.'

It would be wrong to close this discussion on voice in the verbal group without qualifying some of the views we have expressed above. The truth is that for the sake of argument we have oversimplified some of the issues. Our first qualification concerns our opposing style and 'meaning'. Basically, what we would like to say here is that stylistics is not concerned with what we might call primary meaning, but is concerned with secondary meaning with the delicate nuances of meaning that make a language so rich. Stylistics could help us, for example, to differentiate a set of words appearing under one heading in Roget's *Thesaurus*. Stylistics would help us to decide in what varieties of language the use of a particular item was or was not appropriate. Our second qualification concerns the way in which we have tended to dismiss the use of the passive as a stylistic device as being a matter of less interest to us. The fact is that if it were found that the use of the passive co-occurred with the use of a number of features, such as impersonal *one* and *it*, which one would associate with the use of the elaborated code, then the passive would be of considerable interest. For it could then be regarded as a marker of this kind of discourse. Bernstein would predict that the passive is an effective marker of such discourse in the mature speaker. It would be a much less effective marker in the speech of young children. This, then, essentially concludes our discussion of voice in the verbal group: it only remains to explain how we coded the voice system in our analysis.

The voice system was treated as an 'on/off' choice, as were indeed the systems of modality, polarity and sequent tense. As in each of these systems there is one term which is very frequently selected and another which is only rather rarely selected, it is economical not to positively mark the frequent selection, and only to mark the infrequent selection. So in these systems 'active', 'non-modal', 'positive' and 'non-sequent' are not positively marked (the system being regarded as 'off') whilst their opposites 'passive', 'modal', 'negative' and 'sequent' are positively marked (the system being 'on'). The choice of 'passive' is marked by 'V', the choice of 'modal' by 'M', the choice of 'negative' by 'P', and finally the choice of 'sequent' by 'C'.

6.4 Modality

The system of modality has two terms, 'modal' and 'non-modal'. A verbal group which has the feature 'modal' begins with one of the following items:

> can, could, may, might, must, need, dare, ought to, shall, should, will, would, is/was to, and used to.

Modals are items with a limited range of tense. It is possible to recognise a tense distinction between can/could, may/might, shall/should, will/would, is/was to, and used to. But the other modals do not select for tense. As the range of tense is so narrow here, it was decided that for this analysis we would not subdivide the items for tense.

There are some points that should be mentioned concerning the analysis of the modals. A very important point is that *shall, should, will, would* are not always modals: *shall* and *will* are sometimes exponents of future tense, and *should* and *would* are sometimes exponents of sequent future tense. For criteria for recognising when *shall* and *will* are exponents of future tense it is useful to draw on Palmer (1965). (It should be mentioned, however, that Palmer himself does not hold that these items form part of the tense system.) The criteria for *will* now follow:

(a) *Will* may not be used after *if* in a conditional clause:

    (55) He'll be in London tomorrow

but (56) If he is in London tomorrow

(b) It is replaceable by *shall* in the context of *I* and *we*:

    (57) I'll telephone him soon.

    (58) I shall telephone him soon.

(c) Collocation with future time adverbials:

    (59) It'll snow tomorrow.

The criteria for recognising *shall* as exponent of future tense are:

(a) Not after *if*.

(b) Replaceable by *will* with *I* and *we*.

Concerning the analysis of *should* and *would* as exponents of sequent tense we need not add any more here to the description given in section 6.2.

A further point concerns *dare* and *need*. We followed the usual analysis in regarding these as modals only in the negative forms, *daren't* and *needn't*. *Dare* and *need* without *n't* are treated as lexical verbs since they have a full range of tense. Here are some examples:

(60) He needn't come. ⎫ modal
(61) I daren't ask you. ⎭

(62) He did not need to leave. ⎫
(63) I do not dare to ask him many questions. ⎬ lexical
(64) I will need some more paper soon. ⎭

It was decided that it would be better to do a very simple analysis of the modals for the first description and then to perform a more delicate analysis subsequently. The main reason for this decision was that the modals yield much more useful information than can be contained in a table of ten entries: there are fifteen modal items, and most of these may be used in more than one distinct sense; Palmer (1965) distinguishes six different uses of *can*, for instance, which he labels 'ability', 'characteristic', 'permission', 'possibility', 'willingness' and 'sensation'. We decided that the subsequent more delicate analysis would include a consideration of the range of different modals and different senses, making use of the categories and formal criteria provided by Palmer, and a special examination of the modals of possibility and obligation. We shall now discuss the modals of possibility and those of obligation, which we would expect to be used more by the middle-class subjects than by the working-class subjects.

6.4a Modals of 'possibility'

Our interest in modals of 'possibility' stems from them being a useful means of expressing a hypothesis or of indicating tentativeness. Typical examples are:

(65) It might be an aeroplane.

(66) It could be the Eiffel Tower.

(67) He may be bombing the town.

It is thought that there might be a positive correlation between using these modals of 'possibility' and the egocentric sequence 'I think', e.g.

(68) I think it is an aeroplane.

In both cases there is the implication that other interpretations and identifications are possible. One is reminded here of Rackstraw and Robinson's (1967) remark: 'Egocentric sequences paradoxically show an awareness of points of view other than one's own and, hence, imply an objective frame of reference, but sociocentric sequences are tests of similarity of viewpoint, a check on shared subjectivity.'

6.4b Modals of 'obligation'

The modals of 'obligation', that is, certain uses of *must, ought to, needn't* and *should*, are particularly useful for expressing rules, both social rules and game rules. An example of each of these kinds of rule is now given:.

(69) You ought not to play football in the street.

(70) One must hide his eyes, and the others must go and hide.

We said earlier that we expected the middle-class subjects to use more modals of 'obligation'. This was based on the assumption that the speech

113

schedule would tend to elicit rule-stating with reference to games rather than with reference to social control. The reason for this is that there is a whole task devoted to eliciting an explanation of how to play 'Hide and Seek', 'Musical Chairs' or 'Ring a Ring a Roses'. The occasions promoting social control comments, however, are rather more oblique than this, the most likely place being the Picture Story concerned with some boys kicking a football through someone's window. We would expect the middle-class children to use modals of 'obligation' when explaining how to play 'Hide and Seek', etc. because to prescribe the rules seems to be a rather more sophisticated usage than just to describe the sequences. Compare:

(71) One must hide his eyes . . .

and (72) One hides his eyes . . .

The descriptive approach is less abstract than the prescriptive, and is probably more likely to lead to statements of inessential details. It should, perhaps, be mentioned that there are ways of expressing 'obligation' other than by using a modal. A useful account of this topic would have to consider at least *have* + 'to' infinitive and *have got* + 'to' infinitive as well:

(73) You have to hide your eyes.

(74) You've got to hide your eyes.

The question of whether the middle-class would use more modals of 'obligation' in the language of social control is a complicated one. Bernstein in his treatment of social control makes a distinction between 'positional' and 'personal' orientations. We may quote from the coding frame developed by Bernstein and his colleagues: 'a. The sub-category *positional* refers to behaviour seen in terms of the social categories:

	I	age
	II	sex
	III	age relation
or	IV	other

'b. The sub-category *personal* refers to behaviour seen in terms of development, sentiments or special attributes.

'(This positional/personal distinction could be seen as one between "external" social features and "internal" personal/psychological ones: feelings, intentions, abilities.)'

Now it seems likely that modals of 'obligation' are more strongly associated with positional control than with personal control. What Bernstein calls position-oriented appeals include such statements as:

(75) Promises must be kept.

114

(76) You mustn't steal/be naughty.

(77) You must be tidy/clean/careful.

(78) I tell her that all children must go to school at five.

(79) Children of this age ought to be able to . . .

Person-oriented appeals include the following statements, for example:

(80) That makes mummy very angry.

(81) You want to please mummy.

(82) Daddy can't help forgetting sometimes.

(83) You'll feel miserable if you go on doing that.

Some person-oriented appeals may have a modal of 'obligation', as is illustrated by the following:

(84) You must expect mummy to be cross if you do that.

In general, working-class family-role systems are more likely to employ positional modes of social control, and this positional control is likely to be associated with the restricted code. Bernstein (1965), describing the restricted code (lexical prediction), points out that 'the status or positional aspect of the social relationship is important'. Also, we may note: 'The code restricts the verbal signalling of individual difference.' Person-oriented control is probably more likely to be associated with the middle-class and the elaborated code. Personal control concentrates on the feelings, intentions and abilities of the person. The 'elaborated code user comes to perceive language as a set of theoretical possibilities available for the transmission of unique experience. The concept of self, unlike the concept of self of a speaker limited to a restricted code, will be verbally differentiated, so that it becomes in itself the object of special perceptual activity. In the case of a speaker limited to a restricted code, the concept of self will tend to be refracted through the implications of the status arrangements.'

To return to our o-iginal question about modals of 'obligation' in regulatory language we may say that the working-class are more likely to use more modals of 'obligation' associated with positional appeals and the middle-class are more likely to choose modals of 'obligation' associated with appeals of the personal kind. As for the game rules, as we have said above, we would expect the middle-class to use more modals of obligation in contexts where their use is appropriate.

6.5 Polarity

The system of polarity has two terms: positive and negative. Negative is signalled by the presence of *n't* or *not*. The negative item generally follows or is combined with an auxiliary item, the auxiliary items being *be, have, do* and the modals previously mentioned. Examples of negatives are:

(85) He didn't finish it.

(86) He daren't go away.

(87) He hasn't been seen for a long time.

(88) He isn't coming this evening.

(89) He did not show up last night.

There are just two lexical verbs, as opposed to auxiliary verbs, which are associated with negation, these being *be* and *have*, e.g.

(90) It isn't a man.

(91) I haven't any money.

The use of the negative has attracted considerable attention from philosophers and psychologists as well as linguists. Wason (1960), a psychologist who has made a special study of negation, quotes Bertrand Russell (1948):
'When I say truly "this is not blue", there is, on the subjective side, consideration of "this is blue", followed by rejection, while on the objective side there is some colour differing from blue.'

Wason established that it is more difficult (as measured by times and errors) to respond to negative than positive statements, even after practice. This is because when judging whether a negative is true or false, a human being seems to have to convert the negative statement to a positive one, and then invert the appropriate response. The explanation for this type of behaviour lies in the nature of human development. We learn to describe and respond to our environment mainly in positive terms. Negative statements of fact 'generally play only a subsidiary role in communication: they are used to clarify a topic by removing possible misconception'. Wason describes this use of the negative as 'precautionary': 'it breaks down information in order to re-establish it'. Negative statements which are not precautionary can be very vague as to the identification of the referents, e.g. 'That is not a house'. Because of this, negative statements come to be associated with feelings of vagueness and uncertainty.

Wason also points out that the negative is associated in people's minds with prohibitive commands, e.g. 'Do not do that!' He hypothesises that this association of the negative with prohibition affects its use in *statements* of fact. It could slow down a person's responses.

It seems clear that the main divisions that Wason outlines could be of great use in a subclassification of negatives that occurred in a text. The division into those occurring in 'precautionary' statements and those occurring in 'non-precautionary' statements is an important one. We would expect the former to be more typical of elaborated speech, it being a useful way of obtaining clarification by removing possible misconceptions. The suggestion that the negative is associated with prohibitive commands is provocative. Bernstein suggests that frequent use of commands is a feature of the social control exercised by working-class mothers over their children. It seems quite likely that prohibitive commands will not be infrequent. One might guess, therefore, that the association of the negative with prohibition will be stronger in the working-class than in the middle-class. If this is so, one might expect two different reflections of this association in the speech behaviour of the working-class. One, in role-play situations concerned with social control, e.g. the first Picture Story which is about some boys breaking a window with a football, we might expect the working-class to use a higher frequency of negative commands, e.g.

(92) Don't come here again

And, two, we might expect to find that they use negative statements of fact less frequently.

On the subject of negation it is of interest to consider the work of Miller and his fellow researchers (Miller, 1962; and Miller, 1964, for a general discussion). Miller was impressed by Wason's finding that on an evaluation task the positive-negative difference was more important than the difference between true and false sentences. As Miller says, 'syntactic form was more important than semantic content'. Around about the same time Miller (1962) had found on a sentence-matching task that the negative transformation takes about 1 second, the passive about 1½ seconds, and the two together about 2½ seconds, that is, the sum of the times taken individually. Discussing this experiment Miller (1964) writes: 'The significant point . . . was that the time differences observed in Wason's experiments might have been attributable, at least in part, to the time required to perform the grammatical transformations from negative to affirmative statements.' A simple way to test this conjecture, Miller explains, would be to see whether, 'under the conditions used by Wason, passive sentences also took longer to evaluate, since one might expect that a similar kind of grammatical unravelling would be involved in processing them'. This problem was explored by McMahon (1963). He found that it took about 0·1 second longer to evaluate passive than active sentences, and about 0·4 second longer to evaluate negative than affirmative sentences and that negative-passive sentences took the sum of the above two times, thus giving some support to 'the hypothesis that at least part of the difficulty in using negatively-phrased information is attributable to the difficulty in unscrambling its grammatical form' (Miller, 1964).

Miller's work, however, has to be qualified on two grounds. One, according to Bever, Fodor and Weksel (1965) Miller has made a mistake that is common in psychological investigations concerned with generative grammar. The mistake is to assign a privileged status to the simple declarative sentence, and to treat it as the base to which transformations are applied. The base form is not the simple declarative sentence. 'The kernel grammar does *not* produce simple declarative sentences; it does not produce *any* sentences. Rather, the kernel grammar produces abstract structures that are transformed into a variety of different sentence types of which the simple declarative is one.' So according to Bever and his co-authors 'Miller's (1962) discovery that it takes less time to find the passive corresponding to an active than to find the passive corresponding to a question is *not* explained by appeal to the linguistic fact that the active is the underlying form in the production of the passive and the question. There is no such linguistic fact.' This criticism would also apply to Miller's suggestion that the affirmative underlies the negative, that is, that the negative is arrived at by a grammatical transformation from the affirmative.

Second, Wason, convinced that not all the facts concerned with negation could be explained in terms of syntax, performed a further experiment. Pursuing his belief that the chief use of the negative statement is 'precautionary', that is, to correct plausible errors, e.g. you would not say 'John's not coming' unless there was some reason for your listener to think that he might have been coming, Wason designed an experiment to test if it took longer to complete negative statements about unexceptional facts than about exceptional facts. He found that it was as he predicted. Miller (1964) comments: 'Since I know of nothing in the theory of grammar that would lead one to predict such an outcome, I am forced to agree with Wason that there is more to this matter than syntax alone can account for.'

The above suggests that the problem of negation has interesting sociological and psychological implications.

6.6 Aspect

Only non-finite verbal groups select for aspect. This is what distinguishes them from finite ones. Following Halliday, we recognise three terms: 'perfective', 'imperfective' and 'neutral'. For those verbal groups that select 'perfective' there is a further systemic choice, that of 'perfectability'. This system has two terms: 'to' infinitive and 'zero' infinitive. Here are some examples to illustrate these systems (the code names for the terms being given alongside):

(93) perfective 'zero' infinitive, *go* (B = base)

(94) perfective 'to' infinitive, *to go* (S = summed)

(95) imperfective, *going* (I = imperfective)

(96) neutral, *gone* (N = neutral)

The non-finite verbal group has a number of uses which make it of interest to us: it is used in bound clauses (what Sinclair calls P-bound clauses), in rankshifted clauses and in phase relations. Some examples now follow:

(97) He hurt himself, *trying* to climb into the boat.
     (P-bound)

(98) It is difficult *to climb* in the boat from the water.
     (rankshifted)

(99) They're rescuing that man *drowning* in the water.
     (rankshifted)

(100) They're starting *to help* the man *to get out.*
     (phase)

For a fuller description of these categories the reader is referred to Sinclair (1965). In general, it may be said that the non-finite verbal group is associated with complexity and linguistic sophistication.

6.7 Lexical element

The lexical element is normally the last element in verbal group structure. As the name suggests it is the element at which the lexical item in the verbal group operates. We found it useful to recognise several subclasses of lexical items. Each of these subclasses will be described in turn but first a word about the marking of the lexical element itself.

As the lexical element is always present (except in the case of ellipsis), and as the most usual items expounding the lexical element are not the ones we were interested in subclassifying, it was decided that rather than positively putting in, say LO (that is, 'other lexical items') it would be more economical to mark the lexical element negatively – by leaving it out – in these cases.

6.7a Lexical subclasses

O-Legally omitted lexical element

The potentiality for ellipsis is one of the features of the verbal group. The lexical element may be elided, as in the second verbal group in example (101):

(101) John can't go and Mary can't either.

cf.(102) John can't go and Mary can't go either.

Ellipsis is one of the four main ways of achieving grammatical cohesion in a text (Hasan, 1967).

A-Attributive verb

This category was put in so that we could obtain some information about intensive complements. The attributive verb is associated with the intensive complement. In 'scale-and-category' grammar a distinction is made between intensive complements and extensive complements. A description of this distinction is given by Sinclair (1965):

'As a general rule, if C is expounded by an adjective, or if the nominal group expounding it can be replaced by an adjective-head group without change of structural meaning, then that C is a member of a class which we call intensive complements. Its referent (whatever it refers to outside language) is usually the same as that of the subject, whereas in the other class of complement, the extensive, the opposite holds. The reference of an extensive complement is to something other than the subject; it cannot be replaced by adjectives but it can be replaced by pronouns, which the intensive complement is not able to do.' Examples of this class are now given:

(103) The rose smells sweet.

(104) He is fat.

(105) He is a fat man.

Our main interest in this category stemmed from our belief that the middle-class would tend to ascribe attributes to what they were describing more than the working-class.

Halliday (1967c) should be consulted for a more recent description of the intensive complement and also for his analysis of the verb *be*. He distinguishes three lexical verbs *be*, meaning respectively 'can be characterised as, has the attribute of being', 'exists, happens, is found or located' and 'identifies or is identified as, can be equated with'. It is the characterising or attributive *be* that is associated with the intensive complement – the identificatory *be* being extensive. It is thought that our criteria for recognising intensive complements were not detailed enough to distinguish intensive *be* from extensive *be* in all instances and that in fact some extensive *be* occurrences were counted. In some subsequent research on the verbal group, the distinction was made much more rigorously.

Prepositional verbs and phrasal verbs

Prepositional verbs (P) and phrasal verbs (F) have to be distinguished from each other and from simple verbs plus prepositional groups.

A phrasal verb has a particle which is mobile, that is, it may either precede or follow the complement, except when the complement is a personal pronoun, in which case the particle must follow it, e.g.

(106) Look up the book.

(107) Look the book up.

(108) Look it up.

Svartvik (1966), we may mention, also makes use of a further criterion, based on stress and intonation: 'The particle component of the phrasal verb normally (i.e. in unmarked use) bears full stress (and, if at tone unit boundary, nuclear tone), whereas the preposition with the non-phrasal verb is normally unstressed and does not carry a nuclear tone:

(Vph)   He was taken in.   (The particle has a falling nuclear tone)

(Vp)   He was laughed·at.   (The preposition has the "tail" of the nuclear tone).'

In the case of the prepositional verb the particle is not mobile and this distinguishes it from the phrasal verb.

Probably the most useful way of distinguishing the prepositional verb from simple verbs plus prepositional groups is to apply the passive transformation test. Simple verbs plus prepositional groups are intransitive and so do not allow the passive transformation, e.g.

(109) I've been looking for three hours.

(110) Three hours have been looked for.

Prepositional verbs are transitive and therefore the passive transformation is more likely with them, e.g.

(111) I'm looking for my cuff-links.

(112) My cuff-links are being looked for.

R-Verb introducing reported speech

In section 3.3b we differentiated role-play speech into two kinds: direct and indirect. Direct quoted speech was marked by means of the sentence element (see section 3.5) but indirect reported speech by means of the lexical element. So reporting verbs, such as *say, shout, tell, order*, etc., when associated with indirect reported speech, were coded under this category. Here are some examples:

(113) He said that he was tired.

(114) He said he was tired.

(115) He was tired, he said.

121

S-Suspensional verb

In section 6.4a we explained our interest in the modals of 'possibility', which we took to be a useful means of expressing a hypothesis or of indicating tentativeness. There are certain lexical verbs which perform similar functions. We called these the suspensional verbs because they imply a suspension of judgement – an unwillingness to come down firmly in favour of one particular interpretation and a preference for leaving the possibilities open, e.g.

(116) I don't know whether that's a policeman or not.

(117) I wonder if that's an aeroplane there.

E-Egocentric sequence verb

As we explained in section 4.2c the egocentric sequence was coded differently according to whether it was associated with an elliptical clause or not. If it occurred with an elliptical clause it was coded under T3 in the Tag Clause table (see section 4.7). If it did not occur with such a clause, it was marked by means of the present category. Here are some examples which would be coded under LE:

(118) I think that they've just got married.

(119) I think they've just got married.

(120) They've just got married, I think.

6.8 Coding information

TABLE 08 'ELEMENTS OF VERBAL GROUP STRUCTURE'
If 'P' is selected from Table 06, a selection must be made from Table 08 'Elements of verbal group structure'. This table is given below:

Symbol	Element
Y	Missing element
T	Tense
A	Aspect
L	Lexical element
C	Sequent
V	Voice
P	Polarity
M	Modality

122

'ON/OFF' CHOICES

To economise the description, the systems of modality, polarity, voice and sequent tense are regarded as 'on/off' choices. Only if the features 'modal', 'negative', 'passive' or 'sequent' are realised in the verbal group, are these systems marked. They are marked by 'M', 'P', 'V' and 'C' respectively.

TABLE 14 'ASPECT'

If the verbal group is non-finite, 'A' has to be selected from Table 08 and this has to be followed by a selection from Table 14 'Aspect'. This table is presented below:

Symbol	Term
B	Base
S	Summed
I	Imperfective
N	Neutral

TABLE 13 'CLASS OF LEXICAL VERB'

All verbal groups obligatorily have a lexical verb. In our analysis, however, only a few classes of lexical verb are marked *positively*. Verbal groups which have lexical verbs of these classes or an elided lexical verb of any class must select 'L' from Table 06; this 'L' is then subclassified by a selection from Table 13 'Class of lexical verb'. This table is now given:

Symbol	Class
O	Omitted lexical verb (i.e. elliptical)
A	Attributive
P	Prepositional
F	Phrasal
R	Reporting
S	Suspensional
E	Egocentric

TABLE 15 'TENSE'

All verbal groups obligatorily select 'T'. This has to be followed by a selection from Table 15 'Tense'. This table is not reproduced here as it is the same as the major tense table given in section 6.2.

There are three minor tense systems: non-finite and modal tense and sequent tense. Halliday's tables for these tense systems are also given in section 6.2. In our description, however, we do not have separate tables for these minor tense systems. All tense selections are made from Table 15. A selection from a minor tense system is indicated by the presence of 'A', 'M' or 'C' in the verbal group.

SUMMARY

In this chapter we have covered the following choices in the chart of allowable transitions:

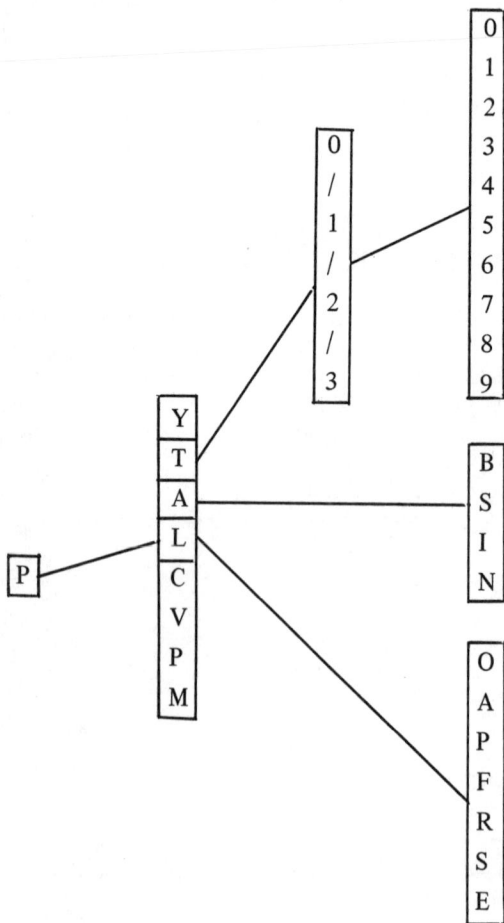

```
                                          ┌───┐
                                          │ 0 │
                                          │ 1 │
                                          │ 2 │
                              ┌───┐       │ 3 │
                              │ 0 │       │ 4 │
                              │ / │       │ 5 │
                              │ 1 │       │ 6 │
                              │ / │       │ 7 │
                              │ 2 │       │ 8 │
                              │ / │       │ 9 │
                              │ 3 │       └───┘
                  ┌───┐       └───┘
                  │ Y │                   ┌───┐
                  │ T │                   │ B │
                  │ A │───────────────────│ S │
                  │ L │                   │ I │
        ┌───┐     │ C │                   │ N │
        │ P │─────│ V │                   └───┘
        └───┘     │ P │
                  │ M │                   ┌───┐
                  └───┘                   │ O │
                                          │ A │
                                          │ P │
                                          │ F │
                                          │ R │
                                          │ S │
                                          │ E │
                                          └───┘
```

124

Example

We may now continue our description of the example sentence (see sections 3.5, 4.7 and 5.9):

That lamp has fallen in front of the television.

Coding

```
1234
10
01S1F1SMD6/HN/1 PT05/1
```

Chapter 7

THE ADJUNCTIVAL GROUP

7.1 Introductory

The adjunctival group is that class of the unit 'group' which operates at clause elements, adjunct (A), linking-conjunction (L) and binding-conjunction (B). Adjunctival groups fall into two types: the prepositional and the adverbial.

7.2 Prepositional group

The prepositional group obligatorily consists of a preposition (P) and a prepositional complement (C). The prepositional complement is always expounded by a rankshifted nominal group. The preposition is optionally modified by a small class of items, which includes *all, far, just, rather, right, straight, very*. We have called the element at which these items occur the temperer (T). Here is, then, the generalised prepositional group structure:

$$(T) \quad P \quad C$$

e.g. (1) all | over | the road

(2) far | beyond the horizon

(3) just | like | what I was telling you about

Because the prepositional complement is always expounded by a rank-shifted nominal group, it was decided that it would be economical to leave out the 'C' element and markers of rankshift, and to insert instead the nominal group elements, direct. So rather than having the following group structure:

$$(T) \quad P \quad C$$

with 'C' expounded by a rankshifted nominal group, (M) H (Q), we have:

$$(T) \quad P \quad (M) \quad H \quad (Q)$$

The objection that might be made to this method of description, namely, that we have lost the information about the nominal group being rank-shifted, does not hold, because we can calculate how many nominal groups were rankshifted in this position simply by referring to the number of prepositions.

To aid recognition of the preposition, we reproduce here the list of these items given by Strang (1962):

about, above, across, after, against, along, amidst, among(st), around, as, at, before, behind, below, beneath, beside, beyond, by, concerning, considering, despite, down, during, except, following, for, from, in, into, like, near, of, off, on, opposite, out, over, per, regarding, round, save, since, then, through, throughout, till, to, towards, under, underneath, unlike, until, up, upon, with, within, without;

across from, along with, alongside of, apart from, away from, because of, down from, due to, except for, inside of, instead of, off of, onto, out of, outside of, over to, together with, up to, up with;

in spite of, on account of, by means of, in addition to, with regard to, in front of, on top of, on behalf of.

It will be observed that almost all of the items which occur in the first list, the one-word items, can also be used as adverbs. For example, we can say:

(4) He walked in.   adverb

(5) He walked in the room.   preposition

The most obvious difference between the adverb use and the preposition use is that the latter is always immediately followed by a nominal group which cannot normally be moved from this position. The only exceptions to this rule are nominal groups containing WH-words, which are auto-matically fronted in certain clauses, e.g.

(6) Whom are you talking to?

cf.   (7) I was talking to John.

Strang (1962) points out that the distinction made above between these items as adverbs and as prepositions is no more than the distinction we make between intransitive and transitive verbs. If we wished, we could speak of intransitive and transitive prepositions. Following Strang, we do not adopt this latter mode of description. For a fuller discussion of the point, the reader is referred to Strang.

Carroll (1964) gives the approximate conceptual meaning of the prepositionals as the class of experience that includes 'relations of spatial, temporal or logical position relative to nominals'. Bernstein (1959) lists among the characteristics he gives of a formal language 'frequent use of prepositions which indicate logical relationships as well as prepositions which indicate temporal and spatial contiguity'. Clearly some subdivision of prepositions is desirable. The difficulty with prepositions is that it is not possible to divide them into groups, so that we can say of each preposition that it is a member of this group and not of any other. An example will illustrate the impossibility of doing this:

(8) He sowed the seeds in the morning.

(9) He sowed the seeds in the garden.

(10) He sowed the seeds in a careless fashion.

Although the same item, *in*, is used in each case, the relationship involved is quite different in each of the above sentences. In traditional terms, the relationship in the first sentence is one of 'time', in the second 'place' and in the third 'manner'. It is clear that the best guide to the nature of the relationship is the noun at the head of the prepositional complement. We decided to subclassify these head-words into four classes: 'time' (H1), 'place' (H2), 'manner' (H3), and 'others' (H4). These classes, especially the first three, are identified by two methods. One, the head-word is related to its lexical set, that is, other words of a similar meaning, which may be substituted for the head-word without the underlying relation being destroyed. The 'time' set includes *second, minute, hour, day, night, morning, afternoon, evening, spring, summer, autumn, winter*, etc. The 'place' set is much larger and includes *inches, feet, yards, miles, garden, field, hedgerow, plantpot, cottonwool*, etc. The 'manner' set of items is very small, the most likely ones being *manner, way* and *fashion*. The 'manner' nouns are often modified by a member of the 'attitudinal' set of adjectives, for example, *careless, angry, amusing, indifferent*. Such adjectives as these may imply that the speaker has made an inference, some subjective assessment of the situation. It is much more difficult to suggest the sets of items which are associated with the 'others' class. Certainly they will include items such as those which can be grouped into 'cause' and 'purpose' sets. It is much easier, however, to make the definition of them negative. In other words, anything that is not covered by the first three classes goes here.

The second method of isolating the classes is to try and determine the relationship involved by asking what underlying question the clause might be regarded as a response to. So the 'time' class covers questions such as 'when?', 'how long?' (duration), 'how often?' (frequency); and the 'place' class covers 'where?', 'how far?' (distance), 'which way?' (direction); and the 'manner' class covers 'how?', 'in what manner?' The 'others' class covers 'why?' both in the sense of 'what reason?' and of 'what purpose?' It also covers any other question not handled by the first three classes.

7.3 Adverbial group

The adverbial group consists of a pivotal element, which may be preceded by a temperer (T) and/or followed by a finisher (F). What value the pivotal element has depends upon which clause element the group is operating at; if the adjunct, then the value 'vortex', if linking-conjunction, then 'linker', and if binding-conjunction, 'binder'. The generalised structure of the adverbial group may be stated as follows:

$$(T) \quad \left\{ \begin{array}{c} V \\ L \\ B \end{array} \right\} \quad (F)$$

The round brackets indicate optional elements and the braces indicate (a) that a selection is obligatory, and (b) that the values, 'V', 'L' and 'B', are mutually exclusive. Each of these obligatory elements will now be considered in turn.

7.4 Vortex

The vortex element is expounded by the adverb. It is possible to recognise several different subclasses of adverb on morphological grounds, but we shall not do this. We shall simply mention some as an aid to identification of this class of word. What may be regarded as the basic or most central adverbs are words such as *here, now, there, seldom, perhaps, still, once, twice, always.* Others include the de-adjectivals, e.g. *wonderfully, cautiously* (these consist of a base adjective + the suffix -*ly*), and the derivatives, e.g. *abroad* (formed with the prefix *a*-), *backwards* (with the suffix -*wards*), *anywhere, nowhere, somehow,* etc. (formed from one of the determiners, *some-, any-, every-, no-,* and one of the following -*how, -way, -where*), and finally *career-wise,* etc. (formed from a noun base + suffix -*wise*). A detailed and useful description of the adverb is to be found in Strang (1962), upon which this present description is based.

Our subclassification of the adverbs parallels the one we made of the prepositional groups. The value of this is that it permits us to collapse across categories if we so wish, and to make more general statements about the expression of 'time' (V1), 'place' (V2), 'manner' (V3), and 'other relations' (V4) at the adjunct.

It is perhaps of use to mention that Strang offers a test-frame for formally establishing three subclasses which are co-extensive with those of 'time', 'place' and 'manner' mentioned above. The basis of the subclassification is the disposition of the adverb, its position relative to the verbal group. Three positions are established and a generic substitute, namely 'there', 'then' and 'thus/so', is given for each. Here is the pattern:

Subject	Predicator		Adjuncts	
		Position 1	Position 2	Position 3
		there-group	then-group	thus/so-group
e.g. (11) I	may go	outside	today	easily

This test-frame is of use but, as Strang points out, most clauses do not seem natural with the three positions occupied. It is more natural to put the 'manner' adverb before the verb, e.g.

(12) I may easily go outside today.

Moreover, it is sometimes possible to advance a different one of the three.

In our analysis the three subclasses of adverb, 'time', 'place' and 'manner', were defined in terms of the underlying questions they might be regarded as responses to. The questions are the same as those given for the prepositions, so there is no need to present them again here. The fourth subclass, 'other adverbs', contains the residual adverbs.

There are two other entries in the vortex table to be described. Stressed *there* was taken out of the 'place' subclass and was coded as V6. It had been noticed that the selection of this word was very frequent in the data, and that it might amount almost to a 'nervous tic' with some children. It seemed better to isolate it then.

Finally, we recognised a class of sentence connectors operating at the adjunct. These are words such as *however, therefore, thus, still, nevertheless* and *indeed*. It was not anticipated that these would be used by many, if any, of the five-year-old children, but provision was made for them in category V5, in case they did occur.

Having outlined the subclasses of adverbs and prepositions that we recognised, we shall discuss them in greater detail, pointing out facts of psychological and sociological interest. We shall begin with a discussion of the 'time' expressions.

What is the relationship between time expressed by the adjunctival group and time expressed by tense in the verbal group? No simple or full answer can be given to this question. We can only touch on the main points here. Sinclair (1965) recognises a system of time-reference which has two terms, 'direct' and 'indirect'. According to Sinclair, there is only one time-reference in the verbal group, and this is the moment of utterance. The direct form of reference relates to the moment of utterance, and it can occur without further details about time, e.g.

(13) I recognise you.

(14) I live in London.

The indirect form cannot occur without further details about time reference. It does not relate to the moment of utterance. It 'can only be used when there is time-reference present or known to the speaker, outside the verbal group', e.g.

130

(15) I recognised you last night.

(16) I lived in London then.

Further details of time-reference can, of course, be given with the direct form, e.g.

(17) I recognise you now.

(18) I live in London all the time.

Sinclair points out that 'these specific references amplify and perhaps partly over-rule the reference of the direct form to the moment of utterance'.

Crystal (1966) quotes Ivić (1962) who writes concerning traditional Serbo-Croatin grammars: 'It has not been realised that the verbal form appears free only if it refers to the actual event, while in other instances it is always bound to the obligatory use of an accessory grammatical element: the non-omissible determiner.' Crystal suggests that any discussion of the 'meanings of English verb forms must also envisage the temporal adverbial (and, in particular, certain kinds of temporal adverbial) as falling within the category of non-omissible determiner'. He refers to this phenomenon as 'specification' (rather than 'non-omissible determination') and he shows how 34 of the 48 time situations he identifies, that is 70% of them, require explicit adverbial specification of some kind. It is intended that future analyses should make use of the descriptive information that Crystal presents. It is thought, for example, that there may be social class differences in the extent to which the children use the temporal adverbials as sentence connectors. Crystal writes: 'It is fairly normal speech practice to introduce a temporal adverbial when switching to a new time-relationship, and not to rely on tense alone. One is readily familiar with the result of using too many tense-forms without specification for variation – temporal vagueness, monotony, even jerkiness because of the unaccustomed brevity. It produces a kind of style very reminiscent of the primitive essays of children, and there may be a case for saying that an important kind of stylistic sophistication is the result of being able to vary one's temporal reference along the two scales, verbal and adverbial.' It would be of interest to see whether middle-class children's speech evinces any evidence of greater sophistication in this respect.

After this brief consideration of the 'time' expressions, we shall now turn to those of 'space'. In our discussion of the 'time' expressions we related them to the system of tense in the verbal group; now we shall relate the 'space' expressions to the system of transitivity in the clause. The relevant feature in the system is that of 'range' (see Halliday, 1967c). Range may be either 'cognate' or 'non-cognate', the former being illustrated by:

(19) He sang a song.

If range is non-cognate, then it may be further distinguished as 'qualitative' or 'quantitative', exemplified respectively by:

(20) He climbed the mountain.

(21) He ran five miles.

We may add that 'quantitative' may be subdivided into 'measure' and 'non-measure', but this distinction need not concern us here. What interests us is the fact that range, especially non-cognate range, often contrasts with a prepositional adjunct of place. This kind of contrast may be illustrated by comparing the following examples with the previous two:

(22) He climbed up the mountain.

(23) He ran for five miles.

Discussing the relation of range to prepositional structures, Halliday comments that 'in general there is no limit on what preposition might be selected'. So for a given range there might be a large number of possible prepositional correspondents. It seems important that future research should attempt to relate range and the prepositional adjunct to see what sort of balance is struck between them in the different social classes.

There are, of course, other relationships between prepositional groups and transitivity features, which we would have to take account of in a more delicate analysis. So, for example, the transitivity feature 'benefactive' may contrast with prepositional adjuncts with *to*, *for*, etc.

(24) He gave John the money.

(25) He gave the money to John.

(26) She poured John some tea.

(27) She poured some tea for John.

The feature 'actor', realised by a nominal group in an active construction, is realised by a prepositional adjunct with *by* in its passive parallel:

(28) John painted the house.

(29) The house was painted by John.

Finally, the attributive may be realised by some prepositional adjuncts, especially those with *in*:

(30) She seemed in pain/in trouble.

cf.   (31) She seemed hurt/worried.

We shall now discuss the 'manner' expressions. These are either adverbial or prepositional. The former usually consists of an adverb of the type, 'adjective' + *ly*, and the latter of the type, preposition (*in*) followed by a nominal group with a noun such as *way, manner, degree* as head; examples are *beautifully* and *in a beautiful manner*. Katz and Postal (1964) call the first type manner adverbials and the second type manner nominals, and they point out the adjectives occurring in the manner nominals are just those occurring before -*ly* in manner adverbials. So the fact that there is no such sentence as:

(32) John sleeps yellowly

follows directly from the absence of

(33) John sleeps in a yellow way.

Because of this relationship between manner adverbials and manner nominals, Katz and Postal propose that they both should be derived from the same source, from a phrase composed of a preposition and a 'dummy' nominal, this latter being realised by *way, manner, degree,* etc., in particular positions.

Lyons (1966) says: 'If this proposal is accepted (that is, Katz and Postal's proposal) . . . we can eliminate "adverbs" from the lexicon and introduce them into sentences as "adjectives" modifying a set of "dummy" nominals.' He argues that the majority of 'adjectives' in English modify both nouns and verbs in 'deep' structure. Halliday (1967c), however, prefers to keep the adjective and the adverb distinct in clauses such as:

(34) She sells them cheap.

(35) She sells them cheaply.

He gives three main reasons for doing this, one of which is particularly interesting from our point of view: 'the semantic distinction between attribution and manner, while in certain instances it may be largely neutralised, is in fact an important one in English; in attribution the focus is on the participant, in manner the focus is on the process.' It may well be that there are social class and sex differences in the extent to which the children tend to focus on the participant or on the process.

Are there any grounds for believing that the three kinds of expressions we have discussed, those of 'time', 'place' and 'manner', are associated with concepts of differing difficulty? Gesell and Ilg (1946), discussing time and space, write: 'Time is in a sense more abstract and inflexible than space. It has only two sectors or dimensions (backward and forward). In an unsophisticated way the infant is aware of the flow of time; but not the units of time. By association he learns to place events in his accustomed surroundings and his accustomed daily schedule. (Note that the word *place* has a spatial connotation.) By experiences of place expectancy, he identifies *times*. By deferments he learns to wait and to appreciate units of time.' The primacy of space language has been commented on by philosophers. Urban (1939) writes that 'Bergson, and other thinkers following him, have maintained that all our words for time had formerly a spatial meaning and that the vulgar notion of time is simply a copy of the notion of space'. Urban thinks that Bergson is right in his main contention, namely that spatial language is primary, and he claims that 'our intellect is primarily fitted to deal with space and moves most easily in this medium'. The suggestions are, then, that space concepts probably present less difficulty than time concepts. What about the concepts that 'manner' expressions are associated with? Are they more difficult than the other two kinds? One would imagine that in general they are. There is not space here to consider the whole range of concepts that the manner expressions are associated with. We shall confine our attention to two types. Firstly, there are those that are concerned with the relationship between space and time, with velocity, for instance, as in:

(36) He's running slowly.

Because of the fact that a relationship between space and time is involved, one would expect that such a concept would be more difficult than one of space or of time. Secondly, there are those that involve making judgements about the psychological states of others, e.g.

(37) She's smiling unhappily.

It is thought that the inferences that are required in order to make such judgements probably present greater difficulty than do inferences about time and space.

So far we have not discussed the adjunctival expressions that are concerned with relationships other than those of time, place and manner. Linguists have subclassified these expressions into several different categories: Jacobson (1964), for example, talks of 'aspect or viewpoint', 'degree', 'restriction, particularisation, and exemplification' and 'mood'. A group of expressions that are particularly interesting from the point of view of our research are those that have been identified by Davies (1967) – the 'comment' adjuncts. These are adjuncts which enable the speaker to add a comment on what he is saying, for example, a comment concerning its probability or truth, as in:

(38) Probably he's saying, 'I'll smack you.'

and (39) Possibly it's a wedding party.

Just as we would expect the middle-class children to use 'I think' and modals of possibility more, so we would expect there to be a similar pattern in these adverbial expressions. That the mothers of these children use more such expressions has been established by Cook (1968), who found differences on a category she called 'adverbs of possibility'. Other comment adjuncts that we would expect to be used by the middle-class, though not by young children, are those that Davies calls the 'passive capacity' adjuncts. Here is an example of such an adjunct:

(40) Understandably he felt very angry.

This clause has a clear correspondence to the following passive clause:

(41) It can be understood that he felt very angry.

The name 'passive capacity' relates to this correspondence. Davies also points out a further correspondence: 'These "passive capacity" adjuncts can in fact, in some respects, be considered related in function to transitive verbs of saying, thinking, knowing, believing, presuming, imagining and so on: that is, verbs which describe the way in which a participant in one situation relates himself to another hypothetical situation, event or state of affairs, as set forth in a following clause.' We would certainly expect the middle-class to reveal a greater tendency than the working-class for expressing hypotheticalness of this sort.

7.5 The temperer and the finisher

The description of the temperer which was given in connection with the prepositional group also holds for the adverbial group, so there is no need to elaborate it further here.

The 'finisher' element does need to be described, however. As the name suggests, it is the element which follows the pivotal element in an adverbial group; it is an optional choice, and only a relatively small number of selections are possible. It may be either a single word such as *enough* and *indeed* or a rankshifted prepositional group, the most usual prepositions being *as, of* and *than*. Here are some examples:

(42) quickly enough

(43) very quickly indeed

(44) as quickly as possible

(45) more quickly than his rival

(46) best of all

The rankshifted nominal group operating within the prepositional group may, of course, have a rankshifted clause operating as head, as in the example which follows:

(47) John ran more quickly than his rival did.

135

7.6 Adverbial and prepositional group complexity

The adverbial and prepositional group structures, like those of the sentence, clause and nominal group, were collected in terms of a combination matrix. The matrix is reproduced below:

V	VF	H	PH
TV	TVF	TP	TPH

There are, in fact, only seven categories, the 'TP' category being an unreal category since a preposition by definition may not occur without an 'H'. It was put in to fill out the pattern and thereby to make the computing more straightforward. The main idea behind this categorisation is that 'T' and 'F' are useful measures of complexity in these groups. They are optional elements: their use involves going beyond the minimal structures.

7.7 Linker

In a compound sentence such as

(48) I went home and I sat down

there are three possible ways of describing *and*, assuming that one wishes to describe it at all. One can describe it as (a) part of the first clause, (b) part of the second clause, and (c) as part of neither clause, just merely a link between them. Actually we did both (b) and (c). In sentence structure we have a '+' sign which shows that a relationship of co-ordination exists between two clauses, but the '+' sign is part of neither clause as such; that is (c). But in clause structure the linker *and* is taken to be part of the second clause; that is (b). It may seem redundant to describe this phenomenon in two ways, but it is not so, because the relationship of co-ordination may exist between clauses without a linker being present, as for example in:

(49) I went home, had my tea and went to bed.

In sentence (49), the second clause is co-ordinately related to the first clause but it displays no linker.

In our analysis the linkers are broken down into four classes. As there are very few items it is possible to set up some one-member classes, thus:

L1	additive, *and*
L2	adversative, *but*
L3	disjunctive and conjunctive, *or*
L4	other linkers

The other linkers include *so, yet* and compounds of these with *and* and *but*, e.g. *and so* and *but yet*.

7.8 Binder

Bernstein (1959) gives among the characteristics of a formal language the following: 'Logical modifications and stress are mediated through a grammatically complex sentence construction, especially through the use of a range of conjunctions and relative clauses.' Certainly the items that operate at the binding-conjunction in clause structure are very useful for achieving the purposes Bernstein outlines. In order to give an idea of the range we reproduce a list of binders:

after	in order (that)/to
although/though	in that
as	once
as if/as though	provided/ . . . ing/on condition (that)
as/so long as	since
because	so that/as
before	such that
considering/seeing (that)	supposing/assuming (that)
directly/immediately	till/until
except (that)	that
for	unless
given/granted (that)	where
if	whereas
inasmuch/insofar as	whether
in case	while/whilst
	with

It could not be expected, of course, that five-year-old children would make much use of this range. The formal logical operations that many of these binders imply are far beyond the conceptual development of children of this age. It was thought, then, that it would be reasonable to divide the binders into four classes, making use of some traditional subdivisions, so: binders of 'time' (B1), 'cause' (B2), 'condition' (B3) and 'other binders' (B4). To a large extent it is possible to specify which items belong to each class. As is usual in language, however, there are some formal items which have more than one use. In the case of these items, particularly *as* and *since*, it is necessary to ask which unambiguous binders (such as *whilst* and *because*) can be substituted for them without unduly distorting the basic relationship.

The 'time' binders are: *after, as, before, directly, immediately, once, since, till/until, while/whilst*. The binders expressing 'cause' are: *as, because, for, since*. The most likely binders of 'condition' are *if, provided/ . . . ing/on condition (that)* and *unless*. All other items are coded under 'other binders'.

It must be stressed that this analysis in terms of 'time', 'cause' and 'condition' is somewhat superficial. These concepts refer to the most usual

137

potential meaning of the items, and not to what a deep semantic analysis might reveal to be their actual instantial* meaning in any particular sentence. The following sentences will illustrate this point:

(50) When I got home, I sat down.

(51) When you squeeze the bulb, the elephant moves his arms.

(52) If you squeeze the bulb, the elephant moves his arms.

(53) Because I squeezed the bulb, the elephant moved his arms.

In the first sentence the relationship between the clauses is one of temporality; *when* here does not carry implications of causality or condition. *When* in the second sentence, in contrast, does carry such implications, perhaps rather more definitely than the implication of temporality, as is shown when it is compared with the other sentences. It was thought, though, that the form of description we adopted was the best we could do in formal grammatical terms.

We may conclude this section, however, with a brief consideration of some of the semantic parallels that exist between linkers, binders and sentence connectors. We shall confine ourselves to the notions of contrast, cause-and-effect and choice.

The notion of contrast or opposition may be expressed by means of a concessive binder (e.g. *although*), an adversative linker (*but*) or a sentence connector (e.g. *however*), as in the following examples:

(54) Although I am busy, I will do it.

(55) I am busy, but I will do it.

(56) I am busy; however, I will do it.

Similarly, the cause-and-effect relationship may be expressed in at least three different syntactic ways:

(57) Tom broke a cup and Mummy was upset.

(58) Because Tom broke a cup, Mummy was upset.

(59) Tom broke a cup; consequently, Mummy was upset.

When a linker or sentence connector is used, the cause clause must precede the effect clause, but when a binder is used, the effect clause may be given before the cause clause, as in the example below:

(60) Mummy was upset, because Tom broke the cup.

Alternatives, like contrast and cause-and-effect, may be expressed in three ways, as may be shown by the following examples:

* A distinction between potential and instantial meaning is made by Ellis (1966).

(61) If you buy that book, there will be no money for the bus.

(62) Don't buy that book or there will be no money for the bus.

(63) Don't buy that book; otherwise, there will be no money for the bus.

If *or* or *otherwise* is used, instead of *if*, a negative imperative clause must be used in order to express this kind of relationship.

In section 4.2b.ii we gave our reasons for believing that the middle-class children would tend to use more cause and condition clauses. In particular we discussed the correlation between the Child-oriented Reasoning Index and Social Class. Now it seems clear that the type of reasoning we described in that section would have an influence not only on the way a child binds clauses together, but also on the way he links them and connects sentences. The middle-class mother is likely to express notions such as cause and condition in a variety of ways, and we can expect to find reflections of this in her child's choice of binders, linkers and sentence connectors.

7.9 Coding information

TABLE 09 'ELEMENTS OF ADJUNCTIVAL GROUP STRUCTURES'

If 'A', 'B' or 'L' is selected from Table 06, then a selection must be made from Table 09 'Elements of adjunctival group structure'. The table is now given:

Symbol	Element
Q	Qualifier
H	Head
M	Modifier
P	Preposition
F	Finisher
V	Vortex
T	Temperer
B	Binder
L	Linker

Adjunctival groups fall into two types: the prepositional and the adverbial.

THE PREPOSITIONAL GROUP

TABLES 07, 10, 20, 19 and 12

A prepositional group always contains a rankshifted nominal group. Because the rankshifting is fully predictable, it is NOT marked, i.e. we do

139

not put in 07 . . . /1, the usual way of marking such rankshifting. We simply enter the description of the nominal group immediately after the 'P' element. There is no need to rehearse the description of the nominal group here. The description is just the same as is set out in Tables 07, 10, 20 and 12 (section 5.9). The only difference is in the subclassification of 'H'. In a nominal group occurring at 'S', 'C', 'Z' or 'V', the 'H' element is subclassified in terms of Tables 11 and 21, but in one occurring elsewhere in the structure of the clause, 'H' is subclassified in terms of Table 19 (Classes of Head II). Here is this table:

Symbol	Class
1	Time
2	Place
3	Manner
4	Other

THE ADVERBIAL GROUP

If 'A', 'L' or 'B' is selected from Table 06 'Elements of clause structure', then 'V', 'L' or 'B' respectively has to be selected from Table 09. If 'V' is selected, then a choice has to be made from Table 18 'Classes of adverb'. This table is given below:

Symbol	Class
1	Time
2	Place, except *there*
3	Manner
4	Other
5	Sentence connector
6	*There*

If 'B' is selected from Table 09, a selection has to be made from Table 16 'Class of binder', which table is now given:

Symbol	Class
1	Time
2	Cause
3	Condition
4	Others

Finally, if 'L' is selected from Table 09, a selection is to be made from Table 17 'Class of linker':

Symbol	Class
1	Additive *and*
2	Adversative *but*
3	Disjunctive and Conjunctive *or*
4	Others

It is possible (theoretically) for 'V', 'B' or 'L' to be preceded by 'T' and followed by 'F'.

'T' simply precedes the element in question: there is no '/' between them.

A '/', however, must come between the subclassified 'V', 'B' or 'L'. If the finisher is one word only, then simply 'F' is entered. If the finisher is a rankshifted group (a rankshifted prepositional group), then an angle bracket, '⟨', is placed immediately after 'F' and this is followed by the number of the 'Elements of adjunctival group structure' table, '09'. The prepositional group is described in the usual way and the end of this group is shown by '/1' and the end of rankshifting by '⟩'.

SUMMARY

With the adjunctival group selections we have now completed the chart of allowable transitions. (See page 142.)

Example

We are finally in a position to complete our description of the example sentence (see sections 3.5, 4.7, 5.9 and 6.8):

That lamp has fallen in front of the television.

Coding

```
1234
10
01S1F1SMD6/HN/1  PT05/1  APMD8/H2/3
```

141

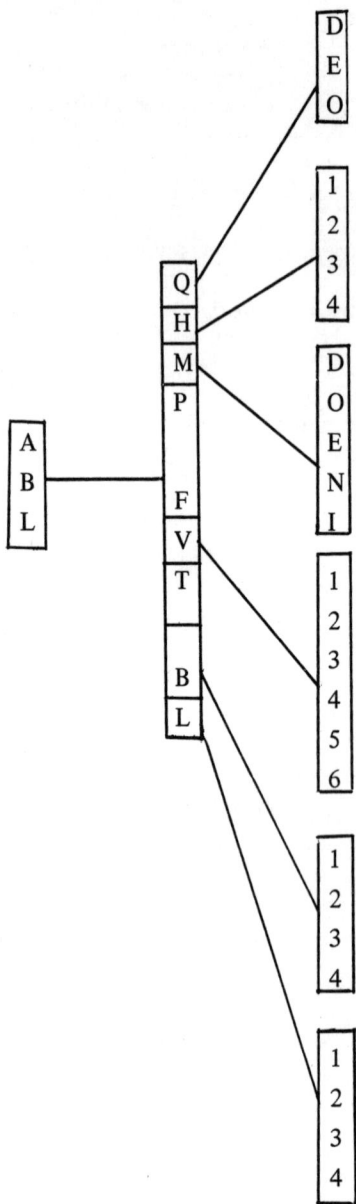

A
B
L

Q
H
M
P
F
V
T
B
L

D
E
O

1
2
3
4

D
O
E
N
I

1
2
3
4
5
6

1
2
3
4

1
2
3
4

Chapter 8

MAZES

8.1 Introductory

Spoken language often contains incomplete utterances, false starts, repetitions, corrections, etc. All such phenomena are classified as examples of maze behaviour. The term 'maze' is taken from Loban (1961), the image behind it being of a person thrashing about trying to find the correct verbal means for expressing what he wants to express. The name is not important, however.

There are many reasons why speakers do not complete sentences, repeat themselves, etc. For one thing language in natural use is a medium which contains a good deal of redundancy. Quirk (1962) writes: 'Indeed, redundancy is a natural and necessary factor in all use of language: without it, any momentary inattention or mispronunciation or misprint or the intrusion of "noise" of any kind would make comprehension impossible; and even without such intrusions, the degree of concentration necessary to understand anything would exhaust most of us.' As Quirk points out, sometimes when we do not complete an utterance we are intuitively acknowledging the existence of redundancy in language. He gives the following rather amusing illustration: A man waits at Oxford Circus and at last his friend turns up; their conversation may begin somewhat as follows:

> 'I'm sorry if I'm er . . . Shall we go and have a bite to . . . ? or have you had your . . . Oh, by the way, we can't go for a drive in my . . . you see, I've failed my . . . Ugh, the examiner was an absolute . . . '

It seems doubtful, though, that five-year-old children will exhibit this kind of redundancy, at least in the novel kind of situation they were put into.

Chomsky (1965) writes: 'Linguistic theory is concerned primarily with an ideal speaker-listener, in a completely homogeneous speech-community, who knows its language perfectly and is unaffected by such grammatically irrelevant conditions as memory limitations, distractions, shifts of attention and interest, and errors (random or characteristic) in applying his knowledge of the language in actual performance.' Later he remarks: 'A record of natural speech will show numerous false starts, deviations from

143

rules, changes of plan in mid-course, and so on.' The fundamental concern of linguistic theory is to characterise the 'competence' (the speaker-hearer's knowledge of his language) underlying actual 'performance' (the actual use of language in concrete situations). It is Chomsky's view that 'investigation of performance will proceed only so far as understanding of underlying competence permits'. He suggests that the only significant work that has been done so far has been based on assumptions about underlying competence.

The above view is also expressed by Wales and Marshall (1966). They do not present a theory of linguistic performance but make a critical survey of a vast amount of literature on the psychology of language, and give many suggestions for future research and theory. We have not space to consider these suggestions in detail here; we will restrict ourselves to general comments. In the first place, the task of isolating the effect that knowledge of the language (that is, underlying competence) has on actual speech behaviour (performance), of separating this effect from the effects of limitations of memory, shifts of attention, differences in perception, social ease or dis-ease in a situation, fatigue etc. is enormous. This is not to suggest that it cannot be done. But it is clear that closely controlled experiments, probably covering a wide range of situations, are demanded. Certainly our survey type of material is not suitable for such inquiry. If we found social class differences in linguistic performance, we could not say with any certainty whether these differences were a result of, say, lack of attention or interest in the working-class, social awkwardness when talking to an adult with superordinate status, or true differences in underlying linguistic competence. The justification for the survey approach as an initial tool is that it can indicate areas of difference which seem worthy of more detailed and tightly controlled inquiry.

There is nothing in Bernstein's writings, in any case, to suggest that there are likely to be social class differences in underlying linguistic competence, apart from dialect differences. And dialect differences, such as the use of *what* in relative clauses, e.g. 'the man what I met', Bernstein is not interested in. What does interest Bernstein, however, is the relative frequency of particular selections in the two social classes. He is also interested in what he calls 'verbal planning' and this might well have some association with maze behaviour. According to Bernstein (1962a) the two codes, that is, Elaborated and Restricted, are considered 'to entail qualitatively different verbal planning orientations which control different modes of self-regulation and levels of cognitive behaviour'. He suggests that verbal planning may be considered in terms of patterns of orientation, association and organisation. Bernstein linked up verbal planning with hesitation phenomena. He found such things as the following: that the working-class used a longer mean phrase length, spent less time pausing and used a shorter word length. Bernstein took this to indicate that the working-class were actually spending less time planning their speech and were making use of previously-learned phrases. He referred to Goldman-Eisler (e.g. 1961) for suggestions why the middle-class should spend more time planning. Goldman-Eisler had found that summarising (that is, abstracting and generalising from perceived events) requires more time in pausing than does giving a description. Bernstein suggested that there may be differences in the organisation of the content of working-class and middle-class speech, but he was cautious about this, as the content had not been analysed.

If hesitation phenomena are associated with planning, it is likely that at least some maze behaviour may also be related to planning. In an article called 'Speech and Thought', Goldman-Eisler (1962) writes: 'The argument ran that if pauses are as much a part of speech as are the sound sequences produced, then they must have a function relevant to the production of speech, and that this function would be the planning of speech, which is a form of thinking.' She concludes her article with the following: 'By learning about the function of pauses in speech we have gained a signal for the occurrence and a yardstick of the level of thought activity and of the complexity of the central processes in the brain.' The possible relationships between different types of maze behaviour and thought, and how these are likely to be associated with social class, will be discussed after we have presented the maze categories.

It should be pointed out that quite apart from our interest in mazes as a possible indicator of thought processes, we had to face the problem of describing them in order that we could give a consistent account of our grammatical categories. There could be no reliable account of the grammatical categories if there were no reliable account of the 'noise' in the speech. Our categories, then, may be viewed as partly a matter of expediency and partly a matter of interest.

8.2 Maze types*

			Code
I.	Fragment (structure)	⌈ incompletely structured	1 1 1 1
		⌊ nonsensical structure	1 2 1 1
II.	Repetition (location)	⌈ immediate	2 1 1 1
		⌊ non-immediate	2 2 1 1
III.	Substitution	Location ⌈ immediate	3 - - -
		⌊ non-immediate	4 - - -
		Structure† ⌈ reduced	- 1 - -
		├ same	- 2 - -
		⌊ expanded	- 3 - -

* We should like to acknowledge our debt in this formulation to Mr. J. N. H. Pellowe's work on what he called 'speech turbulences'.

† The terms 'structure' and 'exponence' are used rather more loosely here than in 2.2.

145

(Continued from page 145)

$$
\text{Exponence} \begin{cases} \text{grammatical change} & - - 1 - \\ \text{lexical change} & - - 2 - \\ \text{grammatical and lexical change} & - - 3 - \\ \text{no change} & - - 4 - \end{cases}
$$

$$
\text{Effect} \begin{cases} \text{improved} & - - - 1 \\ \text{worsened} & - - - 2 \\ \text{neutral} & - - - 3 \end{cases}
$$

I. FRAGMENT

1. Incompletely structured

This type of fragment occurs when a unit consists of one or more units of the rank below, but lacks one or more units that are essential to give it complete structural meaning, e.g.

(1) John hit the

The 'unsatisfactory' intonation that accompanies this type of incomplete structure generally may be taken to indicate that the speaker has abandoned the utterance either because his attention has been distracted (associated with a sharp break in the intonation pattern immediately followed by another utterance) or because he is unable to 'find' the lexical or grammatical item(s) he needs (associated with a faltering breakdown of the intonation pattern usually followed by a pause).

2. Nonsensical

This type of fragment occurs when a unit consists of one or more units of the rank below, but lacks either sufficient units or order to give it structural meaning, e.g.

(2) the off gone

II. REPETITION

1. Immediate

This type of repetition occurs when two instances of the same item are found consecutively and the two instances are not a paratactic relation (co-ordination or apposed) or in a hypotactic relation (e.g. subordinate), e.g.

(3) John John sat down

146

2. Non-immediate

This type of repetition differs from the above type only in that the two instances occur non-consecutively. There is other language material intervening. The non-immediate repetition usually occurs either at the end of a clause where it echoes the subject:

(4) This man was arguing this man.

or near the beginning of a co-ordinate clause where it seems to function as a means of 'buying time' in which to plan the rest of the clause:

(5) and then and he went away.

This latter type of non-immediate repetition is distinguished from substitution (see below) by the accompanying intonation: repetition is normally associated with pausing, whilst substitution is associated with a sharp break in the intonation pattern.

III. SUBSTITUTION

3. Immediate

This type of substitution occurs when an element of structure is expounded by two different units of the rank below which are not in a paratactic relation (co-ordinate or apposed) or a hypotactic relation (e.g. subordinate), e.g.

(6) John kicked the cat dog.

4. Non-immediate

This type of substitution occurs when a stretch of language is repeated in order that a part of it may be altered in some way, e.g.

(7) John kicked the cat kicked the dog.

Both types of substitution may be subclassified on three dimensions: Structure, Exponence and Effect. We shall consider each of these in turn.

Structure

The structure of a substituted item may be either a reduced form of the item it is a substitute for, or the same form as it, or finally an expanded form of it, measured in terms of the number of elements of structure. Here are some examples:

147

(8) John kicked an old dog

(9)   kicked a dog   (reduced)

(10)   kicked an old cat   (same)

(11)   kicked a very old dog (expanded)

Exponence

Exponence refers to items that make up a structure, the exponents of the structure. In a substitution there may be a grammatical change, a lexical change, both a grammatical and a lexical change, or no change at all in the exponents (this latter being in the case of reduced substitution).

The distinction* between grammar and lexis here is that made by Halliday and others (e.g. Halliday, McIntosh and Strevens, 1964). The distinction is based on recognition of the fact that the range of options available varies at different places in the language. At some places there is 'a small fixed number of possibilities and a clear line between what is possible and what is not', for example, we have to choose between 'singular' and 'plural'; 'past', 'present' and 'future'; 'positive' and 'negative'; 'active' and 'passive'; and so on. At other places we make our selection from 'a very large number of possibilities; we cannot count them, or draw a clear line round such as will separate what is possible from what is impossible'. Thus, for example, in the clause

She is very . . .

the blank could be filled by a selection from a huge range of items, young, old, beautiful, attractive, lazy, tired, healthy, etc. Grammar handles the first kind of choice, the 'closed' choice, whereas lexis deals with the second kind of choice, the 'open' one. The range of possibilities in a closed choice is called a 'system' and that in an open one is a 'set'. In language there are certain choices which are clearly closed system choices, and there are others which are equally clearly open set choices, but there are some which are less clear; the prepositions, for example, are intermediate in this respect. In our analysis, only those choices which are clearly closed system choices were handled by grammar, and it is only these that can constitute a 'grammatical' change in our Exponence category. Here are some examples of changes in exponence:

They walked down the street
are walking down the street   (grammatical)

She is speaking to a man
                    woman   (lexical)

* This distinction was introduced in section 2.1 but is repeated here for convenience.

```
She is speaking to a man
                    that woman                          (grammatical and
                                                              lexical)
```

Effect

Our final category is rather more subjective than the others. It is an attempt at evaluating the effect of the substitution. The message may be improved or worsened by the substitution, or it may be unaffected in either direction. The criteria involved are not to do with style or aesthetics but concern grammaticalness, deviation and contextual appropriateness. If a child substitutes a grammatical, non-deviant item for an ungrammatical, deviant item, then this would constitute an improvement, e.g.

```
He catched a fish
   caught a fish    (improved)
```

If, however, he substituted *catched* for *caught*, this would be coded 'worsened'. Contextual appropriateness is a rather more subjective notion. Sometimes it is not difficult to check whether the child has chosen appropriate linguistic items for making reference to the context of situation, e.g.

```
There are three men in that boat
             two men in that boat    (improved)
(on the 3rd Picture Story).
```

At other times the reference is too vague or ambiguous to permit a check on its appropriateness: in cases such as these no decision can be taken as to whether a substitution constitutes an improvement or a worsening and it has to be coded as 'neutral'.

We may mention that the two types of phenomena referred to by Bloomfield (1933) as 'aposiopesis' and 'anacoluthon' (their names in classical rhetoric) are largely covered by the category 'fragment'. Here is Bloomfield's description of them: 'In aposiopesis the speaker breaks off or is interrupted: "I thought he . . .". In anacoluthon he starts over again: "it's high time we − oh, well − I guess it won't matter".'

The categories described above are of a fairly abstract nature: in the category 'repetition', for example, what is repeated could be a clause (complete or incomplete), a group (complete or incomplete), a word, etc. It was not intended that such information should be lost. Our descriptive technique was to describe the maze material in terms of the same categories as were used on the rest of the speech, but to bracket it off, so that on its first run the computer would only operate on non-maze speech. On a subsequent run or by a manual analysis the information about the location and size of a maze could be extracted. The convention adopted was to bracket off maze material by means of pound signs (£) and to follow the second pound sign with the code number of the category of maze, so:

```
      a        a black cat
  £D8£2111     D8
```

After we had analysed our data in terms of the categories described above, we became familiar with the work of Maclay and Osgood (1959). These writers analysed a sample of the spontaneous speech of adult male participants in a university conference. They used four main categories: Repeats, False Starts, which were subdivided into Retraced and Non-retraced, Filled Pauses and Unfilled Pauses. There is a high degree of correspondence between Repeats and our Repetitions, between Retraced False Starts and Substitutions, and between Unretraced False Starts and Fragments. What is of great interest in Maclay and Osgood's work is that they examined the distribution of the hesitation types with respect to Fries' (1952) word classes. They found that False Starts typically involve lexical items (nouns, verbs, adjectives and adverbs), whereas Repeats typically involve function words and occur antecedent to lexical items (the most usual function words being articles, possessive pronouns, numbers, prepositions and words uniting phrases). They also found that the subject personal pronouns appeared to operate with respect to hesitation phenomena like function words rather than lexical items. This is, as it were, an external justification for our treating the personal pronouns as grammatical rather than lexical items. Repeats tended to occur in the same locations as pauses, that is, before lexical items. Moreover, Repeats are most frequently of a single word or several words (71%) and only rarely of units smaller than the word (12%). Further they found that when a False Start is retraced, the retracing usually includes the function word or words immediately prior to and associated with the lexical item which is corrected. We need not consider their findings on Filled and Unfilled Pauses in detail here.

The picture that Maclay and Osgood abstract from these results is as follows. The speaker is operating simultaneously on two levels of choices, lexical and grammatical. He has available 'a "pool" of heavily practised, tightly integrated word and phrase units, but selection from this pool required simultaneous lexical and grammatical determinants'. The larger, the more complex, the less probable the unit the speaker is processing, the greater the tendency for a filled pause or a repeat. The authors associate lexical organisation with sense or semantics and grammatical organisation with form or structure. So: 'Since he is monitoring the sense of his utterances more than their structure, and because errors of sense are more likely than errors of form, he will often halt after a "miss", retrace, and correct it – but the unit of retracing is that of the skill sequence, and this typically includes the function-word context along with lexical core.'

One of the most important points that emerges from the above is the association of hesitation phenomena with the making of lexical choices. False Starts typically involve lexical items: there is a blocking after a lexical choice and the speaker returns to correct it. Repeats and Pauses tend to occur antecedent to lexical items: they seem to provide time for selection among numerous lexical alternatives. Maclay and Osgood point out that their findings are consistent with Lounsbury's (1954) predictions and Goldman-Eisler's work. Lounsbury gave three hypotheses, the first of which is probably most interesting here, namely that 'hesitation pauses correspond to the point of highest statistical uncertainty in the sequencing of units of any given order'. Goldman-Eisler (1958) showed that hesitation pauses preceded a sudden increase of information, estimated in terms of transition probabilities. Maclay and Osgood admit, however, that the interpretation that the hesitation phenomena in their data occur at points of high uncertainty, because they appear more before lexical items than before function words, is 'rather inferential'. They suggest how this could be checked by making use of the Thorndike-Lorge frequencies.

Clearly it would be unwise to generalise widely from the findings of these researchers on the hesitation phenomena exhibited by a small number of professional men speaking at a university conference: one hesitates to say anything about the speech of five-year-old middle- and working-class children. However, there are a couple of points that seem worth making. One, it is likely that young children will have more difficulty with the grammatical level than adults do, and so there will be a stronger association of hesitation phenomena with grammatical choices than in adults. This is not to say that their hesitation phenomena will more frequently be associated with grammatical choices than with lexical choices, for it seems likely that hesitation is more probable when a choice has to be made from a large set of items (lexical) than when it is made from a small set (grammatical). Two, a number of researchers (Ervin, 1961 and Brown and Berko, 1960) have noted that there is a typical shift from syntagmatic to paradigmatic associations as a child's language develops, especially between the ages of six and ten. McNeill (1966) suggests that this shift is associated with the development of the child's semantic system. According to McNeill the child's syntax is reasonably well developed at 4—5 years, whilst his semantic system develops markedly at 6—8 years. Putting things very crudely, then, we may suggest: The more developed the child's semantic system (or at least one aspect of it) the wider the range of paradigmatic choices available to him. And as we have mentioned under the first point above, the larger the set of choices available, the more likely hesitation phenomena.

We have evidence from an analysis performed by one of the researchers in the Sociological Research Unit (Henderson, 1969) that the middle-class five-year-olds used more different nouns, adjectives and verbs on the three tasks of the speech schedule that were examined. By coincidence the

151

criteria used by Henderson for isolating these word classes were those of Fries, that is, the same ones as were used by Maclay and Osgood. It would be of great interest to check whether the middle-class reveal correspondingly more hesitation phenomena associated with these lexical choices, particularly substitutions (Maclay and Osgood's retraced false starts) and repetitions occurring antecedent to the lexical items (their repeats). If it were found that the middle-class children did display more of such phenomena, then a case could be made for saying that not only do the middle-class select a wider range of lexical items in these areas but also the selection is associated with greater verbal planning.

With this suggestion for future research we shall now conclude this section on maze types. The next section gives the coding information.

8.3 Coding information

MAZE INFORMATION

The method of description is to analyse the maze speech with the usual categories but to bracket if off with pound signs, that is, one '£' immediately before it and another immediately after. The second '£' is followed immediately by a four-digit number. These numbers are given at the beginning of section 8.2.

Example

That lamp has fallen in front of the telephone television

Coding

1234
10
01S1F1SMD6/HN/1 PT05/1 APMD1/£H2£3221H2/3

In the code number 3221, the first digit (3) means that *television* is a substitution for *telephone* and that the substitution is 'immediate', that is, *television* occurs immediately after *telephone*; the second digit (2) indicates that the final structure is the same as the original one; the third one (2) marks that there has been a lexical change; and the last digit (2) records that the final version is an improvement on the first one.

Chapter 9

CONCLUDING REMARKS

In the preceding six chapters our aim has been to describe the linguistic categories that we used and to relate them to sociological and psychological categories. The amount of detail with which we have treated these categories has varied: some categories have been discussed in detail; others not. This variation reflects two things mainly: the relevance of the categories for our research and the extent of our knowledge at the present time. Generally, we have regarded as most relevant to our research those grammatical categories which are associated with particular functions, so, for example, in our treatment of the verbal group we considered how it could be used for making various kinds of statements, predictive, hypothetical, precautionary, etc. We were much less concerned about describing the rules for correct English usage (standard English) and showing in great detail where children depart from these rules either as a result of linguistic immaturity or of exposure to non-standard dialects. It is thought that ultimately functional categories will provide the best bridge between linguistic categories on the one hand and sociological and psychological ones on the other.

The linguistic categories we have described are essentially of an exploratory kind. We needed them to explore the data in order to discover which areas seemed worthy of more intensive investigation. They were designed to make broad cuts in the data and to break it down into more easily observable parts. Generally, they were not designed with a view to the eventual synthesis of sets of categories. It is important that subsequent more delicate work should permit such synthesis. An example will make this point clearer. In our initial analysis we looked at negation only in the verbal group. But, of course, we could have examined it in the nominal group (*no, neither, no-one, nobody, not* (a soul) etc.) and in the adjunctival group (*never, nowhere, scarcely, in neither case*, etc.). We chose the verbal group as a starting point because we believed that the choice of negative most frequently occurs there. Now if the results on negation in the verbal group suggest that this topic is worthy of further investigation, then clearly a much more delicate description will have to be made of the determiners, indefinite pronouns, adverbs, etc. so that a complete picture of the use of negation in the children's speech can be established.

That linguistic analysis we have described in this monograph was first performed on a sample of 110 subjects. The sample was of a factorial design: it had a two-way division on sex, social class and communication index and a three-way division on verbal intelligence scores, with five children per cell, two cells being empty. Preliminary results obtained on this sample indicated a number of areas which were worthy of further attention. These areas were particularly associated with the nominal group (e.g. attribution and reference), verbal group (e.g. tentativeness*) and adjunctival group (e.g. manner expressions). It was decided that these areas should be investigated using a more delicate form of analysis and larger samples of children, both random and factorial. The results for these analyses are to be presented in future monographs.

With these brief concluding remarks we end Part One of the monograph. Part Two, which now follows, consists of a description of the computer program which was designed to assist the linguistic analysis.

* See Turner and Pickvance (1969).

PART TWO

**A COMPUTER PROGRAM FOR ASSISTING THE
LINGUISTIC ANALYSIS OF CHILDREN'S SPEECH**

Introduction

Part I of this monograph has described a system of grammatical analysis, due to Michael Halliday, which is potentially sensitive to quite small differences in the grammatical structure of children's speech. As shown in Part I, the system is basically hierarchical in form. And, within each of the main levels in the hierarchy, increasingly fine distinctions can be made among the grammatical categories specified. These categories can be related in several different ways, each way having its own theoretical significance. The result is a complex heterarchical network of micro-categories, which enable highly delicate grammatical analyses to be conducted.

From the point of view of the practical researcher, there is no need to preserve Halliday's system in all its elegant entirety. Although it debases the system, to borrow bits from it and to disregard the rest, certain features of the system are likely to be more relevant than others to the researcher's particular interests. A special advantage of Halliday's system is that many subdivisions are, from the researcher's viewpoint, optional. In other words, the category system can be partitioned according to the researcher's needs.

For certain purposes, a comparatively crude analysis (using only the coarser macro-categories of Halliday's system) may suffice. For other purposes, a highly delicate analysis may be necessary. The theoretical orientation of the Sociological Research Unit called for a selection of grammatical categories that were most likely to have sociological and psychological significance. An account of the categories chosen, and the reasons for choosing them, has already been given (in Part I) and need not be repeated here. For the moment, it is enough to note that *whatever* selection is made, the amount of data generated rapidly becomes unmanageable. Unless the Halliday system is completely trivialised (by selecting only the coarsest categories), its practical application to speech samples yields too much data to be readily manipulable by pencil and paper techniques.

The enormity of the data-processing problem can be savoured in the following way. Imagine a smallish sample of 100 children (e.g. 50 middle-class and 50 working-class children), *each* producing on average 100 sentences consisting of, say, 200 clauses and 1,000 words. If this corpus of 100,000 words is subjected to an abridged form of Hallidayan analysis involving, say, 50 grammatical subdivisions, it is clear that computer assistance is essential. This part of the monograph will therefore describe a computer program that was especially developed, by the writer, to give the assistance required.

Main Objectives of Computer Program

The computer program described in this report is specifically concerned with the problem of handling data for the description of syntax. Much of the recent work done in computational linguistics has been directed towards producing programs which parse an input of natural language text (either in terms of a grammar of categories pre-existing in the program, or in terms of categories determined by means of the program). See J. P. Thorne (1964).

The program described here does not do this. It takes an input, not of natural language, but of a syntactic description of natural language. It then checks the description for errors of notation. Finally, it outputs frequencies of the categories of the description. The business of syntactic description is done by the linguist; the business of checking and counting this description is done by the computer.

This is a fairly modest achievement. And it contributes very little to the important problem of measuring syntactic complexity. But it effectively assembles complex strings of linguistic elements in a form which enables pertinent measures to be made. What is claimed is that a data processing system has been set up (1) which works, (2) which handles the main features of the descriptive theory (namely, Halliday's Scale and Category Grammar) being used, (3) which provides a basis for exploring the relationships among selected sets of linguistic elements, and (4) which is flexible enough to allow further descriptive devices to be easily adjoined. It can be used as it stands, or as a stepping stone to a more elegant or adequate handling of complex data-structures.

Broader Implications

Emphasis has so far been placed on the need for a computer program to assist the kind of grammatical analysis developed by Halliday. It would be a pity, however, to think of the project solely in these rather narrow terms. The computer program described in this report could be readily adapted to handle other kinds of grammatical analysis. And it could be extended, more significantly, to encompass quite different kinds of *serial* phenomena. As Miller and Chomsky (1964) point out, 'If we are to

158

understand something about the nature of human language, the same concepts and methods should help us to understand other kinds of complicated behaviour as well.'

Several examples come to mind. In social psychology and child development studies, it is often desired to break down a complex stream of behaviour into constituent 'episodes'. A typical analytic system is provided by Barker & Wright (1954). In industrial psychology, it is equally important to break down skilled behaviour into smaller and smaller components or 'skill elements' (Seymour, 1966). In both these cases the focus of interest is partly upon the elements that make up the total sequence, and partly upon the temporal and psychological and logical relationships that obtain among the elements. In short, there is a dual problem of (a) characterising the elements of a sequence in informationally-useful ways, and (b) explicating the different relationships that can exist among the elements characterised. More generally, there are numerous serial phenomena whose significance depends not only on the kinds of items making up the sequence but *also* on the kinds of relationships existing among successive sets of items. In this sense, the problems involved in grammatical analysis have important conceptual similarities with problems arising in the analysis of diverse forms of naturally-occurring phenomena. Some obvious examples, in further support of Miller & Chomsky's remark, are music, choreography, ethology, meteorology, econometrics, and systems analysis.

The present report is, of course, concerned solely with the restricted problem of grammatical analysis. It does not pretend to make any significant contribution to the analysis of other sequential phenomena. But anyone who is interested in the deeper theoretical problems might find it instructive to keep the broader view in mind.

The Present Program and the 'General Inquirer' Program

To illustrate the points made in the previous section, it is worth comparing the present program with the 'General Inquirer' program of Hunt *et al.* (1966).

The primary function of the 'General Inquirer' is to identify within a text, instances of words and phrases that belong to categories specified by the investigator. In other words, the investigator decides on what his categories are, and how they are recognised, and puts this information into a 'dictionary' which the program then uses.

By contrast, under the present system, the investigator identifies his categories with a text and writes down a representation of his text in terms of these categories. It is *this* that is input to the computer, *not* (as in the General Inquirer system) the text itself. Under the General Inquirer system the program identifies the categories in the text. Under the S.R.U. system, the investigator identifies the categories in the text.

The important point about the S.R.U. data is that there are complex inter-relationships among the categories. There are categories of categories, organised into hierarchical tree structures – and the program checks whether these combinations are well-formed. By interrogation techniques, it can also be used to search for further regularities or restrictions.

In principle, there is no reason why the program could not *also* have taken over the analyst's task of building up the initial description. In this case, the actual texts (as transcribed) would have been fed into the computer. And, as in the case of the General Inquirer system, a systematic pattern-recognition program would have done the human analyst's job of identifying the selected grammatical categories. The pattern-recognition program would, however, have been extremely complex – especially since the unedited transcripts (which contain innumerable false-starts, unfinished sentences, etc.) were extremely 'messy'. In practice, it was cheaper and quicker to use humans as the pattern-recognisers, since they could mentally discount ambiguities, etc, in ways that would have required very elaborate programming.

Data Characteristics

The main properties of the data, stated informally, and in approximately ascending order of difficulty, were as follows:

(1) *Sequential* – consisting, in the present case, of strings of 'words'.

(2) *Hierarchical* – the 'words' were parts of 'phrases' which were parts of 'clauses' which were parts of 'sentences', and so on.

(3) *Of variable length and format* – a 'sentence' consisted of one *or more* 'clauses', which consisted of one *or more* 'phrases', etc.

(4) *Recursive* – it was possible for the role of a 'word' to be taken over by a 'clause', producing a hierarchy within a hierarchy.

(5) *Discontinuous* – a clause could 'interrupt' another clause.

There are several ways in which a computer can be used to assist the analysis of such data.

At one extreme, the linguist can *simplify* the input to the computer, by abstracting only those properties of the data that are relevant to his immediate needs. For example, he might just count the number of occurrences of different clause elements (as in diagram 1) without bothering to record the order in which the elements occur. Or he might decide to conduct separate analyses on distinct and possibly overlapping sets of grammatical categories – a decision which could lead him to break down the data into the relevant sets, so that the computer can handle it in easy stages. In both cases an attempt is made to simplify the computer's task by pre-computing the data (by hand) so that the input to the computer is more manageable. In both cases, information is lost. In the diagram 1 case, information is lost concerning the placement of the adjuncts. In the second case, information is preserved within each category set. But the 'between set' information is lost, and this removes the possibility of doing certain kinds of configural analysis.

At the other extreme, the linguist might want to preserve all the information in his description, by feeding into the computer the full (unabridged) syntactic description. This complicates the data processing (and the computer program that does it), but leaves all options open.

The first method might be called the method of selective description; the second, the method of non-selective description. The relative merits of the two methods are fairly self-evident. In selective description, it is comparatively easy to transfer the data to punched cards (say) and to process them. But the features not selected for analysis are lost. Their subsequent retrieval would require a further, and possibly lengthy, manual recoding of the original (hand-produced) description. So it is necessary to be certain, in advance, that all relevant features have been incorporated.

In the case of the S.R.U. data, this certainty did not (and could not) exist. It was therefore decided to play safe and to opt for the total non-selective description. This decision gives rise to complicated programming problems, since it is necessary to input a sentence description running from sentence structure down to a number of quite detailed classes at group and word rank. But it has the additional advantage that the full data are available not only for subsequent reanalyses, but also for other linguists who may want to examine the data from other points of view.

Choice of Programming Language

A decision was required concerning the most suitable programming language for handling large amounts of data of complex structure. The major scientific programming languages, ALGOL and FORTRAN, were ruled out as being not well suited to data of such volume and complexity. This left COBOL as a possible candidate. However, it appeared that there was a programming language, A.C.L., available on the ATLAS computer at London University, which represented a considerable advance on COBOL in several ways, and this was the final choice.

It was particularly convenient to use A.C.L. since its designer (Mr. D. Hendry, of the University of London Institute of Computer Science) was willing to supervise the writing of the program in this new language. A revised version of the program has been written in B.C.L., a more recent development in programming languages (see Hendry and Mohan, 1968) which is particularly suitable for the processing of complex data structures. This is discussed towards the end of this report.

Administrative Arrangements

Diagram 3 shows, in summary form, the step-by-step procedure for collecting and analysing the children's speech.

Several hundred children were interviewed. Each interview had 6–7 main sections, and these were tape-recorded. For purposes of the analysis under discussion, a sub-sample of 110 children was extracted from the overall sample. This sub-sample (of factorial design) was chosen to provide comparisons that were of special interest to the S.R.U. The nature of these comparisons, and the reasons for making them, have already been discussed in Part One of this monograph and in Henderson *et al.* (1969). So they do not need to be discussed here. For present purposes, it is enough to note that these multiple comparisons required each child to be identified (in the computer program) by a vector of symbols denoting the social class, school, I.Q. grouping, etc., to which the child belonged.

The tape-recorded speech of the 110 selected children was processed in the following way:

(1) The tape-recordings were transcribed into typewritten form, and sample-checked for accuracy of transcription.

(2) The syntax of the speech was analysed, using both the tape-recordings *and* the transcripts. The tape-recordings were used at this stage (a) to provide a detailed check on the accuracy of transcription, and (b) to help resolve (by reference to hesitation phenomena, patterns of intonation, etc.) inherent ambiguities in the transcribed speech.

(3) Certain syntactic categories were counted. This yielded totals for each child, and for each task.

(4) The resultant figures provided material for statistical processing, the aim of which was to find syntactic correlates of certain parameters of the sample. For example, it was of interest to know what syntactic features distinguished certain pre-selected subgroups ('working-class', as opposed to 'middle-class' children, etc.) of the sample.

As already indicated, it is step (3) – the counting of relevant syntactic categories – that poses the largest administrative problem. Since Halliday's Scale and Category Grammar was not explicitly designed to have sociological or psychological significance, it was necessary to make intelligent guesses about the categories that were most likely to

162

discriminate among the 110 children sampled. A great many variables (and combinations of variables) came under consideration in this way – too many, in fact, to permit the counting to be done by hand. Instead of making an arbitrary selection among the possible variables (a selection which might later have been regretted) it was decided:

(1) to make counts in considerable detail, and

(2) to have the possibility of re-examining certain classes of variable, by changing the counting procedures as the work progressed.

It was felt that using a computer made both (1) and (2) more possible. In fact, objective (2) was a great deal more feasible, once the data were prepared in acceptable form for input, and a program written to handle it. Under these conditions, the difficulties of running alternative counts and exploring contingencies were comparatively small and much less time-consuming.

The decision to use the computer for stage (3) of the analysis, yielded a two-part problem:

(1) to find a way of converting the grammatical descriptions, in the form of trees, into a convenient linear notation;

(2) to write a program which would work through this linear notation, counting the single categories and/or combinations of categories that were thought to be of interest.

Part 1: An appropriate linear notation

The system of grammatical description used was 'Scale and Category Grammar'* and it is initially important to recall that it is a 'rank-scale' grammar. That is, having set up a hierarchy of grammatical units for any one language, it fixes the number of units in the hierarchy for that language.† For example, we might decide that English had four grammatical units: sentence, clause, group and word. We would then say that a 'consists of' or 'inclusion' relation holds between them: a sentence consists of at least one clause, a clause of at least one group and a group of at least one word. The fact that the number of ranks is by definition constant for every sentence described makes the notation problem easier.

Solution
We can convert such trees as these into a linear notation by observing two conventions.

* M. A. K. Halliday, 'Categories of the Theory of Grammar', *Word*, 17.
† ibid., Sect. 3.3

Convention 1

This specifies the order in which each node is to be copied off the tree to form a linear string.

An informal description of the process would be as follows (it is assumed that each node is labelled):

> Start at the top of the tree. Take a path down the tree until you reach a bottom node, copying each label as you go. Do this, working down the paths on the left of the tree first, until you have covered all the branches. Don't copy any label more than once.

The rules for this process are specified in an algorithm in Diagram 3. By application of these rules the tree-description of 'Help me if you can' (Diagram 4) should be converted into the string:

'ABCDEFGHIJKLM'

But notice that this string cannot be converted back unambiguously into its tree. In this form, the original form of the tree is not retrievable.

The ordering of labels that this convention permits can be diagrammed (see Diagram 5). This shows clearly that several possible ranks of label can follow a word rank label. It is therefore necessary to invoke Convention 2.

Convention 2

This specifies what is to follow a word rank label. It could also be thought of as controlling the 'backtracking' instruction of Convention 1, or, more generally, making the original tree recoverable. The marker used for this purpose consists of a '/' symbol plus a digit. The details are as follows:

'/3' means that the following symbol will be a sentence rank label.

'/2' means that the following symbol will be a clause rank label.

'/1' means that the following symbol will be a group rank label.

The *absence* of any marker is used to show that a word rank label follows. The alphabetic string previously mentioned now becomes:

ABCD/1EF/2GHI/1JK/1LM/3

The terminal markers give a convenient demarcation of the units of the data. Thus a word rank label can only be followed immediately by another word rank label within the same group. A word label not followed by another word label has an identifying marker indicating that a higher level unit has begun.

This was the basic form of the linear notation used. The details are incorporated in Diagram 6. In fact, there are several more layers to the trees we actually construct with the corresponding markers, but these are not essential to the exposition.

Part 2: The basic mechanism of the program

Our label diagram requires further comment. Firstly, we are dealing, not with a single label at each rank, but with a set of labels. E.g. B and G are the labels at clause rank in Diagram 4. Each set of labels is written as a table.

Secondly, within a set of labels, one label may be followed by set_1 of labels at the next rank down and another label may be followed by set_2 of labels at the next rank down. So, in diagram 4, B may be followed by either C or E and G may be followed by either H or J or L.

The result is a *network* of tables linked in a specific way. These are written into the program. Each table is made up of a number of entries (11 in our case). Each entry consists of:

a character — representing the label;

a number — which specifies which table is to follow.

In addition, we require a group of locations for storing the occurrences of the symbol, and a number which specifies whether the symbol is to be counted in combination with other specified symbols. The program reads a character from the description, which is punched on paper tape, then compares it with an appropriate table. If it finds a matching character on the table, it scores an occurrence of the character and locates the next table. It reads the next character from the tape and compares it with that table.

The last character on every table is 'X'. If the matching process does not succeed, the character read from the tape is compared with every character on the table down to 'X'. If 'X' is reached, an error routine is called.

When a table corresponding to a bottom-most node is reached, the program looks up the number which specifies which table is to follow and finds a 'dummy' entry. The 'dummy' entry produces a search for a terminal marker. The network of tables is then re-entered at the point indicated by the terminal marker.

When the end of a chosen unit of data is reached, the counts of all the occurrences of symbols for that unit are printed out and the process is repeated with the next unit.

Further Facilities

The system of description so far specified was still inadequate, and called for four further facilities.

1. It was desired to express *relationships* between the elements of the description.

For example, groups of the same class within a clause might be in relationships (with each other) of co-ordination, subordination or apposition. Illustrations of this, for the verbal group, would be:

He *starts and eats* his dinner
    P +   P   *co-ordination*

He *starts eating* his dinner
    P –   P   *subordination*

Apposition is best illustrated in the nominal group:

James Bond, secret agent supreme swung into action
    S   =   S   *apposition*

There was a fourth category, of a rather different type from the others — presupposition. A standard example of this is:

Old men and women [were there].
S M H   + S*MH   *presupposition*

If this is taken to mean 'Old men and <u>old</u> women', then the underlined 'old' — symbolised as *M in the description — is presupposed.

The relations were symbolised as follows:

'+' = co-ordinated
'–' = subordinated
'=' = apposed
'*' = presupposed.

These relation markers can be attached to any symbol after the S which starts each sentence, with the sole exception of the double digit which specifies the tense of the verb.

2. A special type of subordination relation can occur when a unit of higher rank takes the place of a unit of lower rank. e.g.:

'You are eating bread.' 'You are eating *what you are eating*'

This, in effect, creates a clause within a clause, or, to state it in relation to the problem at hand, a tree attached to a tree.

Appropriately, the routine to handle this recursive relation, called 'rankshift' in the grammatical theory, makes a fresh start on the network of tables.

The form for describing this relation is:

'⟨' plus a two-digit number; then the rankshifted item; then '⟩'.

The two-digit number specifies the point of entry to the table network. e.g.:

⟨06 PT02/1 CHN/2⟩ where 'PT02/1 CHN/2' is the rankshifted item.

166

3. It occasionally happens that one unit interrupts another, e.g.:

'When, *may I ask*, did this happen?'

The technical term for this is 'inclusion'.
The form for this is:

'(' plus a two-digit number; then the included element; then ')' e.g.:

(02FIPT02/1 CHN/2) where 'FIPT02/1 CHN/2' is the included item.

Both 2 and 3 require that we temporarily hold information we have about the unfinished tree, the 'parent' item, and that we use fresh areas of store to hold information about the item we are working on. Because of this, an arbitrary limit of five has been set. That is, no more than five of these structures (counting the parent structure as one) are allowed to nest one within the other. This was certainly adequate for our sample of the speech of young children, but would have to be increased for adult speech.

The similarity between the handling of rankshift and inclusion by the computer program should not be allowed to obscure the great difference in their grammatical nature.

4. It is a fact that speech has surprisingly little of the 'finished' quality of writing. Its syntax is full of unfinished attempts, changes of direction, false starts. (These were given the name 'turbulence'.) In order to have some way of representing these, a notation was devised as follows:

'£' plus 'false start' plus '£' plus four-digit code.

The four-digit code expressed the type of turbulence.

At present the symbols between the '£'s are ignored, but the possibility remains of analysing these fragments in relation to their syntactic environment.

'Turbulences' were allowed to nest within each other to a depth which was arbitrarily set at nine.

Layout Details

These facilities and the diagram of the network of tables specify the features of the descriptive system which the program allows. In addition, there are some features which may be used, at the option of the coder, to improve the layout of documentation. These can be specified by two rules:

(1) The character 'space' is allowed, to any number, after every '/1' terminal marker.

(2) The characters 'new line' and 'space', in any combination, and to any number, are allowed after every '/2' terminal marker, or marker of higher rank; and also after code numbers and task numbers.

Practical Features: Verification of Data

The actual use of the program produces certain extra requirements. The amount of data input was fairly large and it was unrealistic to expect it to be error-free. Consequently, some way of handling errors had to be found. A distinction was made between:

(a) errors of *reference*, i.e. errors in 'labelling' the categories of the data correctly, and

(b) errors of *notation*, i.e. errors in writing out the strings of symbols of the syntactic description (such as illegal combinations of symbols).

Errors of type (a) were guarded against by making checks to ensure reliability among the analysts of the data. Errors of type (b) were detected by means of special tests built into the computer program, so that, in practice, almost all were discoverable.

The result was an error routine which was called whenever the procedure of matching a character from the tape with a table failed. The action taken was to move the data tape along to the next terminal marker of sentence rank (or above) and to clear any 'combination counts', so by-passing the unit which was in error. At the same time, a message was printed out, giving the number of the sentence, the character from the data tape, and the reference of the table on which the mismatch occurred. This way, the error could be easily located afterwards.

There are a number of other 'messages' which are printed out if an error occurs within the various 'further facility' routines mentioned above.

Clearly, the overall result here is to keep the program running at the cost of some loss of information. Hence, the aim is to minimise the number of errors in the data. For this purpose, the data were first run through a shortened version of the program, corrected, and then run on the main program. The shortened version (called 'CENTRETESTER') produced a detailed print-out of errors. The full version copied all the counts made on to magnetic tape, and produced a summary of the distributions of these counts.

Present Use of the Program

The program has been used to process the main section of the linguistic data analysed as part of one year's sample at the Sociological Research Unit. In the special sample processed, there were 110 subjects — yielding approximately 15,000 clauses.

These were all checked on 'Centretester' and then run in several batches on 'Grammartracker'. The resulting counts were stored on magnetic tape. A subsidiary program ('Copier') was written which copies the summary

168

counts of given subjects or sets of subjects from the magnetic tape. Details of these programs are given in the Appendix.

Error-checking in B.C.L.

The potential user, considering the A.C.L. programs described here, may feel that two particular shortcomings restrict their usefulness. First, the programs cannot be used on a wide range of machines, since an A.C.L. compiler is available only on the London ATLAS computer. Secondly, although *small* modifications are easy to make, more radical modifications may involve reprogramming.

The successor to A.C.L., a programming language called B.C.L., offered a remedy to these shortcomings. As stated earlier, B.C.L. is currently under development at the University of London Institute of Computer Science. It is to be made available on a wide range of computers and it is particularly well adapted to syntactic problems.

'Centretester', the error-checking program, was re-written in B.C.L. with a considerable reduction in length. See the Appendix. The B.C.L. version was punched on cards, rather than on paper-tape – this choice being also available in A.C.L.

The net result was that radical changes of syntax could be encompassed almost as easily as small modifications. Some large modifications can now be made in the time it takes to punch a new card and insert it in the already existing pack of program cards.

The syntax facilities available in B.C.L. give it greater power than a context-sensitive phrase-structure grammar. Thus a wide range of rules can be written. In particular, it is possible to write easily-read rules, so that one choice may affect one or more other choices. This is a useful facility for recent developments in Halliday's grammar.

An additional bonus of the B.C.L. program was that it could be used for interrogating the data, once this was error-free. Again, this provides a very flexible and general facility, since it is now possible to interrogate the data for, say, any co-occurrence (or mutual exclusion) of symbols, or patterns of symbols, within any unit of data.

Further Use of the Program

Only two sections of the program are tied to the specifications of our particular problem and they are the routine which counts certain combinations of elements, and the routine which builds up summary figures. Apart from this the contents of the tables and their exact pattern of links are parameters of the program and can be easily altered. Alterations involving the number of tables and the number of 'layers' in the table network involve some detail alterations which are specified in the manual of the program.

The program is therefore not limited solely to its present application, but has a degree of flexibility which allows it to be modified for other uses. The program was in fact written with some specific possibilities for extension in mind. These are as follows:

1. Producing a count of the occurrences of each type of string at a particular rank, e.g. patterns of clause elements.
   Procedure: to copy off the symbols belonging to the chosen 'layers' and then sort them in the conventional way, counting the occurrences of similar strings.

2. Producing a lexicogrammatical analysis of the data.
   Procedure: insert the textual items at the terminal nodes of the description. Using the information contained in the pushdown store, attach syntactic information to these items. Copy off the items with their syntactic descriptions attached, and sort them.

Possible alterations of the program to deal with other types of discontinuity, and modifications which would enable it to handle the systemic networks which Halliday has now developed, are discussed in the manual.

A final, long-range, possibility is the accumulation of a 'data-bank' between linguists who are prepared to work within the same system of analysis.

Fully analysed linguistic data is an expensive commodity, both in time and money. At present, the data analysed by one research project is hardly ever used again by other researchers. At the same time, projects spend years building up samples of data that are sufficiently large to work with. One of the difficulties which allows this waste to continue is the lack of general agreement among linguists on the systems of syntactic analysis to be used, plus the fact that the systems themselves are undergoing development. Another difficulty is that the data are seldom in a form which can be manipulated by other researchers for their special purposes.

We hope that the system here described suggests the beginnings of an answer to the second problem, however crude and incomplete it may be. As already indicated, the procedure used splits the analysis of the data into two clearly distinct processes: analysing the general grammatical structure of the data 'by hand', and selecting specific aspects of this structure for investigation by program. Thus researchers with purposes differing from ours can use this data, only modifying the program. Furthermore, where disagreement about the system of syntactic analysis is small, it should be possible to alter the data by procedures similar to the methods of updating files, familiar in commercial data processing. It must be remembered, however, that the use of data from a data-bank has its dangers where the purposes of the investigator differ from those of the original collector of the data. See Baker (1965).

170

Concluding Remarks

It has several times been stressed that the S.R.U. program does not replace the human linguist. Instead, it takes the linguist's analysis, and checks and counts selected features of it. There are good reasons for adopting this procedure. As already indicated, the problems of fully automating the high-quality analysis of linguistic data are very great. At the present stage of development, this initial analysis is best left to human beings. (And difficulties in the way of automatic translation would seem to bear this out.)

If we rule out the possibility of complete automation, man-machine co-operation seems to be the most fruitful compromise. In this case, the man would do the highly complex (e.g. open-ended) tasks, and the computer would follow up with data-handling processes which can be clearly and simply specified, but which require the sort of accuracy and consistency that humans find hard to maintain.

An example of a system of this kind has been developed by the Mitre Corporation (Walker, 1967). It is particularly directed towards information retrieval. Under this system man and machine 'co-operate' in abstracting and storing information from natural language texts. A comparable development along the lines of the present program might allow a linguist to correct errors in the grammatical analysis as the program identified them. He might also ask for simple counts, and then ask for more specialised or more complex counts on the basis of these.

The increasing availability of 'on-line' facilities, where man and machine can interact in a give-and-take 'conversational' mode, gives hope that man might in the future be cast in a more exploratory role, with machines serving a supportive (helping and advising) role in an ongoing process. The present piece of work may be a step in this direction.

APPENDIX TO PART TWO

FLOW DIAGRAMS

Commentary

The program as a whole is a number of sections grouped around a central routine. The central routine deals with the recognition of the grammatical analysis; other routines deal with special cases in this analysis, with errors in the analysis, and with counts made on the analysis.

The routines (or pages) divide as follows:

1. The central routine which matches the symbols on the input tape against the tables in the program. (PAGES 3, 5 and 6).
2. Special cases in this process are handled by sections which
   (i) handle the symbols indicating relationships (PAGE 4)
   (ii) deal with rankshift (PAGE 8) and inclusion (PAGE 9).
3. The error routine, which locates the end of the current sentence by skipping symbols until it reaches a terminal marker which specifies the end of the sentence. It then outputs an error message (PAGE 11).
4. The routine which deals with the descriptions of 'false starts' in the text. These are enclosed in '£' signs and are followed by a four-digit coding. The routine skips what is enclosed in the '£' signs and takes account of the coding. (PAGE 10).
5. The section which counts certain occurrences of symbols (PAGE 7).
6. The routines for assembling all the counts made and printing them out (PAGE 12).

'Centretester' in ACL and BCL

The two versions of the program are closely comparable, but they are not identical. Both versions perform a similar checking function on the input; but the ACL version, because it was developed as a subsection of a larger program, performs some additional operations which are used in the 'counting' parts of the larger program. Strictly speaking they are redundant, but they are so much part of the structure of the program that it is difficult to delete them.

As far as the syntax-checking function is concerned, the two versions may be contrasted as follows: the ACL version sets up tables and has a central routine which inputs a character and searches the tables; in the BCL version these two parts are integrated: the part of the program corresponding to a table not only contains the symbols to be matched, but can also contain the commands which control the matching process.

The structure of the BCL version can be easily grasped by anyone familiar with phrase-structure grammar notation. The main correspondences are tabulated below:

P.S.G.	B.C.L.
Terminal symbol	Symbol in quotes
$A \rightarrow B$	A IS ('B')
$A \rightarrow B + C$	A IS ('B', 'C')
$A \rightarrow \begin{Bmatrix} B \\ C \end{Bmatrix}$	A IS (EITHER 'B' OR 'C')

This is not to suggest that the limitations of phrase-structure grammar conventions necessarily correspond to similar limitations in BCL.

174

BIBLIOGRAPHY

Part One

AUSTIN, J. L., (1962). *How to do things with words.* Cambridge, Mass.: Harvard University Press.

BERNSTEIN, B., (1958). Some sociological determinants of perception: an enquiry into sub-cultural differences. *British Journal of Sociology*, 9, pp. 159–174.

BERNSTEIN, B., (1959). A public language: some sociological implications of a linguistic form, *British Journal of Sociology*, 10, pp. 311–326.

BERNSTEIN, B., (1961). Social class and linguistic development: a theory of social learning. In Halsey, A. H., Floud, J., & Anderson, C. A., (eds.), *Education, Economy and Society*. New York: Free Press, pp. 288–314.

BERNSTEIN, B., (1962a). Linguistic codes, hesitation phenomena and intelligence. *Language and Speech*, 5, pp. 31–46.

BERNSTEIN, B., (1962b). Social class, linguistic codes and grammatical elements. *Language and Speech*, 5, pp. 221–240.

BERNSTEIN, B., (1964a). Family role systems, socialisation and communication. Paper given at the Conference on Cross-cultural Research into Childhood and Adolescence, University of Chicago.

BERNSTEIN, B., (1964b). Elaborated and Restricted Codes: Their origins and some consequences. In Gumperz, J. J., & Hymes, D., (eds.). *The Ethography of Communication.*, *American Anthropologist* (special publication), Vol. 66, No. 6, Pt. 2. Menasna, Wisconsin: American Anthropological Association, pp. 55–69.

BERNSTEIN, B., (1965). A socio-linguistic approach to social learning. In Gould, J. (ed.). *Social Science Survey*, London: Pelican Books.

BERNSTEIN, B., (1969). A socio-linguistic approach to socialisation: with some reference to educability. In Gumperz, J. & Hymes, D. (eds.). *Directions in Sociolinguistics*. New York: Holt, Reinhart & Winston.

BERNSTEIN, B., & BRANDIS, W., (1969). Social class differences in communication and control. In Brandis, W., and Henderson, D. *Primary socialisation, language and education, Vol. I: Social class, language and communication*. London: Routledge & Kegan Paul.

BERNSTEIN, B., & HENDERSON, D., (1969). Social class differences in the relevance of language to socialisation. *Sociology*, 3.

175

BERNSTEIN, B., & YOUNG, D., (1967). Social class differences in conceptions of the uses of toys. *Sociology*, 1, pp. 131–140.

BEVER, T. G., FODOR, J. A., & WEKSEL, W., (1965). On the acquisition of syntax: A critique of "contextual generalisation". *Psychological Review*, 72, pp. 467–482.

BLOOMFIELD, L., (1933). *Language*. London: George Allen & Unwin.

BRANDIS, W., (1969a). Appendix II: A measure of the mother's orientation towards communication and control. In Brandis, W., & Henderson, D. *Primary socialisation, language and education, Vol. I: Social class, language and communication*. London: Routledge & Kegan Paul.

BRANDIS, W., (1969b). Appendix III: The relationship between social class and mother's orientation towards communication and control. In Brandis, W., & Henderson, D. *Primary socialisation, language and education, Vol. I: Social class, language and communication.* London: Routledge & Kegan Paul.

BROWN, R., & BERKO, J., (1960). Word association and the acquisition of grammar. *Child Development*, 31, pp. 1–14.

CARROLL, J. B., (1964). *Language and Thought*. Englewood Cliffs, New Jersey: Prentice Hall.

CAZDEN, C. B., (1966) Subcultural differences in child language: an interdisciplinary review. *Merrill–Palmer Quarterly*, 12, pp. 185–219.

CHOMSKY, N., (1964). 'Formal Discussion' (of 'The development of grammar in child language' by Miller, W., & Ervin, S.) in Bellugi, U., & Brown, R. (eds.). *The Acquistion of Language*. Monographs of the Society for Research in Child Development, Serial No. 92, 1964, Vol. 29, No. 1, pp. 35–39.

CHOMSKY, N., (1965). *Aspects of the theory of syntax*. Cambridge, Mass.: MIT Press.

CHOMSKY, N., & MILLER, G. A., (1963). Introduction to the formal analysis of natural languages. In Luce, R. D., Bush, R., & Galanter, E. (eds). *Handbook of Mathematical Psychology*, Vol. II., New York: Wiley, pp. 269–322.

COOK, J., (1968). *The Mother's Speech in Answering the Child Control Questions*. Unpublished report, Sociological Research Unit.

CRYSTAL, D., (1966). Specification and English tenses. *Journal of Linguistics*, 2, pp. 1–34.

DAVIES, E. C., (1967). Some notes on English clause types. *Transactions of Philological Society*, pp. 1–31.

DAVIS, E. A., (1937). *The development of linguistic skill in twins. singletons with siblings and only children from age 5 to 10 years.* Institute of Child Welfare Monograph Series, No. 14. Minneapolis: University of Minnesota Press.

DAY, E. J., (1932). The development of language in twins: I. A comparison of twins and single children. *Child Development*, 3, pp. 179–199.

DEUTSCH, M. P., (1963). The disadvantaged child and the learning process. In Passow, A. H. (ed.). *Education in depressed areas.* New York: Teachers College Columbia University, pp. 163–179.

ELLIS, J. O. (1966). On contextual meaning. In Bazell, C. E., Catford, J. C., Halliday, M. A. K., & Robins, R. H. (eds.). *In memory of J. R. Firth*, London: Longmans.

ERVIN, S. M., (1961). Changes with age in the verbal determinants of word association. *American Journal of Psychology*, 74, pp. 361–372.

FRAISSE, P., (1964). *The Psychology of Time*. Trans. by Leith, J., London: Eyre and Spottiswoode.

FRIES, C. C., (1952). *The Structure of English*, New York: Harcourt, Brace & Co.

GAHAGAN, D. M., & GAHAGAN, G. A., (1966). *Proposed framework and rationale for a content analysis of the speech schedule and instructions for coding.* Unpublished report, Sociological Research Unit.

GESELL, A., & ILG, F. L., (1943). *Infant and child in the culture of today.* New York: Harper.

GLEASON, M. A., Jr., (1965). *Linguistics and English Grammar.* New York: Holt, Rinehart & Winston.

GOLDMAN-EISLER, F., (1958). Speech production and the predictability of words in context. *Quarterly Journal of Experimental Psychology*, I, Part 3.

GOLDMAN-EISLER, F., (1961). Hesitation and information in speech. *Information theory, 4th London Symposium*, London: Butterworth.

GOLDMAN-EISLER, F., (1962). Speech and thought. *Discovery*, April.

HALLIDAY, M. A. K., (1961). Categories of the theory of grammar. *Word*, 17, pp. 241–292.

HALLIDAY, M. A. K., (1963a). Intonation systems in English. In McIntosh, Angus, & Halliday, M. A. K., *Patterns of Language: Papers in general, descriptive and applied linguistics.* London: Longmans.

HALLIDAY, M. A. K., (1963b). Class in relation to the axes of chain and choice in language. *Linguistics*, 2, pp. 5–15.

HALLIDAY, M. A. K., (1964). Syntax and the consumer. In Stuart, C.I.J.M. (ed.), *Report of the Fifteenth Annual (First International) Round Table Meeting on Linguistics and Language Studies* (Monograph Series on Languages and Linguistics, 17). Washington, D.C.: Georgetown University Press, pp. 11–24.

HALLIDAY, M. A. K., (1965). Types of structure. *Nuffield Programme in Linguistics and English Teaching Work Paper: I.*

HALLIDAY, M. A. K., (1966a). Some notes on 'deep' grammar. *Journal of Linguistics*, 2, pp. 57–67.

HALLIDAY, M. A. K., (1966b). The English verbal group: a specimen of a manual of analysis. *Nuffield Programme in Linguistics and English Teaching Work Paper: VI*

HALLIDAY, M. A. K., (1967a). Language and experience. Paper read to Nursery Schools Association Conference on Children's Problems in Language, Harrogate, 20 May 1967.

HALLIDAY, M. A. K., (1967b). *Grammar, society and the noun.* London: University College.

HALLIDAY, M. A. K., (1967c). Notes on transitivity and theme in English: Pt. I. *Journal of Linguistics*, 3, pp. 37–81.

HALLIDAY, M. A. K., (1967d). Notes on transitivity and theme in English: Pt. II. *Journal of Linguistics*, 3, pp. 199–244.

HALLIDAY, M. A. K., (1967e). *Intonation and Grammar in British English.* The Hague: Mouton (Janua Linguarum Series Practica 48).

HALLIDAY, M. A. K., (1968). Notes on transitivity and theme in English: Pt. III. *Journal of Linguistics*, 4, pp. 179–215.

HALLIDAY, M. A. K., McINTOSH, A., & STREVENS, P., (1964). *The Linguistic Sciences and Language Teaching.* London: Longmans.

HASAN, R., (1964). *A linguistic study of contrasting features in the style of two contemporary English prose writers.* Ph.D. Thesis, Edinburgh.

HASAN, R., (1967). *Grammatical cohesion in spoken and written English, Part I.* London: Nuffield Programme in Linguistics and English Teaching (Papers 7).

HASAN, R., (1968). *Grammatical cohesion in spoken and written English, Part II.* London: Nuffield Programme in Linguistics and English Teaching (Papers 7).

HAWKINS, P. R., (1969). Social class, the nominal group and reference. *Language and Speech* (in press).

HEIDER, F. K., & HEIDER, G. M., (1940). A comparison of sentence structures of deaf and hearing children. *Psychological Monographs*, 52, pp. 42–103.

HENDERSON, D., (1969). Social class differences in form-class usage among five-year-old children. In Brandis, W., & Henderson, D. *Primary socialisation, language and education, Vol. I: Social class, language and communication.* London: Routledge & Kegan Paul.

HUDDLESTON, R. D., (1965). Rank and depth. *Language*, 41, pp. 574–586.

HUNT, J. Mc. V., (1961). *Intelligence and experience.* New York: Ronald Press.

HYMES, D., (1968). On communicative competence. Mimeo.

INHELDER, B., & PIAGET, J., (1958). *The Growth of Logical Thinking.* London: Routledge & Kegan Paul.

IVIČ, M., (1966). The grammatical category of non-omissible determiners. *Lingua*, 11, pp. 199–204.

JACOBSON, S., (1964). *Adverbial Positions in English.* Stockholm: AB Studentbok.

JESPERSEN, O., (1924). *The Philosophy of Grammar.* London: George Allen & Unwin.

178

JONES, Jean, (1966). Social class and the under-fives. *New Society*, 22 December, pp. 935–936.

KATZ, J. J., & POSTAL, P. M., (1965). *An integrated theory of linguistic descriptions*. Research Monograph No. 26. Cambridge, Mass.: MIT Press.

LABOV, W., & WALETZKY, J., (1967). Narrative analysis: Oral versions of personal experience. Mimeo.

LA BRANT, L., (1933). A study of certain language developments of children in grades four to twelve, inclusive. *Genetic Psychology Monographs*, XIV, pp. 387–491.

LAWTON, D., (1963). Social class differences in language development: a study of some samples of written work. *Language and Speech*, 6, pp. 120–143.

LAWTON, D., (1964). Social class language differences in group discussions. *Language and Speech*, 7, pp. 182–204.

LEECH, G. N., (1966). *English in advertising – a linguistic study of advertising in Great Britain*. London: Longmans.

LEES, R. B., (1960). *The Grammar of English Nominalizations*. Bloomington: Indiana University, Research Center in Anthropology, Folklore and Linguistics (12).

LESHAN, L. L., (1952). Time orientation and social class. *Journal of Abnormal Social Psychology*, 47, pp. 589–592.

LEWIS, M. M., (1951). *Infant Speech: A study of the beginnings of language*. (2nd ed. with additional chapters and appendices) New York: Humanities Press., London: Routledge & Kegan Paul.

LOBAN, W. D., (1961). *The language of elementary school children*. Mimeo.

LOBAN, W. D., (1966). *Language Ability: Grades Seven, Eight and Nine*. Washington: U.S. Government Printing Office. Co-operative Research Monograph No. 18, US Dept. of Health, Education & Welfare, Office of Education.

LOUNSBURY, F., (1954). In Osgood, C. E., & Sebeok, T. A. (eds.), *Psycholinguistics: A survey of theory and research*. Baltimore. pp. 98–101.

LURIA, A. R., & YUDOVICH, F. I., (1959). *Speech and the development of mental processes in the child*. London: Staples Press.

LYONS, J., (1966). Towards a 'notional' theory of the 'parts of speech'. *Journal of Linguistics*, 2, pp. 209–236.

LYONS, J., (1968). *Introduction to Theoretical Linguistics*. Cambridge: The University Press.

MACLAY, H., & OSGOOD, C. E., (1959). Hesitation phenomena in spontaneous English speech. *Word*, 15, pp. 19–44.

MARSHALL, J. C., & WALES, R. J., (1966). Which syntax: A consumer's guide. *Journal of Linguistics*, 2, pp. 181–188.

MARTIN, E., & ROBERTS, K. H., (1966). Grammatical factors in sentence retention. *Journal of Verbal Learning and Verbal Behaviour*, 5, pp. 285–291.

MILLER, G. A., (1962). Some psychological studies of grammar. *American Psychologist*, 17, pp. 748–762.

MILLER, G. A., (1964). Language and psychology. In Lenneberg, E. H. (ed.) *New directions in the study of language*. Cambridge, Mass.: MIT Press. pp. 89–107.

McCARTHY, D. M., (1930). *The language development of the pre-school child*. Institute of Child Welfare Monograph Series No. 4, Minneapolis: University of Minnesota Press.

McCARTHY, D. M., (1954). Language development in children. In Carmichael, L. (ed.), *Manual of Child Psychology*, New York: Wiley & Sons; London: Chapman & Hall.

McINTOSH, A., (1966). Predictive statements. In Bazell, C. E., Catford, J. C., Halliday, M. A. K., & Robins, R. H. (eds.). *In memory of J. R. Firth*. London: Longmans, pp.303–320.

McMAHON, E., (1963). Grammatical analysis as part of understanding. (Unpublished doctoral dissertation, Harvard University).

McNALLY, J., & MURRAY, W., (1962). *Key words in literacy: a basic word list*. London: The Schoolmaster Publishing Co.

McNEILL, D., (1966). The creation of language by children. In Lyons, J., & Wales. R. J. (eds.) *Psycholinguistic papers: The proceedings of the 1966 Edinburgh conference*. Edinburgh: Edinburgh University Press, pp. 99–115.

PALMER, F. R., (1965). *A linguistic study of the English verb*. London: Longmans.

PALMER, F. R., (1964). Grammatical categories and their phonetic exponents. In Lunt, H. G. (ed.). *Proceedings of the Ninth International Congress of Linguistics*. The Hague: Mouton, pp. 338–344.

PIAGET, J., (1926). *Language and thought of the child*. London: Kegan Paul.

PIAGET, J., (1946). *Le developpement de la notion de temps chez l'enfant*. Paris: Presses Univers. France.

POLDAUF, I., (1964). The third syntactical plan. *Travaux Linguistiques de Prague* (New Series, I), pp. 241–255.

QUIRK, R., & SMITH, A. H. (eds.) (1959). *The teaching of English*. (Studies in communication, 3). London: Secker & Warburg.

QUIRK, R., (1962). *The use of English*. London: Longmans.

RACKSTRAW, S. J., & ROBINSON, W. P., (1967). Social and psychological factors related to variability of answering behaviour in five-year-old children. *Language and Speech*, 10, pp. 88–106.

ROBERTS, P., (1964). *English Syntax*. New York: Harcourt, Brace & World.

ROBINSON, W. P., & RACKSTRAW, S. J., (1967). Variations in mothers' answers to children's questions, as a function of social class, verbal intelligence test scores and sex. *Sociology*, 1, pp. 259–276.

RUSSELL, B., (1948). *Human knowledge, its scope and limits.* London: Allen & Unwin.

RUSSELL, D. H., (1956). *Children's Thinking.* Boston: Ginn & Co.

SCHATZMAN, L., & STRAUSS, A., (1955). Social class and modes of communication. *American Journal of Sociology*, LX, pp. 329–338.

SINCLAIR, J. McH., (1965). *A course in spoken English. Part 3: Grammar.* Oxford University Press.

SLEDD, J., (1955). Review of FRIES (1952). *Language*, 31, pp. 312–345.

STRANG, B. M. H., (1962). *Modern English Structure.* London: Edward Arnold.

SVARTVIK, J., (1966). *On voice in the English verb.* The Hague: Mouton (Janua Linguarum Series Practica, LXIII).

TEAHAN, J. E., (1958). Future time perspective optimism and academic achievement. *Journal of Abnormal Social Psychology*, 57, pp. 379–380.

TEMPLIN, M. C., (1957). *Certain language skills in children.* Institute of Child Welfare Monograph Series No. 26. Minneapolis: University of Minnesota Press.

THOMAS, O. P., (1965). *Transformational grammar and the teacher of English.* New York: Holt, Rinehart & Winston.

TURNER, G. J., & PICKVANCE, R. E., (1969). Social class differences in the expression of uncertainty in five-year-old children. *Language and Speech* (forthcoming).

URBAN, W. M., (1939). *Language and Reality: The Philosophy of Language and the Principles of Symbolism.* London: George Allen & Unwin.

WAISMANN, F., (1965). *The Principles of Linguistic Philosophy*, ed. R. Harré. London: Macmillan.

WALES, R. J., & MARSHALL, J. C., (1966). The organization of linguistic performance. In Lyons, J., & Wales, R. J. (eds.)., *Papers in Psycholinguistics.* Edinburgh: Edinburgh University Press, pp. 29–80.

WASON, P. C., (1962). *Psychological aspects of negation.* Communication, Research Centre, University College, London.

YNGVE, V. H., (1960). A model and an hypothesis for language structure. *Proceedings of American Philosophical Society*, 104, pp. 444–466.

Part Two

BAKER, F. B., The data bank concept: a dissident point of view. *Journal of Educational Measurement*, 2, pp. 147–149, 1965.

BARKER, R. G., and WRIGHT, H. F., *Midwest and its children: the psychological ecology of an American town.* Evanston, Illinois: Row, Peterson, 1954.

HALLIDAY, M. A. K., Categories of the Theory of Grammar. *Word*, 17, pp. 241–292, 1961.

HENDERSON, D., Social class differences in form-class usage among five-year-old children. In Brandis, W. and Henderson, D., *Primary Socialisation, Language and Education, Vol I: Social Class, Language and Communication*, London: Routledge and Kegan Paul, 1969.

HENDRY, D. F. *A Manual of the Atlas Commercial Language.* London: University of London Atlas Computing Service, 1965.

HENDRY, D. F., and MOHAN, B. A. *BCL1 Manual.* University of London Institute of Computer Science. Internal Document. ICSI 103. 1968.

HUNT, E. B. *Concept learning: an information processing problem.* New York: Wiley, 1962.

MILLER, G., and CHOMSKY, N. Finitary models of language users. In: R. D. Luce, R. Bush, and E. Galanter, (eds.), *Handbook of Mathematical Psychology*, Vol II, pp. 419–492. New York: Wiley, 1963.

SEYMOUR, W. D. *Industrial Skills.* London: Pitman, 1966.

STONE, P. J., DUNPHY, D. C., SMITH, M. S. and OGILVIE, D. M. *The General Inquirer: a computer approach to content analysis.* Cambridge, Massachusetts: The MIT Press, 1966.

THORNE, J. P. Grammars and Machines. *Transactions of the Philological Society*, pp. 30–45, 1964.

WALKER, D. E. On-line text processing: introduction and overview. MTP–57, MITRE Corporation, 1967.

ALC version

OPERATIONAL
NO SOURCE TESTING
FORMAT CHANGE LC

PT-FILE   :   data   :CODE 1
1:    drib   :   :   1N
1:    copper   :   :   1N
1:    sym   :   :   1C
ERROR GO TO help
1:    number   :   :   1N
ERROR GO TO cruncha
1:    digit   :   :   1N
ERROR GO TO creepback
1:    code   :   :   2C
ERROR GO TO crunchb
1:    section   :   :   2C
ERROR GO TO crunchc
1:    figure   :   :   4C
ERROR GO TO crunchd
1:    signpost   :   :   1N
ERROR GO TO gr1
1:    term   :   :   3C
ERROR GO TO final

WS
1:    n   :   :   2N
1:    j   :   :   1N
1:    depth   :   :   1N
1:    r   :   :   1N
1:    holder
2:    now   :   :   2N   :   5
1:    child   :   :   2C
1:    task   :   :   2C
1:    snum   :   :   4C
1:    bank
2:    store   :   :   :   7
3:    pushdown   :   :   2N   :   5
1:    increment
2:    layer   :   :   1N   :   5
1:    pdigit   :   :   1N
1:    tables
2:    table   :   :   :   21
3:    entry   :   :   :   11
4:    tsym   :   :   1C
4:    total
5:    symtot   :   :   3N   :   5
4:    sequence   :   :   2N
4:    nextab   :   :   2N

183

```
TABLE table( 1) = '1',   0, 0, 0, 0, 0, 1, 2,
                  '2',   0,0,0,0,0,1,2,
                  '3',   0,0,0,0,0,2,2,
                  '4',   0,0,0,0,0,2,2,
                  'G',   0,0,0,0,0,0,0,
                  'G',   0,0,0,0,0,0,0,
                  'G',   0,0,0,0,0,0,0,
                  'G',   0,0,0,0,0,0,0,
                  'G',   0,0,0,0,0,0,0,
                  'G',   0,0,0,0,0,0,0,
                  'X',   0,0,0,0,0,0,0

TABLE table( 2) = 'F',   0, 0, 0, 0, 0,10, 3,
                  'B',   0,0,0,0,0,11,4,
                  'T',   0,0,0,0,0,0,5,
                  'G',   0,0,0,0,0,0,0,
                  'G',   0,0,0,0,0,0,0,
                  'G',   0,0,0,0,0,0,0,
                  'G',   0,0,0,0,0,0,0,
                  'G',   0,0,0,0,0,0,0,
                  'G',   0,0,0,0,0,0,0,
                  'G',   0,0,0,0,0,0,0,
                  'X',   0,0,0,0,0,0,0

TABLE table( 3) = '1',   0, 0, 0, 0, 0, 0, 6,
                  '2',   0,0,0,0,0,0,6,
                  '3',   0,0,0,0,0,0,6,
                  '4',   0,0,0,0,0,0,6,
                  'G',   0,0,0,0,0,0,0,
                  'G',   0,0,0,0,0,0,0,
                  'G',   0,0,0,0,0,0,0,
                  'G',   0,0,0,0,0,0,0,
                  'G',   0,0,0,0,0,0,0,
                  'G',   0,0,0,0,0,0,0,
                  'X',   0,0,0,0,0,0,0

TABLE table( 4) = '1',   0, 0, 0, 0, 0, 0, 6,
                  '2',   0,0,0,0,0,0,6,
                  'G',   0,0,0,0,0,0,0,
                  'G',   0,0,0,0,0,0,0,
                  'G',   0,0,0,0,0,0,0,
                  'G',   0,0,0,0,0,0,0,
                  'G',   0,0,0,0,0,0,0,
                  'G',   0,0,0,0,0,0,0,
                  'G',   0,0,0,0,0,0,0,
                  'G',   0,0,0,0,0,0,0,
                  'X',   0,0,0,0,0,0,0
```

184

```
TABLE table( 5) = '1',   0, 0, 0, 0, 0, 0,0,99,
                  '2',   0,0,0,0,0,0,99,
                  '3',   0,0,0,0,0,0,99,
                  '4',   0,0,0,0,0,0,99,
                  'G',   0,0,0,0,0,0,00,
                  'G',   0,0,0,0,0,0,00,
                  'G',   0,0,0,0,0,0,00,
                  'G',   0,0,0,0,0,0,00,
                  'G',   0,0,0,0,0,0,00,
                  'G',   0,0,0,0,0,0,00,
                  'X',   0,0,0,0,0,0,00

TABLE table( 6) = 'B' ,  0, 0, 0, 0, 0, 0, 9,
                  'L',   0,0,0,0,0,0,9,
                  'Z',   0,0,0,0,0,0,7,
                  'S',   0,0,0,0,0,5,7,
                  'P',   0,0,0,0,0,6,8,
                  'C',   0,0,0,0,0,0,7,
                  'A',   0,0,0,0,0,12,9,
                  'V',   0,0,0,0,0,0,7,
                  'G',   0,0,0,0,0,0,0,
                  'G',   0,0,0,0,0,0,0,
                  'X',   0,0,0,0,0,0,0

TABLE table( 7) = 'M',   0, 0, 0, 0, 0, 0,10,
                  'H',   0,0,0,0,0,9,11,
                  'Q',   0,0,0,0,0,14,12,
                  'Y',   0,0,0,0,0,0,99,
                  'G',   0,0,0,0,0,0,0,
                  'G',   0,0,0,0,0,0,0,
                  'G',   0,0,0,0,0,0,0,
                  'G',   0,0,0,0,0,0,0,
                  'G',   0,0,0,0,0,0,0,
                  'G',   0,0,0,0,0,0,0,
                  'X',   0,0,0,0,0,0,0

TABLE table( 8) = 'M',   0, 0, 0, 0, 0, 0,99,
                  'P',   0,0,0,0,0,0,99,
                  'V',   0,0,0,0,0,0,99,
                  'C',   0,0,0,0,0,0,99,
                  'A',   0,0,0,0,0,0,14,
                  'L',   0,0,0,0,0,0,13,
                  'T',   0,0,0,0,0,0,15,
                  'Y',   0,0,0,0,0,0,99,
                  'G',   0,0,0,0,0,0,0,
                  'G',   0,0,0,0,0,0,0,
                  'X',   0,0,0,0,0,0,0
```

185

```
TABLE table( 9) = 'T',   0, 0, 0, 0, 0, 3,99,
                   'B',   0,0,0,0,0,0,16,
                   'L',   0,0,0,0,0,0,17,
                   'V',   0,0,0,0,0,4,18,
                   'F',   0,0,0,0,0,7,99,
                   'P',   0,0,0,0,0,8,99,
                   'M',   0,0,0,0,0,0,10,
                   'H',   0,0,0,0,0,9,19,
                   'Q',   0,0,0,0,0,14,12,
                   'Y',   0,0,0,0,0,0,99,
                   'X',   0,0,0,0,0,0,0

TABLE table(10) = 'D',   0, 0, 0, 0, 0,13,20,
                   '0',   0,0,0,0,0,13,99,
                   'E',   0,0,0,0,0,13,99,
                   'N',   0,0,0,0,0,13,99,
                   '1',   0,0,0,0,0,13,99,
                   'Y',   0,0,0,0,0,13,99,
                   'G',   0,0,0,0,0,0,0,
                   'G',   0,0,0,0,0,0,0,
                   'G',   0,0,0,0,0,0,0,
                   'G',   0,0,0,0,0,0,0,
                   'X',   0,0,0,0,0,0,0

TABLE table(11) = 'D',   0, 0, 0, 0, 0, 0,99,
                   '0',   0,0,0,0,0,0,99,
                   'E',   0,0,0,0,0,0,99,
                   'N',   0,0,0,0,0,0,99,
                   'P',   0,0,0,0,0,0,21,
                   'S',   0,0,0,0,0,0,99,
                   'T',   0,0,0,0,0,0,99,
                   'W',   0,0,0,0,0,0,99,
                   'Y',   0,0,0,0,0,0,99,
                   'G',   0,0,0,0,0,0,99,
                   'X"   0,0,0,0,0,0,0

TABLE table(12) = 'D',   0, 0, 0, 0, 0, 0,99,
                   'E',   0,0,0,0,0,0,99,
                   '0',   0,0,0,0,0,0,99,
                   'Y',   0,0,0,0,0,0,99,
                   'G',   0,0,0,0,0,0,0,
                   'G',   0,0,0,0,0,0,0,
                   'G',   0,0,0,0,0,0,0,
                   'G',   0,0,0,0,0,0,0,
                   'G',   0,0,0,0,0,0,0,
                   'G',   0,0,0,0,0,0,0,
                   'X',   0,0,0,0,0,0,0
```

```
TABLE table(13) = '0',    0, 0, 0, 0, 0, 0,99,
                  'A',    0,0,0,0,0,0,99,
                  'P',    0,0,0,0,0,0,99,
                  'F',    0,0,0,0,0,0,99,
                  'R',    0,0,0,0,0,0,99,
                  'S',    0,0,0,0,0,0,99,
                  'E',    0,0,0,0,0,0,99,
                  'G',    0,0,0,0,0,0,0,
                  'G',    0,0,0,0,0,0,0,
                  'G',    0,0,0,0,0,0,0,
                  'X',    0,0,0,0,0,0,0

TABLE table(14) = 'B',    0, 0, 0, 0, 0, 0,99,
                  'S',    0,0,0,0,0,0,99,
                  '1',    0,0,0,0,0,0,99,
                  'N',    0,0,0,0,0,0,99,
                  'G',    0,0,0,0,0,0,0,
                  'G',    0,0,0,0,0,0,0,
                  'G',    0,0,0,0,0,0,0,
                  'G',    0,0,0,0,0,0,0,
                  'G',    0,0,0,0,0,0,0,
                  'G',    0,0,0,0,0,0,0,
                  'X',    0,0,0,0,0,0,0

TABLE table(15) = '0',    0, 0, 0, 0, 0, 0,99,
                  '1',    0,0,0,0,0,0,99,
                  '2',    0,0,0,0,0,0,99,
                  '3',    0,0,0,0,0,0,99,
                  '4',    0,0,0,0,0,0,99,
                  '5',    0,0,0,0,0,0,99,
                  '6',    0,0,0,0,0,0,99,
                  '7',    0,0,0,0,0,0,99,
                  '8',    0,0,0,0,0,0,99,
                  '9',    0,0,0,0,0,0,99,
                  'X',    0,0,0,0,0,0,0

TABLE table(16) = '1',    0, 0, 0, 0, 0, 0,99,
                  '2',    0,0,0,0,0,0,99,
                  '3',    0,0,0,0,0,0,99,
                  '4',    0,0,0,0,0,0,99,
                  'Y',    0,0,0,0,0,0,99,
                  'G',    0,0,0,0,0,0,0,
                  'G',    0,0,0,0,0,0,0,
                  'G',    0,0,0,0,0,0,0,
                  'G',    0,0,0,0,0,0,0,
                  'G',    0,0,0,0,0,0,0,
                  'X',    0,0,0,0,0,0,0
```

187

```
TABLE table(17) = '1',    0, 0, 0,0, 0, 0,99,
                  '2',    0,0,0,0,0,0,99,
                  '3',    0,0,0,0,0,0,99,
                  '4',    0,0,0,0,0,0,99,
                  'Y',    0,0,0,0,0,0,99,
                  'G',    0,0,0,0,0,0,0,
                  'G',    0,0,0,0,0,0,0,
                  'G',    0,0,0,0,0,0,0,
                  'G',    0,0,0,0,0,0,0,
                  'G',    0,0,0,0,0,0,0,
                  'X',    0,0,0,0,0,0,0

TABLE table(18) = '1',    0, 0, 0, 0, 0, 0,99,
                  '2',    0,0,0,0,0,0,99,
                  '3',    0,0,0,0,0,0,99,
                  '4',    0,0,0,0,0,0,99,
                  '5',    0,0,0,0,0,0,99,
                  '6',    0,0,0,0,0,0,99,
                  'Y',    0,0,0,0,0,0,99,
                  'G',    0,0,0,0,0,0,0,
                  'G',    0,0,0,0,0,0,0,
                  'G',    0,0,0,0,0,0,0,
                  'X',    0,0,0,0,0,0,0

TABLE table(19) = '1',    0, 0, 0, 0, 0, 0,99,
                  '2',    0,0,0,0,0,0,99,
                  '3',    0,0,0,0,0,0,99,
                  '4',    0,0,0,0,0,0,99,
                  'Y',    0,0,0,0,0,0,99,
                  'G',    0,0,0,0,0,0,0,
                  'G',    0,0,0,0,0,0,0,
                  'G',    0,0,0,0,0,0,0,
                  'G',    0,0,0,0,0,0,0,
                  'G',    0,0,0,0,0,0,0,
                  'X',    0,0,0,0,0,0,0

TABLE table(20) = '1',    0, 0, 0, 0, 0, 0,99,
                  '2',    0,0,0,0,0,0,99,
                  '3',    0,0,0,0,0,0,99,
                  '4',    0,0,0,0,0,0,99,
                  '5',    0,0,0,0,0,0,99,
                  '6',    0,0,0,0,0,0,99,
                  '7',    0,0,0,0,0,0,99,
                  '8',    0,0,0,0,0,0,99,
                  'Y',    0,0,0,0,0,0,99,
                  'G',    0,0,0,0,0,0,0,
                  'X',    0,0,0,0,0,0,0
```

```
TABLE table(21) =  '1',   0, 0, 0, 0, 0, 0,99,
                   '2',   0,0,0,0,0,0,99,
                   '3',   0,0,0,0,0,0,99,
                   '4',   0,0,0,0,0,0,99,
                   '5',   0,0,0,0,0,0,99,
                   '6',   0,0,0,0,0,0,99,
                   '7',   0,0,0,0,0,0,99,
                   '8',   0,0,0,0,0,0,99,
                   '9',   0,0,0,0,0,0,99,
                   'G',   0,0,0,0,0,0,0,
                   'X',   0,0,0,0,0,0,0

REPORT:report1
LINE    :ln1
1:10:    'errorprint'
WS
1:   ranktab
2:   chunk      :    :    :   6
3:   item       :    :  1C
3:   value      :    :  1N
2:   chunkb     :    :    :   6
3:   noit       :    :  1N
3:   noval      :    :  1N
3:   nolay      :    :  1N
1:   cod        :    :  1N
TABLE ranktab = 'M', 1, 'H', 2, 'Q', 3, 'V',4,'O',0.'R',5,
                2,1,2,6,2,4,7,3,5,8,3,5,9,3,5,0,4,0
```

189

PROCEDURE DIVISION

newchild:	DO skipboth
	IF NEXT CH = B1000101 GO TO finish
	READ code FROM data
	PUT code → child DO skipboth
	PRINT 'child', child, CR ON report1
newtask:	DO skipboth READ section FROM data
	PUT section → task DO skipboth
	PRINT 'task', task, CR ON report1
	PUT 1 → r
begin:	IF r > 1 DO [PUT 1 → r PRINT 'BRACKET+LEFT+OPEN',
	CR ON report1]
	PUT 1 → now(r) PUT 1 → layer(r) READ figure FROM data
	PUT figure → snum DO skipsp SKIP CH data DO skipsp
top:	CLEAR n PUT 1 → j
	IF r < 1 DO help IF r > 5 DO help
	READ sym FROM data
nearly:	IF now(r) = 15 GO TO tense
	IF sym = '<' DO rankshift
	IF sym = '(' DO included
	IF sym = '+' DO [PUT 2 → j READ sym FROM data
	GO TO again]
	IF sym = '–' DO [PUT 3 → j READ sym FROM data
	GO TO again]
	IF sym = '=' DO [PUT 4 → j READ sym FROM data
	GO TO again]
	IF sym = '*' DO [PUT 5 → j READ sym FROM data]
again:	PUT 1 + n → n
	IF now(r) = 0 GO TO boob
	IF n = 11 GO TO boob
	IF tsym(now(r),n) ≠ 'X' GO TO ok
boob:	DO help GO TO begin
ok:	IF sym ≠ tsym(now(r),n) GO TO again
forgetit:	PUT now(r) → pushdown(layer(r),r)
	IF nextab (now(r),n) = 99 GO TO changeup
	PUT layer(r) + 1 → layer(r)
	IF j = 5 GO TO changeup
	IF TRANS CH = '<' DO [SKIP CH data DO rankshift]
	PUT nextab (now(r),n) → now(r)
	GO TO top

```
tense:          IF sym = '0' DO[ PUT 2 → j READ sym FROM data
                GO TO again]
                IF sym = '1' DO [PUT 3 → j READ sym FROM data
                GO TO again]
                IF sym = '2' DO [PUT 4 → j READ sym FROM data
                GO TO again]
                IF sym = '3' DO [PUT 5 → j READ sym FROM data
                GO TO again]
                DO help
skipboth:       ROUTINE
x:              IF NEXT CH = B0000010 DO [ SKIP CH data GO TO x ]
y:              IF NEXT CH = B0010000 DO [ SKIP CH data GO TO x ]
END
skipsp:         ROUTINE
y:              IF NEXT CH = B0010000 DO [ SKIP CH data GO TO y ]
END
changeup:       CLEAR n PUT 1 → j READ sym FROM data
                IF sym = '/' GO TO ahead
                IF layer(r) > 6 DO [ PUT 6 → layer(r) PUT pushdown
                (layer(r),r) → now(r) ]
                GO TO nearly
ahead:          READ digit FROM data PUT digit → pdigit
                IF TRANS CH = '>' DO [SKIP CH data GO TO shiftout ]
                IF TRANS CH = ')' DO [ SKIP CH data GO TO out ]
pushup:         IF pdigit > 3 GO TO print
                IF pdigit = 3 DO [ DO skipboth GO TO begin ]
                IF pdigit = 2 DO [ PUT 2 → layer(r) DO skipboth GO TO
                hp ]
                IF pdigit = 1 DO [ PUT 4 → layer(r) DO skipboth GO TO
                hp ]
hp:             IF r < 1 DO [ PUT 1 → r DO help ]
                PUT pushdown (layer(r),r) → now (r) GO TO top


creepback:      PUT 5 → layer(r)
return:         PUT pushdown(layer(r),r) → now(r) GO TO top


help:           ROUTINE
DATA
WS
1:   cycle            :    : 1N
PROCEDURE DIVISION
                IF r < 1 PUT 1 → r
                IF r > 5 PUT 5 → r
                IF cycle > 3 DO [ CLEAR cycle PRINT CR ON report1 ]
                PUT 1 + cycle → cycle
```

PRINT 'ERRSENT', snum, ' ', 'TABLE', now(r), ' ', 'DATA+CH',
sym, ' ' ON report1
washout: CLEAR n
h1:   DO moreout
              END
gr1:   SKIP CH data
more: DO skipboth READ sym FROM data DO moreout
moreout: ROUTINE

              IF sym = '(' DO [PUT 1 + r → r   GO TO more]
              IF sym = '<' DO [PUT 1 + r → r PUT 1 + depth → depth
              GO TO more]
              IF sym = ')' DO [PUT r − 1 → r TEAD sym FROM data
              GO TO more]

              IF sym = '>' DO [PUT r − 1 → r PUT depth − 1 → depth
              READ sym FROM data GO TO more]

              IF sym ≠ '/' GO TO more
leap: READ signpost FROM data
              IF signpost < 3 GO TO more

              IF signpost > 3 DO [PUT signpost → pdigit GO TO print]
              DO skipboth PUT 1 → r
              GO TO begin
              END
rankshift: ROUTINE
DATA
WS

1:    rlet   :   :   1C
1:    coder   :   :   1N
1:    sort
2:    i   :   :   1N   :   2

PROCEDURE DIVISION
PUT tsym → rlet
CLEAR coder CLEAR sort
trick: PUT 1 + coder → coder
              IF coder = 6 DO [PUT value (6) → i (1) GO TO out1]
              IF rlet ≠ item(coder) GO TO trick
              PUT value (coder → i(1)
out1:   SKIP CH data
              READ number FROM data CLEAR coder

192

```
return1:      PUT 1 + coder → coder
              IF coder = 6 DO [ PUT noval (6) → i (2) GO TO out2 ]
              IF number ≠ noit (coder) GO TO return1
              PUT noval(coder) → i (2)
out2:         PUT 1 + depth → depth PUT 1 + r → r
              PUT nolay(coder) → layer(r)
              PUT number → now(r) GO TO top
              END
included:     ROUTINE
              PUT 1 + r → r
              SKIP CH data
              READ number FROM data
              CLEAR coder
sn1:          PUT 1 + coder → coder
              IF coder = 6 GO TO hu1
              IF number ≠ noit(coder) GO TO sn1
hu1:          PUT nolay(coder) → layer(r)
next:         PUT number → now(r) GO TO top

              END


shiftout:     PUT depth −1 → depth PUT r −1 → r DO canny
              GO TO changeup
out:          CLEAR saved CLEAR pacifier PUT r −1 →r DO canny
              GO TO top
canny:        ROUTINE
              IF r < 1 DO [ PUT 1 → r DO help ]
END


cruncha:      PRINT CR, 'INCLUSION NUMBER WRONG', CR ON
              report1
              GO TO gr1
crunchb:      PRINT CR, 'CODE NUMBER WRONG', CR ON report1
              GO TO gr1
crunchc:      PRINT CR, 'SECTION NUMBER WRONG', CR ON
              report1
              GO TO gr1
crunchd:      PRINT CR, 'SENTENCE NUMBER WRONG', CR ON
              report1
              GO TO gr1
print:        PRINT   1n67
              IF pie < 5 DO [ DO skipboth GO TO newtask]
              IF pie < 6 DO [ DO skipboth GO TO newchild]
              GO TO final
finish:       READ term FROM data
              IF term ≠ 'END' PRINT 'childerror', CR ON report 1
final:        CLEAR child
STOPRUN
END OF PROGRAM
***Z
```

193

BCL version

```
MISC IS(AB DIGIT
        2C RANKNO
        2C INCNO
        AB SENTNO
        AB BOUND
        AB DEPTH
        AB INTERRUPT
        AB MARKER
        A   CODE
        A   SECTION
        1C CHARACTER
        1C SYMBOL )
NEWCHILD IS (A CODE, NLS., NEWTASK
                EITHER IF BOUND = 5, NEWCHILD
                OR 'END'
                OR O/P('CHILDERROR', NL.))
NEWTASK IS (A SECTION, NLS, REPEAT)
REPEAT IS (EITHER SENTENCE OR NIL.
            BMARK
            EITHER IF BOUND = 3
                ,(EITHER IF DEPTH GT 0
                    ,O/P('EXTRA OPEN RS BRACKET', SENTNO,
                        NL.)
                  OR   IF DEPTH LT 0
                    , O/P('EXTRA CLOSING RS BRACKET',
                        SENTNO, NL.)
                  OR  NIL.)
                ,(EITHER IF INTERRUPT GT 0
                    , O/P('EXTRA OPEN INCL BRACKET',
                        SENTNO, NL.)
                  OR   IF INTERRUPT LT 0
                    ,O/P('EXTRA CLOSING INCL BRACKET',
                        SENTNO, NL.)
                  OR  NIL.)
                ,NLS, REPEAT
            OR IF BOUND = 4, NEWTASK
            OR  NIL.)

BMARK IS (EITHER '/', BOUND, IF BOUND GT 2, IF BOUND LT 6
            OR HELP)
SENTENCE IS (NEWLINES
            ,SENTNO
            ,'S'
            ,DIGIT, IF DIGIT LT 4
            ,CLAUSE)
```

194

```
CLAUSE IS      (EITHER '*', SYMBOL
                OR   (EITHER RELATOR
                       OR     NIL.
                              (EITHER 'F'
                                OR     'B'
                                OR     'T')
                              ,DIGIT, IF DIGIT LT 4
                              ,ELEMENT)
                EITHER '/2', NEWLINES, CLAUSE
                   OR NIL.)

ELEMENT IS (EITHER    (EITHER '*', SYMBOL
                OR       (EITHER RELATOR
                          OR    NIL.
                          EITHER   (EITHER 'B'
                                     OR     'L'
                                     OR     'A')
                                   ,(EITHER RANKSHIFT
                                     OR     ADVERBGP)
                          OR       (EITHER 'Z'
                                     OR     'S'
                                     OR     'C'
                                     OR     'V')
                                   ,(EITHER RANKSHIFT
                                     OR     NOMGP)
                          OR     'P', VERBGP)
                EITHER '/', '1', NEWLINES, ELEMENT
                   OR  NIL.)
           OR   INCLUSION, NEWLINES, ELEMENT)
ADVGP IS    (EITHER '*', SYMBOL
             OR    (EITHER RELATOR
                    OR    NIL.
                    EITHER    'T'
                    OR        'F'
                    OR        'P'
                    OR        'B'
                              ,(EITHER RANKSHIFT
                                OR     DIGIT, IF DIGIT
                                       LT 5)
                    OR        'L'
                              ,(EITHER RANKSHIFT
                                OR     DIGIT, IF DIGIT
                                       LT 5)
                    OR        'V'
                              ,(EITHER RANKSHIFT
                                OR     DIGIT, IF DIGIT
                                       LT 7)
```

195

```
                        OR        'M'
                                  ,(EITHER  RANKSHIFT
                                        OR        MODPOSS)
                        OR        'H'
                                  ,(EITHER  RANKSHIFT
                                       OR  DIGIT, IF DIGIT
                                            LT 5)
                        OR        'Q'
                                  ,(EITHER  RANKSHIFT
                                       OR  QUALPOSS))
            EITHER  (EITHER        '/'
                        OR         NIL.)
                     ,ADVGP
              OR     NIL.)

NOMGP IS    (EITHER '*',  SYMBOL
              OR        (EITHER   RELATOR
                          OR      NIL.
                        EITHER    'M'
                                  ,(EITHER  RANKSHIFT
                                     OR     MODPOSS)
                          OR      'H'
                                  ,(EITHER  RANKSHIFT
                                     OR     HEADPOSS)
                          OR      'Q'
                                  ,(EITHER  RANKSHIFT
                                     OR     QUALPOSS))
            EITHER '/',  NOMGP
              OR       NIL.)
VERBGP IS   (EITHER '*',  SYMBOL
              OR        (EITHER   RELATOR
                          OR      NIL.
                        EITHER    'M'
                          OR      'P'
                          OR      'V'
                          OR      'C'
                          OR      'Y'
                          OR      'A', ASPECT
                          OR      'L', LEXTYPE
                          OR      'T', TENSE)
            EITHER    VERBGP
              OR      NIL.)
```

```
MODPOSS IS  (EITHER      RELATOR
              OR          NIL.
              EITHER      'D', DIGIT
              OR          'O'
              OR          'E'
              OR          'N'
              OR          'I'
              EITHER      MODPOSS
              OR          NIL.)
HEADPOSS IS(EITHER        RELATOR
              OR          NIL.
              EITHER      'P', DIGIT
              OR          'D'
              OR          'O'
              OR          'E'
              OR          'N'
              OR          'S'
              OR          'T'
              OR          'W'
              OR          'Y'   )
QUALPOSS IS(EITHER   RELATOR
              OR          NIL.
              EITHER      'D'
              OR          'E'
              OR          'O'
              EITHER      QUALPOSS
              OR          NIL. )
ASPECT IS   (EITHER       'B'
              OR          'S'
              OR          'I'
              OR          'N'
              EITHER      '/'
              OR          NIL.)
LEXTYPE IS  (EITHER       'O'
              OR          'A'
              OR          'P'
              OR          'F'
              OR          'R'
              OR          'S'
              OR          'E'
              EITHER      '/'
              OR          NIL.)
```

```
TENSE IS  (A TENSENO, IF TENSENO LT 37)
RANKSHIFT IS ('<', RANKNO
              ,DEPTH =  DEPTH + 1
              EITHER    IF RANKNO = '09', ADVGP, '/1'
                OR      IF RANKNO = '08', VERBGP, '/1'
                OR      IF RANKNO = '07', NOMGP, '/1'
                OR      IF RANKNO = '06', ELEMENT, '/2'
              EITHER    '>', DEPTH = DEPTH − 1
                OR      O/P('CLOSING RANKSHIFT BRACKET
                              NEEDED IN ',SENTNO,NL.))
INCLUSION IS ('(',INCNO
              EITHER    IF INCNO = '06', ELEMENT, '/1'
                OR      IF INCNO = '02', CLAUSE, '/2'
              EITHER    ')'
                OR      O/P('CLOSING INCLUSION BRACKET
                              NEEDED IN ',SENTNO,NL.))
RELATOR IS     (EITHER  '+'
                OR      '−'
                OR      '='   )
NLS IS  (EITHER  SP., OSP., NLS
          OR     NL., NLS
          OR     NIL.)
CHSET IS  (EITHER CHARACTER ,O/P(CHARACTER)
          OR     '/', MARKER = 1,O/P('/')
          OR     SP.,OSP.,O/P(SP.)
          OR     NL.,O/P(NL.)
          OR     '+', O/P('+')
          OR     '−', O/P('−')
          OR     '=', O/P('=')
          OR     '*', O/P('*')
          OR     '<', O/P('<')
                 ,DEPTH5DEPTH+1
          OR     '>' O/P('>')
                 ,DEPTH=DEPTH−1
          OR     '(', O/P('(')
                 ,INTERRUPT = INTERRUPT + 1
          OR     ')', O/P(')')
                 ,INTERRUPT = INTERRUPT − 1 )
NUMCHAR IS (EITHER  '1' OR '2' OR '3' OR '4' OR '5'
            OR      '6' OR '7' OR '8' OR '9' )
```

```
HELP IS (CHSET    ,EITHER   IF MARKER = 1, MARKER = 0,
                            BOUND, IF BOUND GT 2
                            ,O/P(BOUND, '____', 'SENTENCE'
                            'SENTNO,' FAILED', NL.)
                  OR        HELP
                  OR        O/P('FAILED IN HELP', NL.))


INPUTGROUP IS (SELECT INPUT 1
                  ,I/P(NLS,CODENO,NLS,NEWCHILD))


*ENTER(INPUTGROUP)
```

LINEAR TYPEOUT OF GRAMMATICAL ANALYSIS

40
01S3F1PLF/YT01/3
02S1F1AV5/1 SHP3/1 PT03/1 AV4/1 CMD8/HN/2
    +F1LL1/1 *S/1 PLF/T03/1 CHP9/Q0/1   AV4/3
03S1F1SHP3/1 PT01/1 AV2/2
    +F1£LL1/1£2111LL1/1 *S/1 PT01/1 AP/MD8/H4/3
04S2F2PT02/1 CMD8/HN/3
05S1F1AV5/1 SMD8/HN/1 PT01/3
06S2F1AP/H1/3
07S1F1AV5/1 SMD8E/HN/1 PT01/3
08S2F1AP/H1/1 VHN/3
09S1F1£AV5/1£2111AV5/1 SMD8/HN/1 PT01/3
10S2F2AV4/1 PPT02/1 AP/MD8N/H4/3
11S2F1AV5/1 SMD8/HN/1 PT01/2
    B1PAS/T02/1 £CMD8/HN/1−PAN/T02/1£4223CMD8/HN/1
    −PAN/T01/2
    +F1£LL1/1£2111LL1/1 SHP3/1 PT01/1 AP/MD8/H4/2
    +F1LL1/1 SHP3/1 PT02/1 CMD6/HN/2
    +F1LL1/1 SHP3/1 PT01/1 CHP9/1 AP/H2/1 =CMDY/HN/3
12S1F1SMD8/HN/1 PT01/1 AP/H2/2
    +F1LL1/1 SMD8/HN/1 £PT01/1CHP9/1AV2/1£4223PT02/1
    CHP9/1 AV2/2
    +F1LL1/1 PLF/T01/1 CHP9/3
13S1F1SHP3/1 PT08/2
    +F1LL1/1 SHP3/1 PT02/1 CMD8/HN/3
14S1F1AV5/1 SHP3/1 PT01/1 AV2/1 =SMDY/HN/2
    +F1LL1/1 £SHP3/1£2111SHP3/1 AV4/1 PT01/1 CMD3/HN/2
    +F1LL1/1 SHP3/1 PT01/1 AV2/3
15S1F1AV5/1 SHP3/1 PT01/1 AV2/2
    +F1LL1/1 SHP3/1 PT01/1 AV2/1 AP/MD3/H2/2
    +F1SMD8/HN/1 PT01/2
    +F1LL1/1 £SHP3/1PT02/1CHP9/1£2111SHP3/1 PT02/1 CHP9/3
16S1F1AV5/1 SHP3/1 PT07/1 AP/MD8/H2/2
    +F1LL1/1 £SHP3/1£2111SHP3/1 PLF/T01/1 CHP9/2
    +\F1SMD8/HN/1 PL0/T01'/2
    +F1LL1/1 SHP3/1 PT01/1 AMD8N/H4/1 AP/H2/2
    +F1LL1/1 £SHP3/1PT01/1£4223SHP3/1 PT01/1 CMD8/HN/2
    +F1£LL1/1£2111LL1/1 £SHP3/1PT01/1£4211SHP3/1 PT01/1
    CMDY/HN/1 AV1/2
    +F1LL1/1 SHP3/1 PT02/1 −PAS/T02/1 CHP9/2
    +F1LL1/1 SHP3/1 PLF/T01/1 CMD8/HN/1 AV1/3
17S1F1SHT/1 PLE/T02/1 CMD8/HN/4

53
01S1F1SHY/1 PT02/1 AV3/+V3/1 AP/H4/2
 +F2LL1/1 SHP5/1 PT02/1 −PAS/T02/1 CHP9/3
02S1F1SHP2/1 AV4/1 PT02/1 CMD8/HN/2
 +F1LL1/1 *S/1 PT02/1 ATP/MD8EN/H2/2
 +F1LL1/1 SHT/1 PLE/T02/1 CH<06AV3/1SHP2/1PT02/2>/4

60
01S1F1\\SHP3/1 PT02/3
02S1F1SHP2/1 PT02/1 PAS/T02/1 CHS/1 =C£MD5£2111MD5E/HN/2
 +F1LL1/1 SHP2/1 PT02/1 CHP9/1 AP/H4/2
 +\\F1LL1/1 SHP4/1 PT02/3
03S3F1ZMD5E/HN/3
03S3F1ZHS/3
04S1F1AV5/1 SHP8/1 PT02/1 =SMD8E/HN/1 AV6/2
 +F1LL1/1 SHP2/1 AV4/1 PYT02/3
05S1F1SHN/1 PLE/T02/1 CMD8/HN/2
 T1/4

70
01S1F1SMD1/HN/1 PT02/1 AV4/1 PLF/AI/T02/1 CMD8/HN/1
 AP/MD1/H2/3
02S1F1SHP1/1 PPT05/1 AP/MD6/H4/1 AV1/2
 B1BB1/1 SHP1/1 PT02/1 AP/H4/2
 B1BB1/1 SHP1/1 PT02/1 AV2/5

COMPUTER PRINTOUT OF RESULTS
TOTAL FOR CHILD 2111

BASE 160

IDENTIFIER	VALUE 1	VALUE 2	VALUE 3	VALUE 4	VALUE 5	VALUE 6	VALUE 7	VALUE 8	VALUE 9	VALUE 10
SENTENCE++TYPE+	40	17	3	0						
CLAUSE++TYPE+++	147	12	7							
FREE+++CLAUSE+	134	7	6	0						
BOUND+++CLAUSE+	7	5								
TAG++++CLAUSE+	1									
CLAUSE+ELEMENT+	11	71	9	152	159	75	103	1		
NOMINAL+GROUP++	68	225	8	0						
VERBAL++GROUP++	4	2	5	0	2	17	158	2		
ADVERB++GROUP++	11	11	71	56	1	47	33	48	0	10
MODIFIERS+++++	99	2	9	1	0	0	0			
HEADS+NOMINAL++	1	0	4	77	131	0	8	5	0	
QUALIFIERS++++	7	0	0	0						
VERB++LEXICAL++	1	11	0	5	0	0	0			
ASPECT+OF+VERB+	0	1	1	0	0	0				
TYPE+OF+BINDER+	6	5	0	0	0					
TYPE+OF+LINKER+	71	0	0	5						
TYPE+OF+VORTEX+	5	27	9	2	8	4	0			
HEAD+OF+ADVERB+	1	36	0	10	0	0				
DETERMINERS++++	2	0	9	0	1	4	0	83	0	
TYPE+OF+PRONOUN	5	3	28	15	2	4	39	2	33	
TENSE+SUBTYPES+	0	22	101	5	0	7	0	1	21	10
	0	0	0	0	0	0	0	0	0	10
	0	0	0	0	0	0	0	0	0	10
	0	0	0	0	0	0	0	0	0	10
OPERATOR+SYMBOL1	93	2	5	11						

	VALUE 1	VALUE 2	VALUE 3	VALUE 4	VALUE 5	VALUE 6	VALUE 7	VALUE 8	VALUE 9	VALUE 10	VALUE 11	VALUE 12
TURBULENCE+TYPE												
1	2 2	0 3	0 4	0 5	0 6	0 7	0 8	0 9	0 10	0 11	0 12	0
1	0 2	0 3	0 4	0 5	0 6	0 7	0 8	0 9	0 10	0 11	0 12	0
1	0 2	0 3	0 4	0 5	0 6	0 7	0 8	0 9	0 10	0 11	0 12	0
1	19 2	0 3	0 4	0 5	0 6	0 7	0 8	0 9	0 10	0 11	0 12	0
1	0 2	0 3	0 4	0 5	0 6	0 7	0 8	0 9	0 10	0 11	0 12	0
1	0 2	1 3	0 4	0 5	0 6	0 7	0 8	0 9	0 10	0 11	0 12	0
1	0 2	0 3	0 4	0 5	0 6	0 7	0 8	0 9	0 10	0 11	0 12	0
1	0 2	0 3	0 4	0 5	0 6	0 7	0 8	0 9	0 10	0 11	0 12	0
1	0 2	0 3	0 4	0 5	0 6	0 7	0 8	0 9	0 10	0 11	0 12	0
1	0 2	0 3	0 4	0 5	0 6	0 7	0 8	0 9	0 10	0 11	0 12	0
RANKSHIFT+SIZE+												
1	0 2	0 3	0 4	0								
1	0 2	1 3	0 4	0								
1	0 2	0 3	1 4	0								
1	0 2	0 3	0 4	0								
1	0 2	2 3	1 4	0								
SENTENCE+MATRIX												
1	0 2	7 3	2 1	23 2	1 3	0 1	23 2	0 3	0			
SENTENCE+MATRIX												
1	0 2	0 3	0 1	3 2	0 3	0 1	0 2	0 3	0			
CLAUSE++MATRIX+												
1	7 2	1 3	0 4	0 1	2 2	8 3	0 4	0 1	70 2	59 3	11 4	4
ADVERB+MATRIX++												
1	51 2	0 3	3 4	40 1	3 2	1 3	0 4	6				
NOMINAL+MATRIX+												
1	166 2	88 3	11 4	0 1	7 2	1 3	1 3	0 1	0 2	0 3	0 4	0

Diagram 1

Sentence: OFTEN I JUST LEFT THE BAG THERE

Syntactic description: A   S   A   P   C   A
(Much simplified and only given for
clause elements)

A possible selective count:

S	P	C	A
1	1	1	3

The selective count omits certain information. In this case, the positioning of the As (Adjuncts) is omitted.

Type of description	Input to computer	Action to retrieve omitted information
Selective description	Selective count	Manually recode data
Non-selective description	Syntactic description	Alter computer program.ne

Diagram 2
Data collection and processing

Process

Product

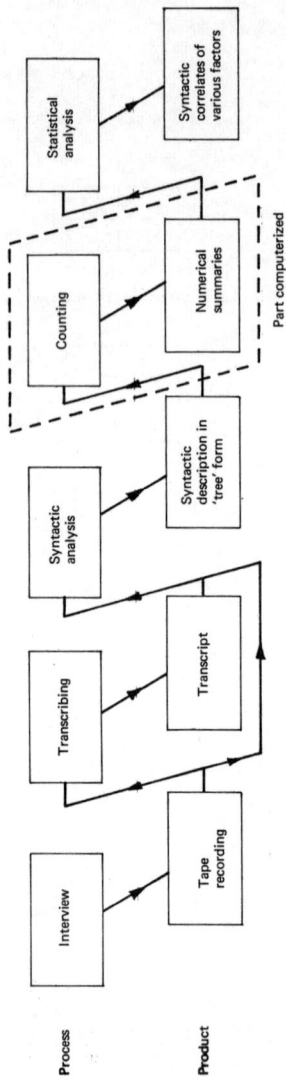

| Interview | → | Transcribing | → | Syntactic analysis | → | Counting | → | Statistical analysis |

Tape recording → Transcript → Syntactic description in 'tree' form → Numerical summaries → Syntactic correlates of various factors

Part computerized

Diagram 3
An algorithm for converting tree structure into linear form

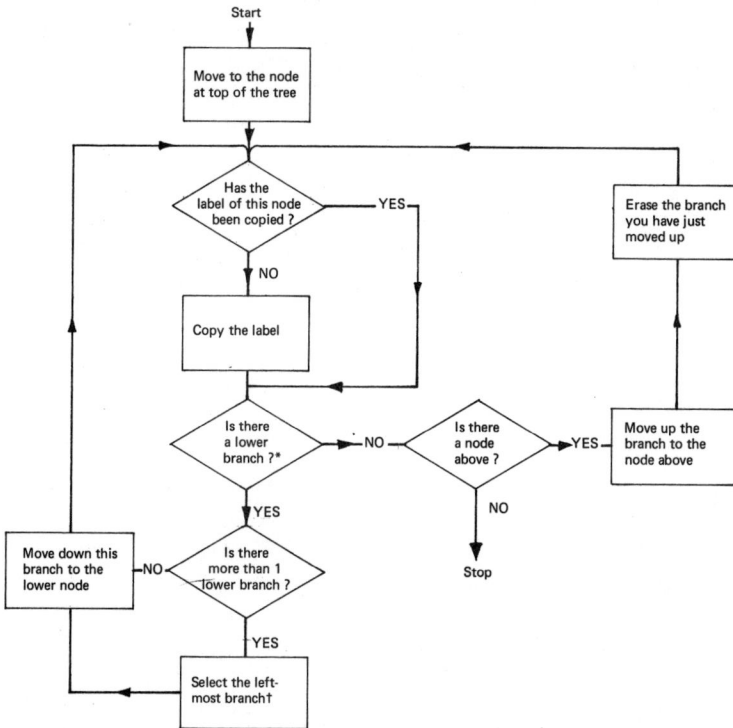

Start

Move to the node
at top of the tree

Has the
label of this node
been copied ? — YES

Erase the branch
you have just
moved up

NO

Copy the label

Is there
a lower
branch ?* — NO

Is there
a node
above ? — YES

Move up the
branch to the
node above

YES

NO

Move down this
branch to the
lower node — NO

Is there
more than 1
lower branch ?

Stop

YES

Select the left-
most branch†

---

*Branch — A line between *two* nodes, and only two.
†Leftmost — Leftmost to an observer looking at the tree from the bottom of the page.

Diagram 4
An illustrative tree structure

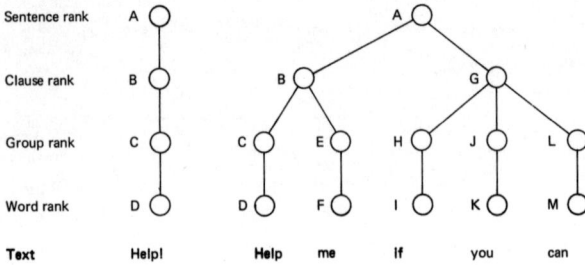

Sentence rank	A		A	
Clause rank	B		B	G
Group rank	C		C E	H J L
Word rank	D		D F	I K M
Text	**Help!**		**Help me**	**if you can**

Diagram 5
Possibilities of recursion

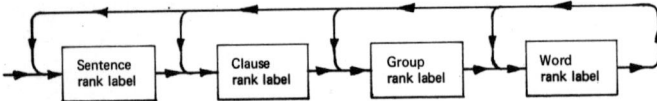

| Sentence rank label | Clause rank label | Group rank label | Word rank label |

Diagram 6
Labelling convention for preserving structure

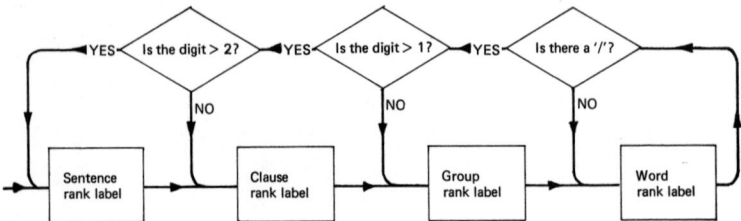

YES — Is the digit > 2?   YES — Is the digit > 1?   YES — Is there a '/'?

NO   NO   NO

| Sentence rank label | Clause rank label | Group rank label | Word rank label |

Diagram 7
Data processing flow chart

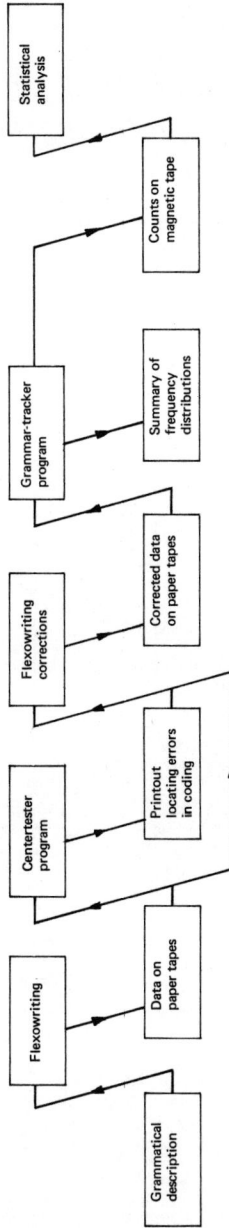

Grammatical description → Flexowriting → Data on paper tapes → Centertester program → Printout locating errors in coding → Flexowriting corrections → Corrected data on paper tapes → Grammar-tracker program → Summary of frequency distributions · Counts on magnetic tape → Statistical analysis

Diagram 8
A Chart of Allowable Transitions

CODE NO — TASK NO — SENT TO — S1 S2 S3 S4 — F B T — 1 2 — P S C Z V A B L — Q H M

Y T A L C V P M

0 / 1 / 2 / 3

0 1 2 3 4 5 6 7 8 9

B S I N

O A P F R S E

D E O

D O E N P S T W Y

D O E N I

1 2 3 4 5 6 7 8 9

1 2 3 4

Q H M P

1 1 2 3 4

F V T

1 2 3 4 5 6

B

L

1 2 3 4 5 6 7 8 Y

1 2 3 4

1 2 3 4

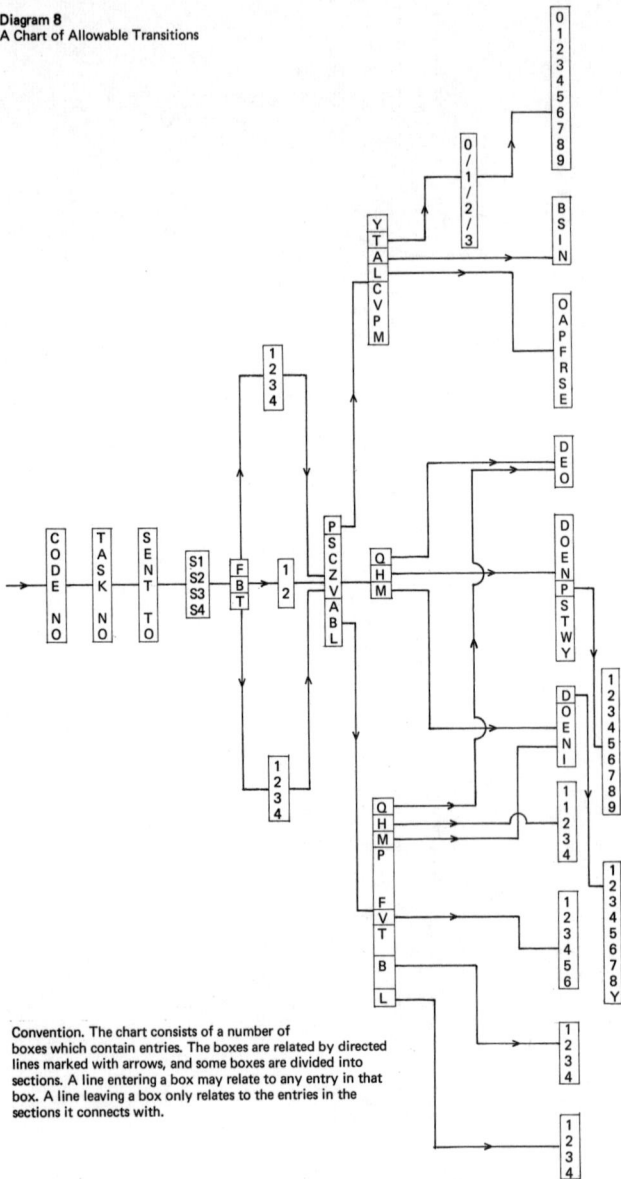

Convention. The chart consists of a number of
boxes which contain entries. The boxes are related by directed
lines marked with arrows, and some boxes are divided into
sections. A line entering a box may relate to any entry in that
box. A line leaving a box only relates to the entries in the
sections it connects with.

**Diagram 9
Central routine***

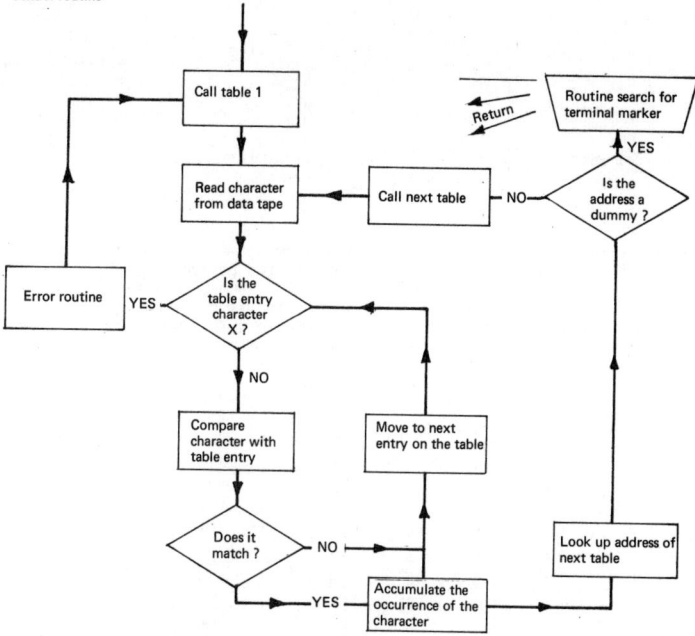

Call table 1

Read character from data tape ← Call next table ← NO ←

Routine search for terminal marker

Return

Is the address a dummy ?

YES

Error routine ← YES ← Is the table entry character X ?

NO

Compare character with table entry

Move to next entry on the table

Look up address of next table

Does it match ? → NO →

YES → Accumulate the occurrence of the character →

*A simplified version, see p. 3ff. of the flow diagrams.

Diagram 10
The pushdown store

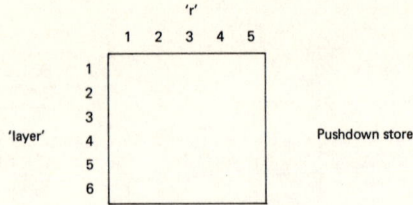

'r'

	1	2	3	4	5
1					
2					
3					
'layer' 4 ... Pushdown store
| 5 | | | | | |
| 6 | | | | | |

The pushdown store is a 2-dimensional array with a pointer (called 'layer') to the value i and a pointer (called 'r') to the value j. Layer (the i pointer) is advanced by each movement down the tree and moved back by the boundary markers. R (the j pointer) is moved forward by the *opening* rankshift and inclusion brackets and moved back by the *closing* rankshift and inclusion brackets. The two pointers together indicate the current cell (i, j) in the pushdown store. When a symbol has been matched on a given table the number of that table is copied into the current cell. It is thus possible to retrace the path back 'up the tree', The bottom nodes are not copied since they have no value for 'retracing'.

Each symbol of a simple example is shown in relation to the state of the relevant parts of the pushdown store.

Example: S 3 F I A M D 5 / H I / Q < 0 9 P H 4 / 1 > / 3
                'T h i s   t i m e   o f d a y'

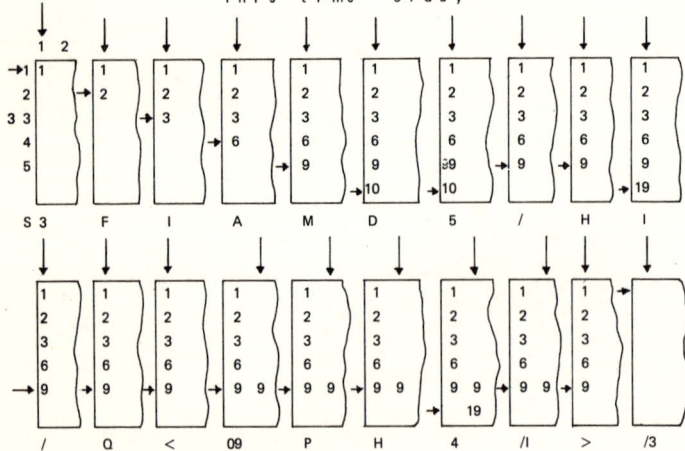

N.B. The arrows represent the values of the two pointers.
N.N.B. Where a cell is shown as blank, this does not imply that it is 'empty' but rather that it is available to be overwritten.

Diagram 11
Identification & counting of symbols

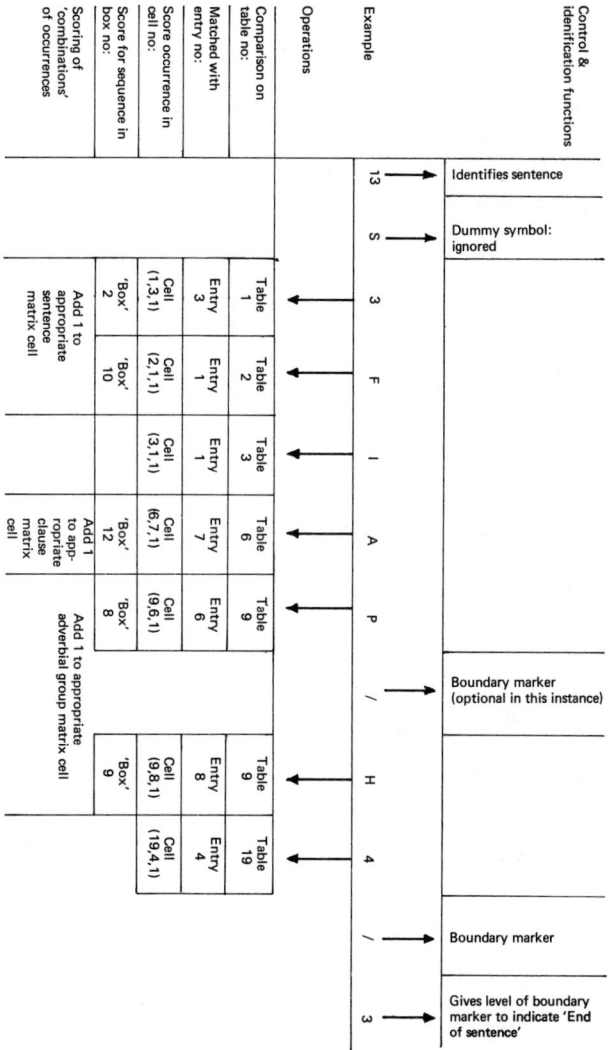

Control & identification functions	13	S	3	F	I	A	P	/	H	4	/	3
	Identifies sentence	Dummy symbol: ignored						Boundary marker (optional in this instance)			Boundary marker	Gives level of boundary marker to indicate 'End of sentence'
Example			3	F	I	A	P	/	H	4	/	3
Operations												
Comparison on table no:			Table 1	Table 2	Table 3	Table 6	Table 9		Table 9	Table 19		
Matched with entry no:			Entry 3	Entry 1	Entry 1	Entry 7	Entry 6		Entry 8	Entry 4		
Score occurrence in cell no:			Cell (1,3,1)	Cell (2,1,1)	Cell (3,1,1)	Cell (6,7,1)	Cell (9,6,1)		Cell (9,8,1)	Cell (19,4,1)		
Score for sequence in box no:			'Box' 2	'Box' 10		'Box' 12	'Box' 8		'Box' 9			
Scoring of 'combinations' of occurrences			Add 1 to appropriate sentence matrix cell			Add 1 to appropriate clause matrix cell			Add 1 to appropriate adverbial group matrix cell			

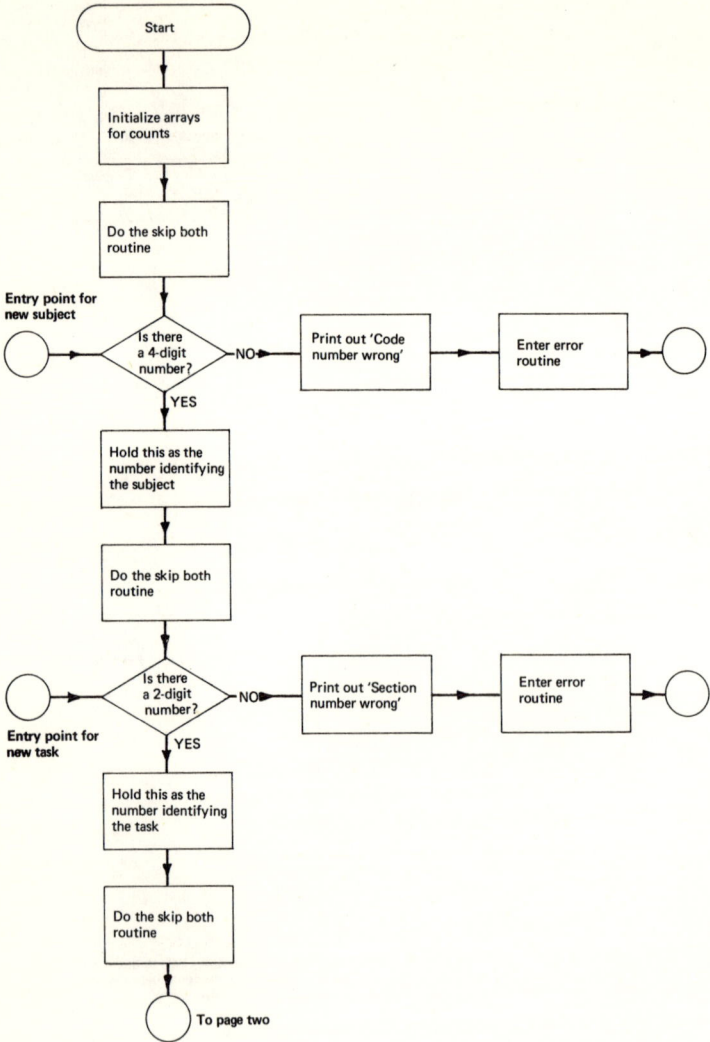

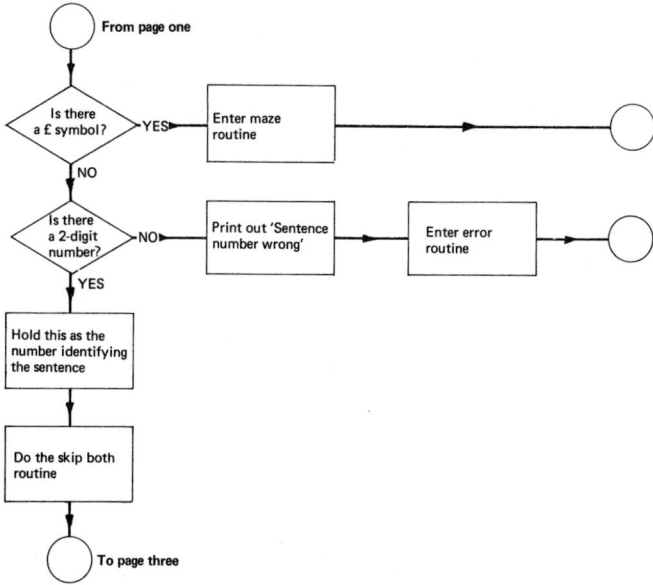

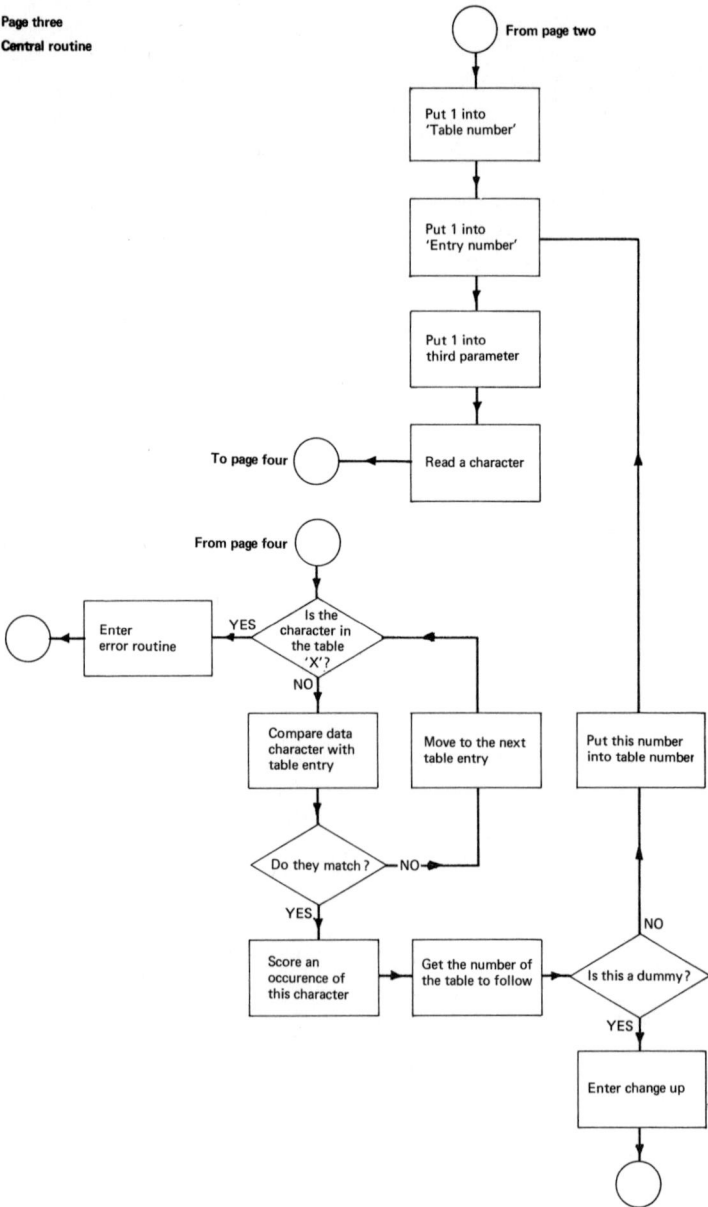

Page three

Central routine

( ) From page two

Put 1 into 'Table number'

Put 1 into 'Entry number'

Put 1 into third parameter

Read a character → To page four ( )

From page four ( )

Is the character in the table 'X'? —YES→ Enter error routine → ( )

NO

Compare data character with table entry

Move to the next table entry

Put this number into table number

Do they match? —NO→

YES

Score an occurence of this character → Get the number of the table to follow → Is this a dummy?

NO

YES

Enter change up

( )

Page four

Modifies the third parameter of the main routine
(Initially = 1)

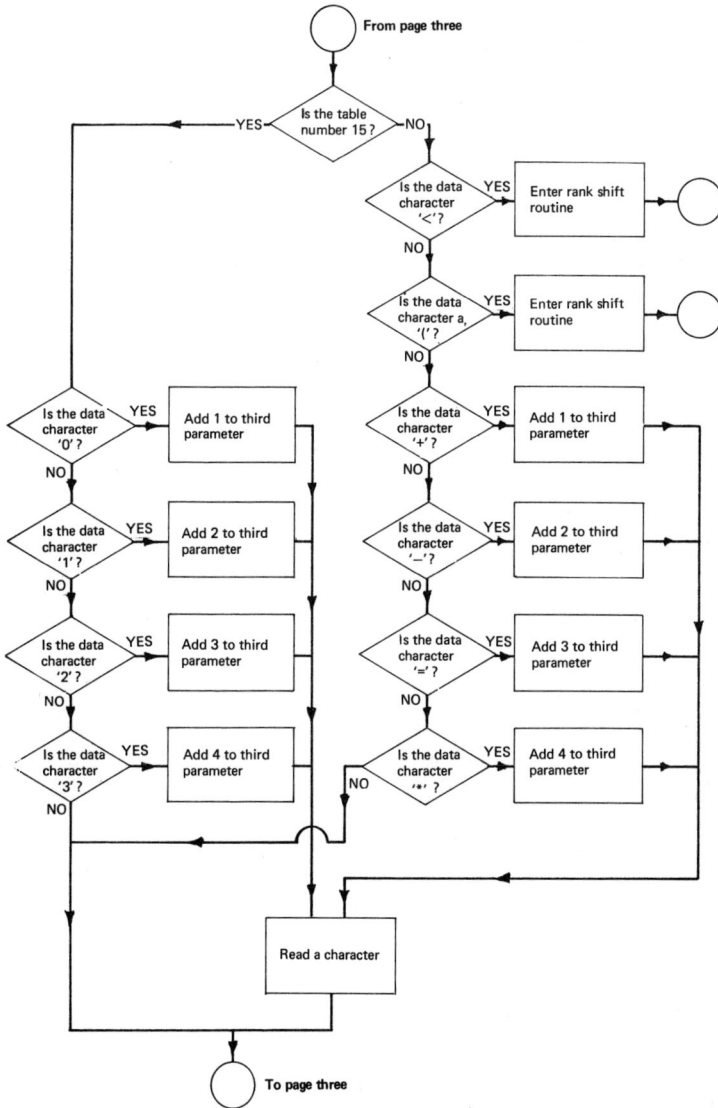

From page three

Is the table number 15?

YES

NO

Is the data character '<'? — YES → Enter rank shift routine

NO

Is the data character a, '('? — YES → Enter rank shift routine

NO

Is the data character '0'? — YES → Add 1 to third parameter

NO

Is the data character '1'? — YES → Add 2 to third parameter

NO

Is the data character '2'? — YES → Add 3 to third parameter

NO

Is the data character '3'? — YES → Add 4 to third parameter

NO

Is the data character '+'? — YES → Add 1 to third parameter

NO

Is the data character '−'? — YES → Add 2 to third parameter

NO

Is the data character '='? — YES → Add 3 to third parameter

NO

Is the data character '*'? — YES → Add 4 to third parameter

NO

Read a character

To page three

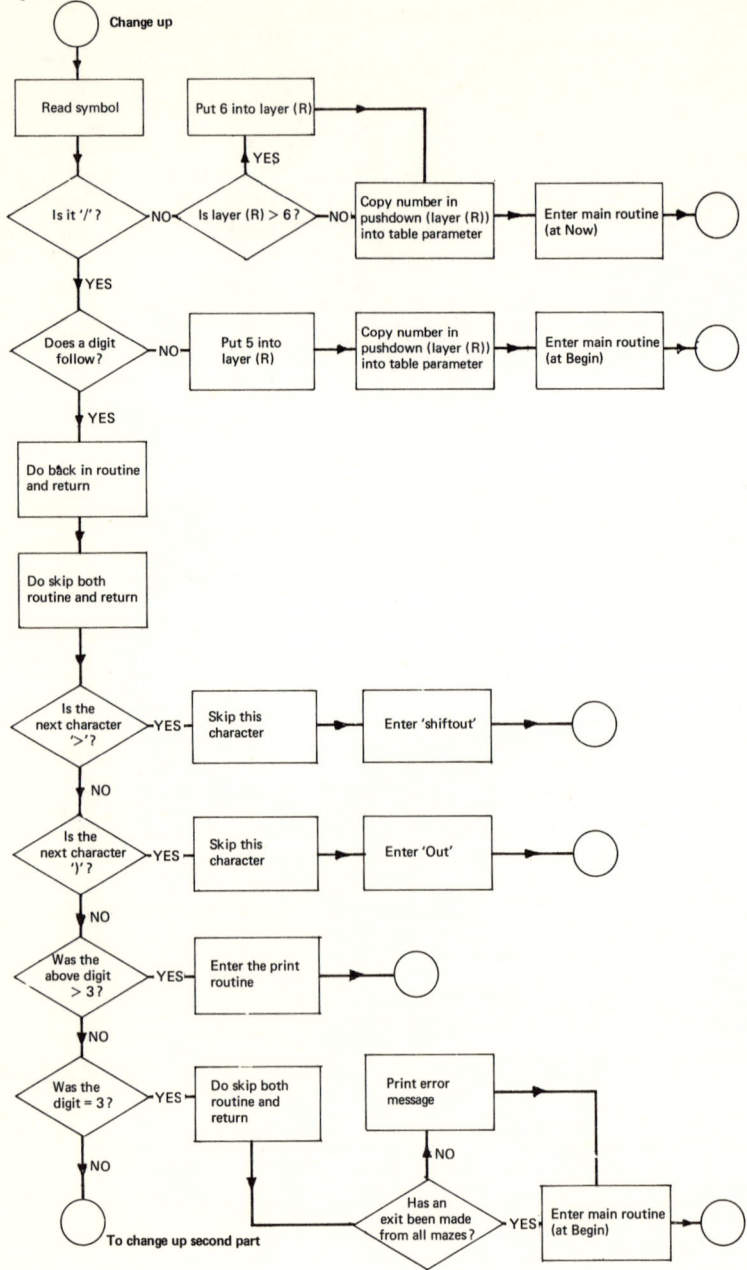

Change up

Read symbol

Put 6 into layer (R)

Is it '/' ? —NO→ Is layer (R) > 6 ? —NO→ Copy number in pushdown (layer (R)) into table parameter → Enter main routine (at Now)

YES (from Is layer (R) > 6?)

YES (Is it '/')

Does a digit follow? —NO→ Put 5 into layer (R) → Copy number in pushdown (layer (R)) into table parameter → Enter main routine (at Begin)

YES

Do back in routine and return

Do skip both routine and return

Is the next character '>' ? —YES→ Skip this character → Enter 'shiftout'

NO

Is the next character ')' ? —YES→ Skip this character → Enter 'Out'

NO

Was the above digit > 3 ? —YES→ Enter the print routine

NO

Was the digit = 3 ? —YES→ Do skip both routine and return → Print error message → Enter main routine (at Begin)

NO

To change up second part

Has an exit been made from all mazes? —NO→ (to Print error message) / —YES→ Enter main routine (at Begin)

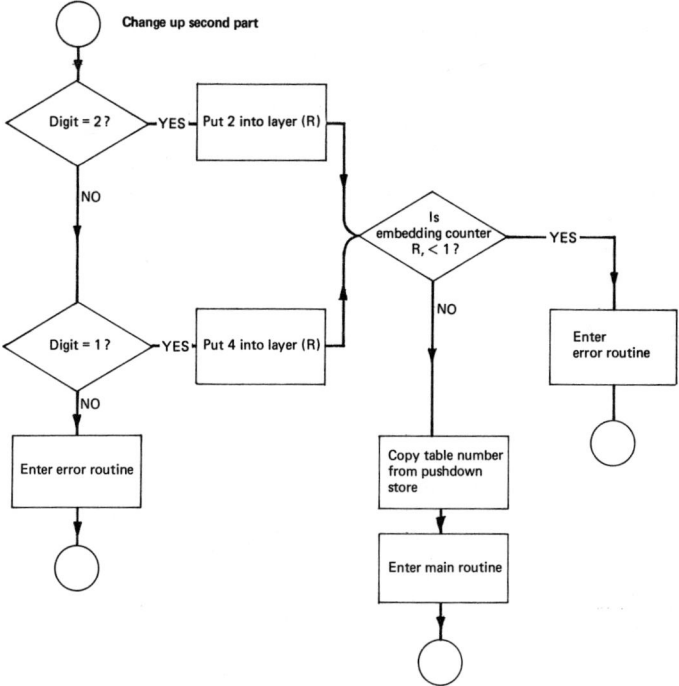

Change up second part

Digit = 2? — YES — Put 2 into layer (R)

NO

Digit = 1? — YES — Put 4 into layer (R)

NO

Enter error routine

Is embedding counter R, < 1? — YES — Enter error routine

NO

Copy table number from pushdown store

Enter main routine

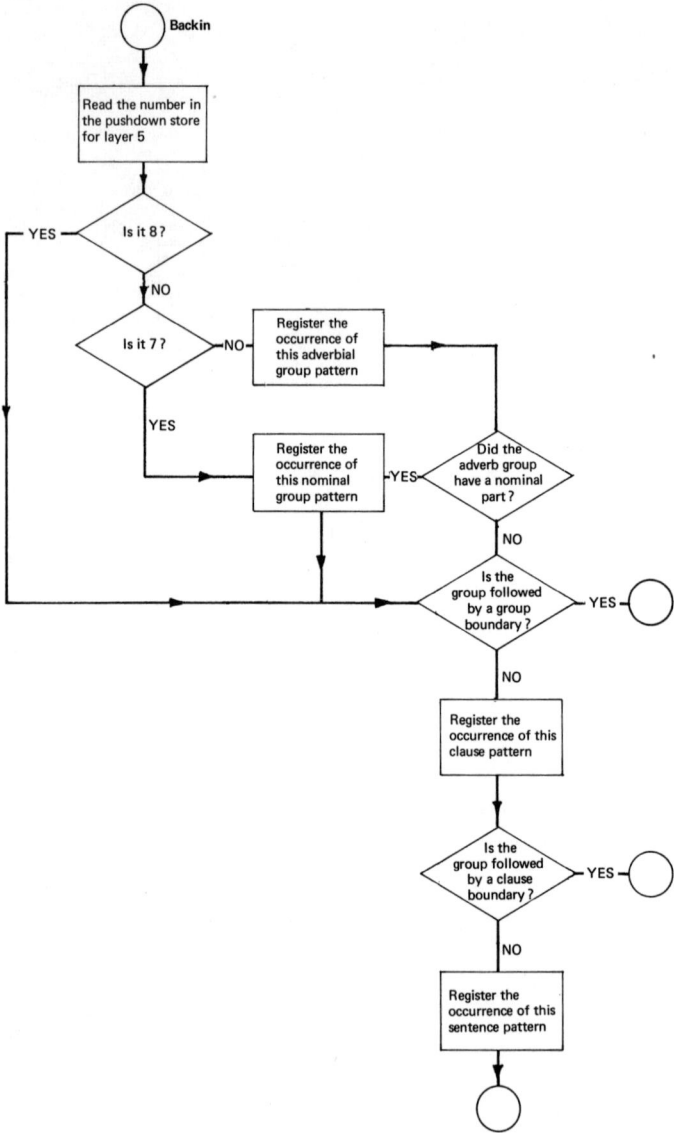

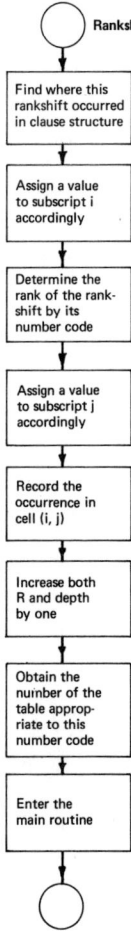

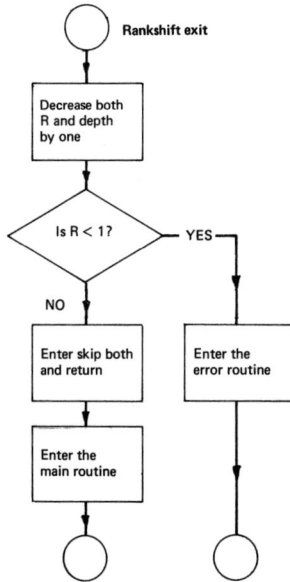

Rankshift entry

Find where this rankshift occurred in clause structure

Assign a value to subscript i accordingly

Determine the rank of the rank-shift by its number code

Assign a value to subscript j accordingly

Record the occurrence in cell (i, j)

Increase both R and depth by one

Obtain the number of the table appropriate to this number code

Enter the main routine

Rankshift exit

Decrease both R and depth by one

Is R < 1?

YES

NO

Enter skip both and return

Enter the error routine

Enter the main routine

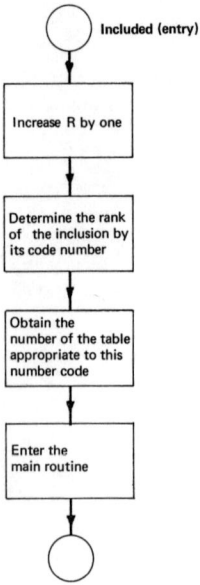

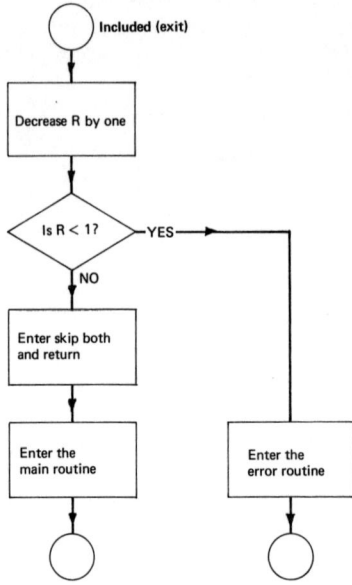

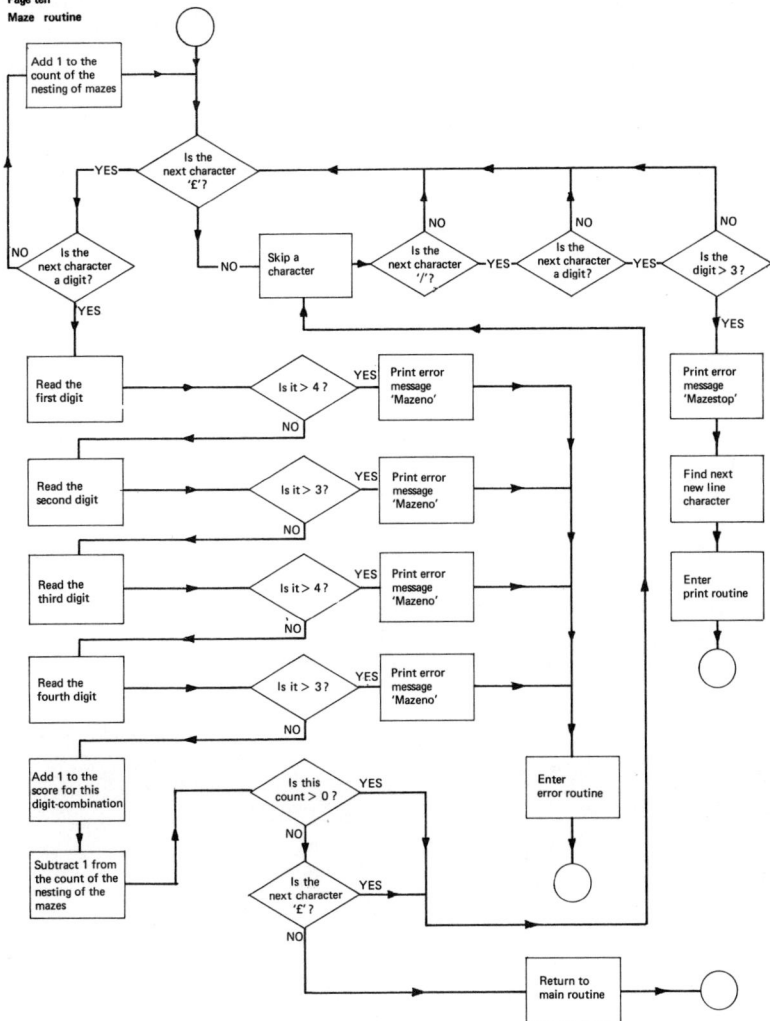

Add 1 to the count of the nesting of mazes

Is the next character '£'? — YES

Is the next character a digit? — NO / YES

NO

Skip a character

Is the next character '/'? — NO / YES

Is the next character a digit? — NO / YES

Is the digit > 3? — NO / YES

Read the first digit — Is it > 4? — YES — Print error message 'Mazeno' / NO

Read the second digit — Is it > 3? — YES — Print error message 'Mazeno' / NO

Read the third digit — Is it > 4? — YES — Print error message 'Mazeno' / NO

Read the fourth digit — Is it > 3? — YES — Print error message 'Mazeno' / NO

Add 1 to the score for this digit-combination

Is this count > 0? — YES / NO

Subtract 1 from the count of the nesting of the mazes

Is the next character '£'? — YES / NO

Enter error routine

Print error message 'Mazestop'

Find next new line character

Enter print routine

Return to main routine

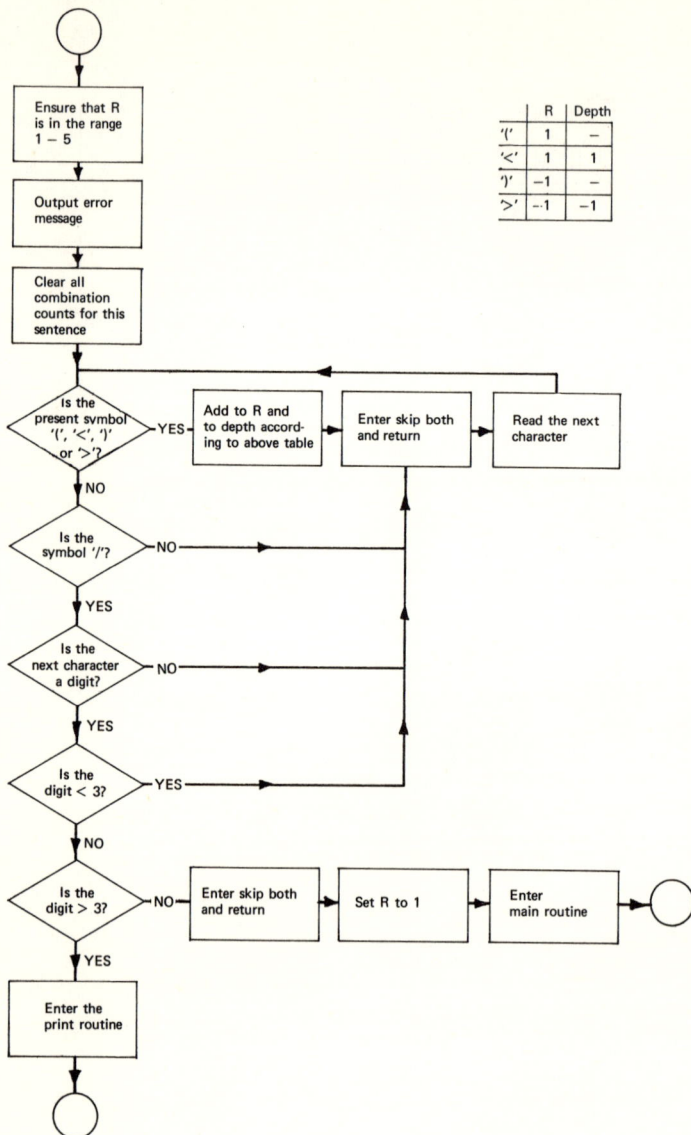

	R	Depth
'('	1	—
'<'	1	1
')'	−1	—
'>'	−1	−1

Ensure that R is in the range 1 − 5

Output error message

Clear all combination counts for this sentence

Is the present symbol '(', '<', ')' or '>'? — YES → Add to R and to depth according to above table → Enter skip both and return → Read the next character

NO

Is the symbol '/'? — NO →

YES

Is the next character a digit? — NO →

YES

Is the digit < 3? — YES →

NO

Is the digit > 3? — NO → Enter skip both and return → Set R to 1 → Enter main routine

YES

Enter the print routine

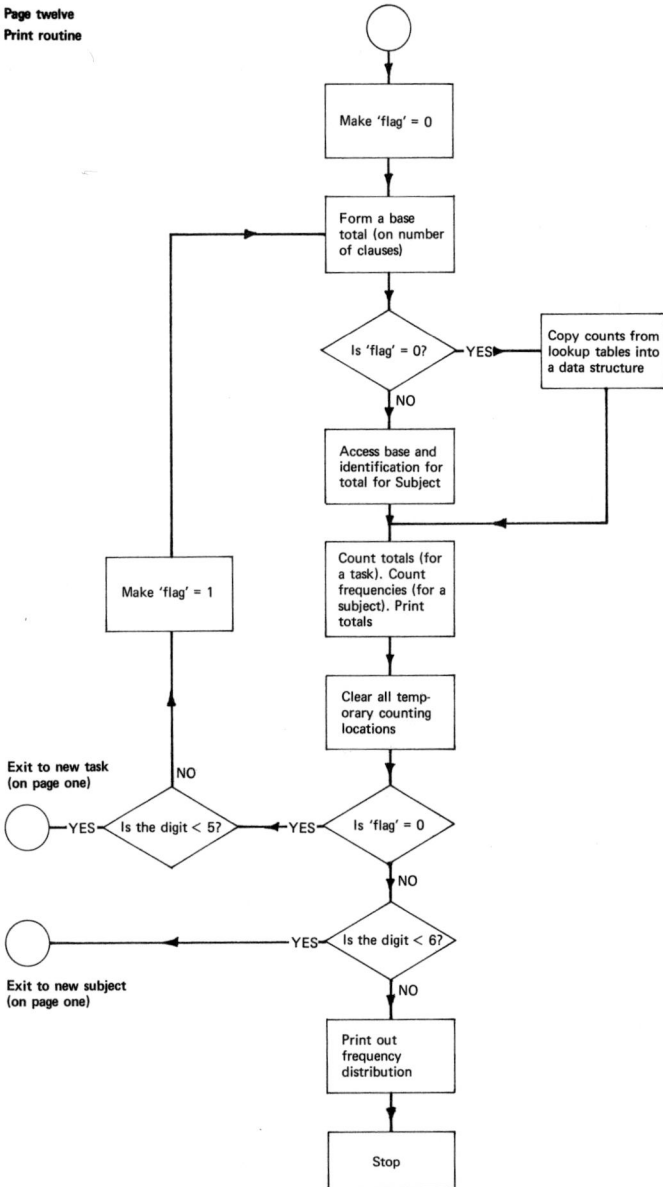

Page twelve
Print routine

```
                                    ( ◯ )
                                     │
                                     ▼
                          ┌────────────────────┐
                          │  Make 'flag' = 0   │
                          └────────────────────┘
                                     │
                                     ▼
        ┌───────────────▶┌────────────────────┐
        │                │  Form a base       │
        │                │  total (on number  │
        │                │  of clauses)       │
        │                └────────────────────┘
        │                          │
        │                          ▼
        │                    ◇ Is 'flag' = 0? ◇──YES──▶┌──────────────────┐
        │                          │                   │  Copy counts from │
        │                          │ NO                │  lookup tables into│
        │                          ▼                   │  a data structure │
        │                ┌────────────────────┐        └──────────────────┘
        │                │  Access base and   │                 │
        │                │  identification for │                │
        │                │  total for Subject │                 │
        │                └────────────────────┘                 │
        │                          │◀──────────────────────────┘
        │                          ▼
        │                ┌────────────────────┐
 ┌──────────────┐        │  Count totals (for │
 │ Make 'flag' = 1│      │  a task). Count    │
 └──────────────┘        │  frequencies (for a│
        ▲                │  subject). Print   │
        │                │  totals            │
        │                └────────────────────┘
        │                          │
        │                          ▼
        │                ┌────────────────────┐
        │                │  Clear all temp-   │
        │                │  orary counting    │
        │                │  locations         │
        │                └────────────────────┘
        │                          │
        │ NO                       ▼
◇ Is the digit < 5? ◇◀──YES──◇ Is 'flag' = 0 ◇
  │                                │
  │ YES                            │ NO
  ▼                                ▼
( ◯ )                        ◇ Is the digit < 6? ◇
                                   │
( ◯ )◀──────────YES───────────────┤
                                   │ NO
                                   ▼
                          ┌────────────────────┐
                          │  Print out         │
                          │  frequency         │
                          │  distribution      │
                          └────────────────────┘
                                   │
                                   ▼
                          ┌────────────────────┐
                          │       Stop         │
                          └────────────────────┘
```

Exit to new task (on page one)

Exit to new subject (on page one)

TURNER & MOHAN   45505,